Twenty Writing
Assignments in Context

Twenty Writing Assignments in Context

An Instructor's Resource for the Composition Classroom

Edited by MELISSA BENDER *and* KARMA WALTONEN

McFarland & Company, Inc., Publishers
Jefferson, North Carolina

LIBRARY OF CONGRESS CATALOGUING-IN-PUBLICATION DATA

Names: Bender, Melissa, 1967– editor. | Waltonen, Karma, 1975– editor.
Title: Twenty writing assignments in context : an instructor's resource for the composition classroom / edited by Melissa Bender and Karma Waltonen.
Description: Jefferson, North Carolina : McFarland & Company, Inc., Publishers, 2016 | Includes bibliographical references and index.
Identifiers: LCCN 2016048198 | ISBN 9781476665092 (softcover : acid free paper) ∞
Subjects: LCSH: English language—Rhetoric—Study and teaching (Higher) | English language—Composition and exercises—Study and teaching. | English language—Composition and exercises—Ability testing. | Writing—Standard. | Writing—Technique.
Classification: LCC PE1404 .W69435 2016 | DDC 808/.0420711—dc23
LC record available at https://lccn.loc.gov/2016048198

BRITISH LIBRARY CATALOGUING DATA ARE AVAILABLE

ISBN (print) 978-1-4766-6509-2
ISBN (ebook) 978-1-4766-2729-8

© 2017 Melissa Bender and Karma Waltonen. All rights reserved

No part of this book may be reproduced or transmitted in any form or by any means, electronic or mechanical, including photocopying or recording, or by any information storage and retrieval system, without permission in writing from the publisher.

Front cover image © 2017 iStock

Printed in the United States of America

McFarland & Company, Inc., Publishers
  Box 611, Jefferson, North Carolina 28640
    www.mcfarlandpub.com

For our University Writing Program colleagues,
whose generosity and creativity are a daily inspiration.

Table of Contents

Introduction   1

The Rhetoric of Everyday Objects: An Assignment Sequence
 MELISSA BENDER   7

Writing and Designing Informational Booklets for
 International Exchange Students
 M. ANN BRADY   20

Framing the Personal Narrative: Composition and
 Documentary Film
 JODIE CHILDERS   34

Blogging Advanced Composition
 ELISA COGBILL-SEIDERS, ED NAGELHOUT *and* DENISE TILLERY   45

Proposal Writing in Technical Communications
 BARBARA J. D'ANGELO   60

Past Meets Present: Exploring the University Archives to
 Compose and Connect
 CHRISTINE DENECKER   75

Writing the Brain: A Multimodal Assignment Sequence
 JASON W. ELLIS   92

Making Financial Contracts User-Friendly: Conducting
 Research, Redesigning Documents and Proposing Changes
 in the Workplace
 SARA K. GUNNING   106

Geobiographies: A Place-Based Assignment Sequence
  Jim Henry — 118

The Discipline Resource Guide Website
  Dalyn Luedtke — 131

Global Urban Centers: A Rhetorical Analysis of Street Art
  Gerald Maki — 143

The Academic Discourse Project
  Gracemarie Mike — 153

Political Cartoons and Multimodal Composition: The Visual Argument Assignment
  Erin Dee Moore — 164

Researching and Writing a History of Composition-Rhetoric
  Lori Ostergaard — 179

Critical Analysis of a *Wikipedia* Entry
  Gwendolynne Reid — 190

"In the Year": Using Website Design for ePortfolios
  Katherine Robbins — 204

Workplace Document Analysis and Evaluation
  Melissa Vosen Callens — 216

The Partner Project: Advanced Argument
  Karma Waltonen — 226

Captain Discourse and Other Heroes: Learning about Writing Research through Comic Books
  Courtney L. Werner *and* Nicole I. Caswell — 244

Critical Analysis of Student Ethnography
  Abby Wilkerson — 257

About the Contributors — 271
Index — 275

Introduction

We two editors consider ourselves fortunate to work in a large, robust writing program and with many outstanding colleagues who generously share their wisdom. Each time one of us begins to teach a course that is new to us, or to re-design a class that we have taught many times before, we have a font of resources to draw upon—model syllabi, writing assignments, and scaffolding activities. The instructors who created these materials are only a few doors down the hallway or an email away; they are always willing to spend some time explaining the design rationale that informs their course materials and to offer practical insights into how they used these materials in the classroom. Thus we rarely find ourselves at a loss when class planning time rolls around.

As writing instructors with 43 years of combined classroom experience, we have also frequently found ourselves on the mentoring side of this exchange, sharing our materials and advising colleagues about how they can adapt them for their own courses. Having designed many courses from the ground up—from the course proposal, to the writing assignments and rubrics—we acknowledge both the gratification that comes from having planned every nut and bolt of a course on one's own and the impracticality of doing so each time one is presented with the prospect of teaching a new course. We have yet to meet a seasoned writing instructor who has never been asked at zero hour to take on a new course or who has not realized, upon anticipating a new semester of teaching, that the writing assignments she has relied upon for years are either irrelevant to a new generation of students or are lagging behind the best current practices. At times like these, having classroom-tested resources and advice from colleagues about how to use them can make the difference between foundering and sailing smoothly through the semester. For novice instructors, such resources are indispensable. *Twenty Writing Assignments in Context* presents our effort to gather and share a collection of pedagogically-sound assignments within the context of each author's classroom practices.

Twenty Writing Assignments in Context brings together original, classroom-tested writing assignments in the form in which they have been presented to students. We selected these twenty from the large number of submissions we received based on several criteria. First, each of the assignments reflects the current state of knowledge on best practices in writing assignment design. For example, many of the assignments incorporate multimodal elements and problem-based learning, or call students' attention to the components of rhetorical situation. Others offer students opportunities to write in collaborative groups, to practice professional genres, and to compose for specific, real-world audiences. Second, the assignments are designed for a range of classes that writing instructors might lead throughout their careers, from first-year composition to upper-division writing in the disciplines courses. Finally, we selected assignments that inspired us with their creativity or fresh approaches to familiar writing forms. We hope that they will also inspire our readers and, in turn, our readers' students.

While there is no shortage of composition textbooks available today, many of which include writing assignments, *Twenty Writing Assignments in Context* offers readers something different. Intended as a resource book for instructors, rather than a textbook aimed at an audience of students, it provides readers with a context for understanding both the pedagogical foundation and the practical application of each assignment contained therein. In addition to the original assignment, each essay also includes the author's design rationale and a number of other supplemental materials such as grading rubrics, scaffolding assignments, and tips for avoiding pitfalls common to the assignment. These materials will assist readers to adapt and use these assignments effectively in their own courses. There are also a number of excellent resources available that discuss effective writing assignment design. John Bean's *Engaging Ideas* (Jossey-Bass, 2011) comes immediately to mind. While such works are invaluable resources when an instructor is preparing to construct his or her own assignments, *Twenty Writing Assignments in Context* provides another option—building upon the resources of other experienced instructors. Overall, *Twenty Writing Assignments in Context* presents composition instructors with a range of assignments that reflect best practices in assignment design and also draw upon the knowledge of the instructors who have designed and implemented the assignments. Both practical and inspiring, the assignments in this collection will be useful for writing instructors at any stage of their careers—from graduate students making their first forays into planning their own courses, to experienced instructors looking for new approaches to courses that they have taught for years.

Our Essays

Melissa Bender has created an upper-division assignment sequence in which students learn to craft original arguments and take a more sophisticated approach to research and revision in this assignment sequence focusing on analyzing material culture. The sequence culminates in a research project in which students analyze an everyday object of their choice.

M. Ann Brady has designed an assignment in which students collaborate on creating a brochure designed to introduce international exchange students to the campus culture. The assignment gives students experience in rhetorical problem solving, writing and design, usability testing, and teamwork.

Jodie Childers' assignment draws upon the lexicon of photography and cinematography to encourage students to analyze how images work to create meaning. Students apply photographic techniques—such as zooming in on a subject—to their written work, an autobiographical essay.

Students in advanced composition courses taught by Elisa Cogbill-Seiders, Ed Nagelhout, and Denise Tillery create a blog as part of their semester-long course—a full blog, with widgets, contact information, etc. Students draft, revise, and publish at least eight blog posts, learning how to write for a real audience and to use internet publishing tools effectively.

Many of our students will struggle to produce solid grant proposals once they're out in the world. Barbara J. D'Angelo's assignment will help them. Students collaborate to produce grant proposals directed at existing funding organizations that support a variety of fields, such as health care, technology, and the social sciences. The sequence of assignments leading up to the proposal, which is also included in this essay, introduces students to sophisticated research strategies.

First-year students in Christine Denecker's class develop connections to the campus environment through this multimodal assignment that requires them to conduct primary research into a specific place or organization on campus. By learning and writing about the history of these campus organizations, students understand how they are connected to previous generations of students as well as their own.

Jason W. Ellis describes a five-week-long, multipart assignment designed around the theme of neuroscience and writing. It gives students an opportunity to experiment with WOVEN (written, oral, visual, electronic, and non-verbal) multimodal communication using overlapping new and traditional media: Twitter, Storify, the poster, and the written essay. Its secondary purpose is to reinforce proven methods of learning success: learning over time (process) and learning through evaluation (reflection).

We could probably all benefit from doing Sara K. Gunning's assignment, in which students analyze the financial and legal contracts that surround them daily and write formal business proposals to make contracts easier to understand via usability testing. In groups of three, over four weeks, students select a financial contract/application—such as student loan, mortgage, credit card, cell phone, payday loan, apartment leases, or rent-to-own applications—and test the contract with potential users. Students use primary research to gather information from users via focus groups, interviews, and surveys, and secondary research by learning about the contracts and financial abuses in the news.

Jim Henry offers two linked writing assignments in which students explore the relationship between place and identity. For one assignment, students create a geo-biography that explores how their lives have been shaped by the geographies in which they live. A second assignment positions students as fieldworkers exploring the place of the campus, reporting from observations, and conducting interviews with upper-class students and instructors.

Dalyn Luedtke's students work in small groups on a semester-long project to build a discipline-specific website aimed at new or prospective students. With effective and engaging multimodal composing techniques, the websites aim to inspire people to pursue education and/or work in the group's chosen field and give viewers the resources they will need to do so. This assignment works well in both lower- and upper-division courses.

Students should be excited about Gerald Maki's assignment, in which they learn to critique and write about visual texts by looking at graffiti from various cities around the world. The assignment is designed to help students develop a stronger awareness of our increasingly globalized world and simultaneously develop visual rhetoric skills. This essay also includes a number of in-class activities tailored to helping students become comfortable writing about visual texts and street art.

In Gracemarie Mike's assignment, first-year students create an annotated bibliography of scholarly articles from their major disciplines, write a brief paper analyzing the discourse and writing style prevalent in this discipline, and create a website introducing others to this discourse community. Through this assignment sequence, students learn to identify the characteristics of academic discourse in their own fields (thus preparing them for their majors), practice analyzing texts, develop primary and secondary research skills, and learn the basics of visual design.

Those of us who teach visual rhetoric will enjoy Erin Dee Moore's assignment, which requires that students research and analyze a print advertisement or a political cartoon and compose a short essay addressing the cartoon's audience, purpose, and use of rhetorical appeals. After students have completed their essays, they are asked to compose their own print advertisement or political cartoon on the same topic.

Many students in the writing major at Lori Ostergaard's university undertake "the study of a single moment, movement, individual, or theory in [comp-rhet's] history" in one of the core courses. Students are required to conduct significant research, including using primary sources, as they write.

Gwendolynne Reid's assignment challenges both student and instructor assumptions about the usefulness of *Wikipedia* in academic writing. Students choose a particular *Wikipedia* entry and analyze it, using intertexts and academic sources, thus exploring its potential utility in academia.

Students in Katherine Robbins' first-year writing course write several papers related by a history theme, which are then graded via portfolio. At the end of the course, as they're preparing the portfolio, they also create a website to showcase their essays. This can be done individually or in groups. This project asks the students to revise their work in a new way, as they create an interactive, user-friendly site.

As part of her Writing in the Health Professions course, Melissa Vosen Callens assigns a Workplace Document Analysis. Students choose an actual piece of healthcare literature to analyze in detail, using elements of document design and rhetoric. She also uses this assignment in other discipline-specific courses.

One of Karma Waltonen's most successful assignments in her upper-division courses is the Partner Project. Each student writes an argumentative essay; they trade these and write formal evaluative essays about each other's papers, arguing whether the paper was a successful piece of persuasion. Students then write a third piece—a formal response to their partner's part 2. Students find the project challenging, but ultimately rewarding, as they learn to apply rhetorical strategies for an actual audience.

Comic book fans will rejoice in Courtney L. Werner and Nicole I. Caswell's group project, used as the culmination of a two-semester first-year writing requirement: "For this project, students were asked to collaboratively produce comic books that teach future college writing students how to conduct writing and rhetoric research." In fulfilling the assignment, students prove that they have grasped the lessons in first-year writing, learn to collaborate, create multimodal work, and perhaps produce a useful tool for future students.

Abby Wilkerson's assignment allows students to critically analyze another student's writing. Many first-year courses have a literacy narrative or its equivalent—here, students have written an ethnography about food. Students are then asked to formally critique each other's ethnographies, using additional scholarly resources. It's a sophisticated assignment, designed to give students valuable insight into writing, reviewing, and scholarship.

Key to Types of Assignments

Type of Assignment	*Relevant Essays*
Advanced Composition	Bender; Cogbill-Seiders, Nagelhout and Tillery; D'Angelo; Gunning; Luedtke; Ostergaard; Reid; Callens; Waltonen
First-Year Composition	Childers; Denecker; Ellis; Henry; Luedtke; Maki; Mike; Reid; Robbins; Werner and Caswell; Wilkerson

6 Introduction

(Type of Assignment)	*(Relevant Essays)*
Group/Partner Composition	Brady; Gunning; Henry; Reid; Robbins; Waltonen; Werner and Caswell; Wilkerson
Meta-Writing/Textual Analysis	Cogbill-Seiders, Nagelhout and Tillery; Ellis; Henry; Maki; Reid; Ostergaard; Reid; Waltonen; Wilkerson
Multimodal Composition	Childers; Cogbill-Seiders, Nagelhout and Tillery; Denecker; Ellis; Gunning; Mike; Reid; Robbins; Werner Caswell
Writing in Disciplines/Professions	Brady; D'Angelo; Gunning; Mike; Callens

The Rhetoric of Everyday Objects
An Assignment Sequence

Melissa Bender

Supplemental Materials

- Rationale
- Scaffolding Assignment 1: Proposal
- Scaffolding Assignment 2: Object Inventory
- Scaffolding Assignment 3: Theoretical Foundation
- Pitfalls and Avoidance Strategies

Assignment Sequence Overview

 Over the course of the next ten weeks, you will be working on a single course project, focused on interpreting an everyday object of your choice. The project is divided into four different components: the Proposal, the Object Inventory (a text collage that is designed to help you simultaneously explore your topic and experiment with your writing style), the Theoretical Foundation, and, finally, the Object Analysis, which will look more like the type of analytical argument that you are accustomed to producing for academic situations. The Object Analysis will draw upon the work that you have done in composing the three previous components. I have organized the course in this manner for several reasons.

 First, because this is an advanced composition course, I want to give you the opportunity to do something advanced, that is, to work on a sustained writing project. Although all writers have their own methods for completing writing tasks, one thing that they cannot do without is time—time to develop sophisticated and original ideas, to explore topics, to conduct the research needed to develop effective arguments, to select evocative examples, to rethink, and to revise. The analysis that you will be aiming to present at the end of the quarter cannot be written overnight or even in a week's time, which is why I refer to this as a sustained writing project.

Second, because you need time to develop this analysis, I have broken the project down into four different components, each with a different due date. Thus, you will be developing your project in manageable increments that are designed to help you build your analysis gradually and to coincide with the various stages of the writing process.

Third, I am asking you to focus your project on analyzing an everyday object because it is a significant but not insurmountable challenge, appropriate for the level of this course. It is unlikely that any of you have ever been asked to write a paper with such a focus; consequently, you each begin the course on equal footing. Nonetheless, the overall assignment is flexible enough that you can choose an object that interests you or a line of inquiry that is related to your disciplinary field.

Writing Assignment: Object Analysis (1800–2000 words)

For *Assignment 4*, the culmination of your course project, you will be writing an argumentative analysis of an everyday object of your choice. To compose your analysis, you may draw upon the material that you generated in Assignments 1–3. The primary objectives of Assignment 4 are to *give your reader a new way of looking at an everyday object* and to go about doing that by answering one of the following two *Core Questions*:

- What purpose—other than the function for which it was designed—does this object serve in U.S. culture or in another culture with which you are familiar?
- What does the use/possession of this object reveal about U.S. culture in general or about the culture or subculture in which the object is most widely circulated?

The object you choose as your focus can be:

- a specific object (such as the Nike Air Jordan).
- a type of object (such as sunglasses or coffee).
- a collection of a single kind of object (such as baseball cards or postage stamps).

- an object that has disappeared (such as the eight-track tape) or seems to be in danger of disappearing (such as globes or books).

The object cannot be:

- an art object or something that was designed to be of purely aesthetic value.
- an animal, a person, a part of a person, or an intangible element, such as pride or intelligence.

Tip: As you make your selection, you should avoid choosing an object simply because it is your favorite possession or you think it is really cool and take into consideration how the object you have chosen might allow you to address one of the two *Core Questions* above.

Although Assignment 4 is not due until the end of the quarter, you will need to choose your object soon because you will begin to write about it in Assignment 1. You are welcome to contact me via email or to visit my office hours to discuss potential topics.

Criteria for Evaluation

When grading Assignment 4, I will be looking for:

- an original analysis of the object that goes beyond stating the obvious.
- a compelling introduction that engages the reader.
- a well-crafted thesis statement.
- a unified focus and sustained development of ideas in the analysis.
- a theoretical foundation that grounds your analysis (this is a resource that presents a theory through which you will be examining your topic).
- references to at least five resources in addition to any you may be using from the assigned course readings.
- clear and correct writing style in both the paper and the self-assessment memo.
- use of MLA style for in-text citations and the works cited page.

Rationale

Designer toys, cruiser bicycles, refrigerators, and neckties are among the many objects that students have chosen as the focus of their course projects in my advanced composition course, which I have dubbed "The Rhetoric of Everyday Objects." I designed the course with the primary goals in mind of teaching students to manage a sustained writing project, to adopt more sophisticated conceptions of research and revision, and, above all—though this seems contrary to the notion of "everydayness"—to compose complex, intellectually-engaging essays.

Although I have been impressed by much of what my students have written in this course, the instructor who wishes to adopt this assignment sequence should be forewarned that students may express anxiety or resistance when first presented with the project. Some students fear that they will not find enough to say about an everyday object to fulfill the word count requirements for each component in the sequence. To some others the project initially seems like a trivial pursuit given all the evidently serious social subjects that a writer might engage today, not to mention the particular intellectual debates that might be brewing in the students' own disciplines. While these objections dissipate as students move through the sequence, I've come to believe that this initial discomfort is a crucial part of the process of moving from merely competent writing to something that approaches the advanced.

Just as first-year composition instructors may encourage their students to drop the security blanket of the three-point thesis statement or the five-paragraph essay, the advanced composition instructor might also have to press students to drop certain writing crutches that they have come to rely upon. The crutch that I aim to convince my upper-division students they can do without is the habit of formulating a thesis before they have gone through a period of research and reflection, an issue that I encountered when I first began teaching advanced composition courses several years ago. I had wanted to grant my upper-division students some autonomy in choosing their own writing projects and also engage them in a single, longer project over the course of the quarter, broken down into smaller components. The rationale for the latter was to allow for a period of exploration and invention, and to encourage a more substantive revision based on that exploration.

However, before I created the object analysis sequence as a framework within which the students could develop their topics, I typically found their final papers disappointing. Because I had allowed the students complete freedom in their choice of topic, most of them had chosen the first controversial topic that came to mind, about which much ink had already been spilt and over which they had already formed very strong opinions. Consequently, extending the project over the course of the quarter lost its purpose. Further, when the students conducted research, they tended to look only for authorities who either agreed or disagreed with their already-formed opinions, thereby limiting their explorations to only two different ways of looking at the given topic. When the course was organized in this fashion, the majority of students were able to produce essays that were competent but, quite frankly, not very interesting or inventive. As a result of this experience, I began to consider how to create an environment of intellectual engagement that both provided a writing context and introduced an ill-structured problem that would force the students to delay thesis formulation.

As defined by a number of composition scholars, a "messy" (Carrithers, Ling, and Bean 153), "ill-structured" (Wardle), or "wicked" problem (Marback 399) "lack[s] a single, knowable solution but instead [is] ambiguous, contingent, and recursive" (Purdy 613). An ill-structured problem cannot be resolved by "finding" a single "right" answer. Struggling to address such problems leads students to take a more thoughtful and active approach to invention and composition.

In "The Rhetoric of Everyday Objects," the ill-structured problem that I present to students is thus: choose an everyday object and, by the end of the course, produce an analytical essay that gives readers a new and unexpected way of viewing that object. Naturally, this means that the students themselves must first learn to look *at* the object, as opposed to *through it*, which is what we do with most everyday objects. As museum curator Ray Batchelor points out, we may see many kettles in our everyday lives, but most of the time we are not consciously "looking at kettles" (139). The initial challenge for the students—the thinking aspect of the ill-structured problem—is one of redirecting their attention: to see for the first time stuff their eyes have passed over thousands of times. The writing aspect of the problem is to get their readers also to see these objects from a new perspective. The assignment sequence overall provides the students with the space in which they can experiment with a variety of possible solutions to this ill-structured problem, while the two core questions, noted in the assignment prompt above, provide the students with a structure within which they will eventually formulate a thesis.

The written components of the sequence include the following:

- Proposal, First Draft
- Object Inventory
- Theoretical Foundation
- Proposal, Final Draft
- Object Analysis

While the proposal and analysis assignments are fairly typical in their forms, the Object Inventory is less conventional and is designed specifically to encourage that period of exploration that is essential to writing thought-provoking essays. Before the Inventory, the students write a first draft of the proposal, which I read, comment on, but do not grade. In this first draft of the proposal, I ask them only to present their chosen object, explain why they think it is suitable for the project, and how they might use it to address one of the two core questions.

Then, in the Inventory assignment, they compose text collages, the primary goal of which is to demonstrate that they've observed their object from a variety of different points of view. To write this essay, the students begin to conduct research and include at least three sources in their final draft. The research that the students conduct during this stage tends to be of a different nature than that performed by students in the open-topic class in that most students do not go into this assignment with a preformed argument in mind; therefore, they don't seek out particular points of view. Instead, they discover such things as the history of the object, how it is made, who invented it, or how it has changed over time. In many instances, they will not find any academic or analytical articles about their objects, because they haven't been written. This can be an unnerving but productive discovery for many students. Instead of relying on the authority of a published writer, they learn that they can fill this critical void with their own original approach to the topic, and, after passing through a period of information gathering and exploration, they have the authority to do so.

Because the Object Inventory assignment requires students to steer away from a thesis or direct argument and to explore, students often bring together remarkable collections of writing, such as real or hypothetical anecdotes that involve the object, analyses of how the object is presented in advertising or popular culture, quotations from blogs, or commentary on the social context in which the object is most often used. As Peter Elbow has noted, "Collage and parataxis are important [...] for the sake of thinking. If we ask our [...] students to spell out their thinking, they often limit themselves to what's dull. If we invite them to use parataxis and collage [...] they often capture more sophisticated thinking" (36). This has certainly been the case for many of the students who have completed the Object Inventory assignment in my course. Indeed, while seeking out multiple points of view and aiming for contrast as opposed to cohesion, students often generate original and compelling ideas that can be developed further as they are working on their Theoretical Foundation paper and revising their Proposals. Spending the time exploring their topics while working on Assignment 2 is an essential step that the students must take to meet the primary goal of Assignment 4, giving readers a new and unexpected view of an everyday object.

Finally, I would like to note that students are also often delighted to find that they too have invented a new way of looking at something while working on their projects in this course. Although it is not always evident to them at the beginning of the quarter, this assignment sequence allows for a great deal of flexibility, especially in terms of how the students construct their arguments in Assignment 4. They are nearly always able to bring their own interests to bear on their projects, whether these interests involve broader social concerns or their own disciplinary points of view. As a conclusion, I offer the following brief list of some of the arguments my students have presented in Assignment 4.

- The Persian rug, like the word Persian itself, serves as a buffer for Iranians who have relocated to cultures hostile to Iran or the Middle East in general.
- The marketing of the Ford Mustang, from the vehicle's introduction to the present, reveals that Americans' romance with individualism is really just another form of social conformity.
- The liberatory politics embodied by the Rainbow Flag are compromised by the fact that most of these flags are produced under unsavory labor conditions in developing countries.
- The lifecycle of the plastic water bottle illustrates the efficiency and the pitfalls of the U.S. capitalist economic system.
- The high-heeled shoe, when worn by drag queens or femme lesbians, subverts the sexual objectification often associated with this object.
- The worldwide market for kimchi demonstrates that globalization flows from east to west as well as west to east.

Scaffolding Assignment 1: The Proposal (350–450 words)

In the Project Proposal, you will propose and describe the topic you intend to pursue for Assignment 4, the Object Analysis. You will write two drafts of the Proposal.

In the first (ungraded) draft of the Project Proposal, you will:

- present your topic (object of choice).
- demonstrate why it will be a suitable object to analyze in Assignment 4 (Object Analysis).
- speculate on the non-functional purposes the object serves, or speculate about what the use/possession of this object reveals about U.S. culture in general or about the culture or subculture in which the object is most widely circulated.
- begin to assess what you need to learn about the object to write about it effectively.

At this stage, I do not expect you to have a thesis statement or detailed outline of how you are going to analyze your topic. Rather, I want to see that you have put some thought into selecting your object. In my feedback on your first draft, I will give you some idea of how feasible your proposal seems as a project. Then you will go on to write Assignments 2 and 3. After you've completed Assignments 2 and 3, you will revise your Proposal and turn it in for a grade.

In the revision of the proposal (which is graded), you will:

- present a thesis statement (even though it may change as you continue to write).
- declare which of the two Core Questions you will be answering in Assignment 4.
- give a brief summation of the argument you intend to pursue in Assignment 4. The summation should include the major points you intend to present, the connections between those points (how they build on or work in conjunction with one another), and an indication of how you will use your theoretical foundation.
- express the limits of your argument in Assignment 4 (explain what your argument will not cover and why).

Criteria for Evaluation

When evaluating your proposal, I will be looking for:

- an effective presentation of all four points above (thesis, core question, summation, limitations).
- a summation that demonstrates the links between the points you will raise.
- a feasible projection (in the summation) of an analysis that will be appropriate for Assignment 4.

Scaffolding Assignment 2: Object Inventory (1500+ words)

The Object Inventory is a collage essay about your topic. It does not present a direct argument on the topic and therefore should not include a thesis statement. The collage is held together by the fact that each of its sections is about your object. *The goal of the assignment is to give your reader multiple, different points of view (not a single unified argument) of your object.* In your assigned reading, you will find three examples of collage essays, one written by a former student in this class and two written by professional writers, Peter Elbow and Linton Weeks. You may use these essays as formal models.

While composing the Object Inventory, you will have the opportunity to explore your topic without yet committing to a particular line of argument or analysis, to immerse yourself in your topic by looking at your object from a variety of points of view, to begin to conduct some research on your object, and to experiment with different writing styles and with a form, the collage, that may be new to you.

The Object Inventory must:

- include five or more distinct sections, each of which has something to do with your object.
- create clear divisions between sections. (Experiment with such things as subtitles, dingbats, textboxes, footnotes, or columns to do this.)
- integrate at least one image.
- organize your sections in a manner that will be appealing to the reader.
- use the organization of the collage, as opposed to direct argumentation, to raise questions about your object.
- make reference to at least three resources (in addition to any you may be using from the assigned course readings. Please note that you *are not required* to use any resources from the reader).*
- avoid allowing quotation to take over your essay.

*Resource Requirements: As you work on the Object Inventory, you will begin to conduct research on your object; include findings from at least three resources in your collage. While you will need to allow your particular object to define the terms of your research, here are a few questions you might consider:

- What is the history of this object? (When was it first made? Who invented/designed it?)
- Where is it made and of what material?
- Since it was first introduced, has its design, form, or value changed?
- What impact might this object have on the environment?
- Is this object constructed under fair labor conditions?
- What have other writers had to say about this object?
- What might experts in different disciplines (e.g., economics, sociology, psychology, gender studies) have to say about this object?

Formatting Guidelines

You are encouraged to experiment with form in this assignment. Your only formatting requirements are to:

- submit your essay electronically as a Word document.
- use MLA style for in-text citations and the work-cited page.
- put your name, the date, and the word count in the upper left corner of the first page.
- include a word count beneath the name/date heading.

Criteria for Evaluation

When evaluating Assignment 2, I will be looking for evidence that you have observed your object thoughtfully and from multiple points of view and that you have put some thought into how to organize the material in a manner that appeals to readers. *Aim to give your readers something new to think about when they look at an object that they have probably taken for granted in the past.*

When evaluating your essays, I want to see that you have made an effort to:

- meet the seven "Object Inventory Requirements" noted above.
- grab and maintain the reader's attention.
- present the reader with multiple perspectives on the object.
- integrate source material effectively into your own writing.
- eliminate most grammar, mechanical, and typographical errors.
- use MLA style for in-text citations and the works cited page.

Scaffolding Assignment 3: Theoretical Foundation

A theoretical foundation is what it sounds like: a theory or an established cultural concept that writers use as a basis from which they can develop a strong argument and substantiate their claims. A well-chosen and integrated theoretical foundation will make your argument more persuasive for two reasons.

First, it will lend ethos (or credibility) to your argument; that is, by making reference to respected authors or scholars or to well-established and accepted concepts, you establish your own reliability as a scholarly writer.

Second, it gives you a tool for developing your argument. In other words, by working a theory or a complex concept into your argument, you will be pressed to develop your own argument in tandem with it. Thus, your argument will become more complex and sophisticated.

To make this writing strategy more concrete for you, I offer below a few examples of how students have used theoretical foundations to support their arguments in Assignment 4.

- A student used sociologist C. Wright Mills' idea of the historical influence on individual lives to explain why youths of the millennial generation are slower to obtain a drivers' license than youths of previous generations.
- Using the concepts of Fordist and Taylorist production, a student argued that the common daily planner divides time into increments that are complementary to a capitalist economic system.

- Another student used the concept of "rugged individualism" and its history in American culture to make an argument for why many Americans continue to own pocket knives even though they have no practical use for them.
- Using Pierre Bourdieu's concept of cultural capital, a student writer offered an argument for why the banjo has recently become a popular instrument in the hipster subculture.

Please note that, in all the examples cited above, the theoretical foundation (Mills, Bourdieu, Fordism, rugged individualism), came from sources that did not directly address the student writer's chosen object. Instead, the students applied these more general concepts to their own analysis of the objects. This is what you will need to do as well.

Assignment Description

For Assignment 3, you are going to find your theoretical foundation and briefly explain how you will use it to develop your argument in Assignment 4. Here are the steps:

- Locate at least one, but no more than three, resources that you will use to help you develop a theoretical foundation for your argument in Assignment 4. The resource *should not directly address your object*; it should, rather, provide a concept or theory that you intend to apply to your own analysis of this object.
- Write a 750-word paper in which you do two things:
  1. Briefly summarize the source(s). Summarize the key concepts presented in the source(s) clearly and primarily in your own words. Limit quotation to a minimal amount (no more than two to three sentences total).
  2. Explain how you will use the source(s) to develop your argument in Assignment 4.

Criteria for Evaluation

When evaluating Assignment 3, I will be looking for:

- one to three resources that appear to be feasible theoretical foundations for your topic.
- clear, concise summary of the resource(s), primarily composed in your own words.
- minimal use of quotation.

- rational explanation for how you will use this resource(s) to develop your argument in Assignment 4.
- clear and correct writing style.
- MLA style for in-text citations and works cited page.

Pitfalls and Avoidance Strategies

After overcoming their initial resistance or anxiety, my students typically appreciate the fact that this sequence allows them to develop their ideas over time and to "recycle" some of the materials that they have composed for the first three assignments when drafting the final assignment. I encourage students to consider such recycling as a part of the revision process. However, without guidance, some students will take this invitation to recycle material as an excuse to do little more than paste together bits and pieces of the previous assignments and present a patchwork for Assignment 4 instead of a unified analysis. This may be particularly tempting for students who enjoyed working on the collage assignment.

To help students avoid this mistake, I devote at least one whole class meeting to discussing what it means for a piece of writing to have a unified focus, which I include in the Criteria for Evaluation for Assignment 4. To facilitate this discussion, I distribute several anonymous student writing samples from previous classes. Reading successful responses to Assignments 2, 3, and 4, written by the same author, often helps students to see how a writer may select, develop, and arrange previously composed material and incorporate it into a new piece. Discussing a less successful example of Assignment 4 can also be instructive. I time this discussion to follow a class period in which we've worked on transition and cohesion strategies and ask the students to begin working on the sample paper by marking awkward transitions. This segues well into a discussion of the fact that frequent disjunctions may signify that something more than mechanics is amiss within an essay. I also recommend reinforcing the lessons learned in these discussions when composing peer review questions. For example, in the peer review for Assignment 4, I ask students to mark awkward transitions, to compare the main point of each paragraph with the thesis statement, and to comment on how unified the analysis is overall.

Clearly, an instructor who uses this sequence for the first time will not have a stock of student writing samples to draw upon. However, essays that were written for other assignments might be used to illustrate unity of focus or lack thereof. Professional essays may also be used to demonstrate this concept while simultaneously introducing students to different approaches to writing about material culture. Selections such as Roland Barthes's "Toys,"

Mihaly Csikszentmihalyi's "Why We Need Things," Fred Davis's "Blue Jeans," Daniel Miller's "Why clothing is not superficial" (in *Stuff*), Ellen Ruppel Shell's "Death of a Craftsman" (in *Cheap*), and Abby Clouse's "Narratives of Value and the Antiques Roadshow" (in the *Journal of Popular Culture*) have all worked well in my classroom.

Works Cited

Batchelor, Ray. "Not Looking at Kettles." *Interpreting Objects and Collections*. Ed. Susan M. Pierce. New York: Routledge, 1996. 139–143. Print.

Carrithers, D., T. Ling, and J. C. Bean. "Messy Problems and Lay Audiences: Teaching Critical Thinking Within the Finance Curriculum." *Business and Professional Communication Quarterly* 71.2 (2008): 152–170. Print.

Elbow, Peter. "Collage: Your Cheatin' Art." *Writing on the Edge* 9.1 (Fall/Winter 1998): 26–40. Print.

Marback, Richard. "Embracing Wicked Problems: The Turn to Design in Composition Studies." *College Composition and Communication* 61.2 (2009): 397–419. Print.

Purdy, James. "What Can Design Thinking Offer Writing Studies?" *College Composition and Communication* 65.4 (2014): 612–641. Print.

Wardle, Elizabeth. "Problem Solving with Prior Knowledge: Influences, Affordances, and Constraints." University Writing Program Conference, University of California, Davis. 18 October 2013. Keynote Speech.

Writing and Designing Informational Booklets for International Exchange Students

M. Ann Brady

Supplemental Materials

- Rationale
- General Assignment Description
- Clients
- Users
- Student Teams
- Scaffolding Activities
- Scaffolding Assignments

To: Students: Introduction to the Field of Scientific and Technical Communication (HU 2600)
From: M. Ann Brady
Re: Writing and designing an informational booklet for International Exchange Students

Purpose: This client project is designed to give you experience in rhetorical problem solving, writing, design, usability testing, and teamwork.

Objectives:
- Appreciation for complex problem solving
- Understanding of rhetorical theories

Goals:
- Move from ill-defined to well-defined problems

- Assess audience, purpose, context, and persona
- Manage multiple tasks, over extended time, with diverse team members

Context: Technical communicators must be critical and creative problem solvers. They need to know the difference between ill-defined and well-defined problems and have insights about the process of moving from the first to the second. They must know, in other words, how to use a variety of research methods to identify, define, assess, and address a range of conflicting and competing needs, including those of clients and users. They should be able to come up with good ideas about how to work with clients and users to "translate" those needs into deliverables. They must also understand how to work in teams—not groups—that is, how to manage a project by distributing tasks equitably, supporting each other constructively, and holding each other to mutually agreed upon standards of performance.

Parameters: For this assignment, we'll function as a communication-consulting firm, comprised of autonomous teams, consulting with each other and reporting to me.

Client: Our client is the Assistant Director, International Programs and Services (IPS), Michigan Technological University.

Specifically, our client says: "I want to develop a handbook for exchange students coming to Michigan Tech."

Here are examples she sent:

www.strath.ac.uk/media/ps/rio/exchange/pdfs/Study_Abroad_at_Strathclyde!.pdf

www.studyabroad.purdue.edu/resource/preparing.pdf

Users: The primary users of these documents are international exchange students, new to the U.S. and the Upper Peninsula. IPS may also use the deliverables to advise and recruit.

Deliverables: The entire document cycle includes the following deliverables, all of which are to be sent to me and to our client on the due dates that follow:

- Project proposals that confirm our client's expectations and the work you will complete (November 1);
- Usability test reports that detail the strengths and shortfalls of your prototypes, as well as plans to apply this information to your final products (November 22);
- Informative and persuasive presentations of your deliverables (December 9, 11, and 13);
- Professionally written and designed handbooks for international exchange students, contextualized by a cover letter (December 13).

22 Twenty Writing Assignments in Context

Date	What We're Doing	What's Due Next
October 23	Our client answers your questions and discusses her goals and expectations, as well as resources.	
October 25		For 10/28, read Thrush, "Multicultural Issues in Technical Communication." Read "3120 Demographic & Needs Assessment Reports." By Sunday, 10/27, 11:59 pm EST, each student posts to our Canvas discussion board re: Thrush (1) a useful takeaway; (2) a question or criticism of her article.
October 28	Discuss Thrush and 3120 assessment reports, identifying gaps and goals.	For 10/30, read Markel, ch 11. Read "3120 Recommendation Reports." By Tuesday, 10/29, 11:59 pm EST, each team posts to our Canvas discussion board summaries of 3120 recommendation reports' noteworthy points and concepts.
October 30	Discuss 3120 recommendation reports, identifying gaps and goals. Discuss proposals.	By Friday, 11/1, 11:59 pm EST, each team emails our client, copying me, a proposal for deliverables.
November 4		For 11/6, read usability principles and strategies (pdfs on Canvas).
November 6	Discuss usability principles and strategies.	For 11/8, each team reviews IGTAAP brochures for usability.
November 8	Discuss IGTAAP brochures' usability in terms of successes and shortfalls.	For 11/11, read "3120 Usability Reports." Review client feedback re: your proposals.
November 11	Discuss gaps and goals, based on 3120 reports. Discuss usability report genre. Discuss client feedback re: proposals.	For 11/13–11/17, prepare to carry out usability testing.
November 13	Hands-on usability testing.	Prepare to carry out usability testing.
November 15		Prepare to carry out usability testing.
November 18	Usability testing work day.	Usability testing work day. For 11/22, prepare written usability testing reports.

Informational Booklets for Exchange Students (Brady) 23

Date	What We're Doing	What's Due Next
November 20	Usability testing work day.	For 11/22, each team also prepares informal oral reports summarizing testing results and next steps. Usability testing work day. For 11/22, prepare written usability testing reports. For 11/22, each team also prepares informal oral reports summarizing testing results and next steps.
November 22	Present informal oral reports summarizing testing results and next steps.	By tonight, 11:59 pm EST, each team emails our client, copying me, their written usability report.
November 25	Holiday	No Class
November 27	Holiday	No Class
November 29	Holiday	No Class
December 2	Discuss cover letter to our client.	For 12/2, read Markel, ch 9.
December 4	Work Day	For 12/9–12/13, each team prepares for client presentations.
December 6	Work day	For 12/9–12/13, each team prepares for client presentations.
December 9	Client presentations	For 12/13, each team prepares final deliverable and cover letter.
December 11	Client presentations	
December 13	Client presentations	By tonight, 11:59 pm EST, each team emails our client, copying me, their final deliverable introduced and contextualized by a cover letter.

Rationale: Institutional and Programmatic Contexts

Scientific and Technical Communication (STC) is located in the Humanities Department at Michigan Technological University (MTU). The program's approximately forty majors complete lower-division, foundational courses in writing and media, as well as a year-long requirement in modern languages and culture, before electing to pursue concentrations in one of four emphasis areas: Rhetoric and Writing; Writing in the Sciences; Business Communication; and Digital Rhetorics and Design. Each of the emphasis areas offers students a suite of interdisciplinary electives drawn from humanities, engineering, natural and computer sciences, and business. At the same time as they are pursuing one of these concentrations, students are often also engaged in client work. They may be on internships, sponsored by non-profit or industry partners, or working on interdisciplinary and international academic projects.

Preparing students to succeed in this advanced work begins in a first-year STC writing course, "Introduction to the Field of Scientific and Technical Communication" (HU 2600). Here students are introduced to rhetorical concepts, such as audience, context, and purpose. While concepts like these are often taught in writing courses across the country, in MTU's technical communication classes, they play a central role as students use them to develop user-centered solutions to problems as they write and design in print and digital contexts. Problems and problem solving that are a-rhetorical and instrumental—identify a problem, design a solution, test it, implement it, and then evaluate it—have little value in any writing class for one reason: they are de-contextualized. They do not suggest particular audiences or users for whom these problems are to be solved. And they do not indicate why these audiences or users want these problems solved or what they will do with the solutions. Technical communicators, on the other hand, work with problems that are highly contextualized in that they are "tied to the interests of diverse stakeholders" (Mirel 22) and are related to the needs of those stakeholders whose interests infuse the solutions the technical communicators are being asked to generate. Moreover, these solutions depend on "many possible and equally legitimate moves and strategies" that can be used to accomplish a range of workable solutions (Mirel 16). Whether writing instructions for a hand-held device or testing the usability of a website, few simple solutions exist, so STC students learn how to develop multiple strategies for addressing "complexity, instability, and uncertainty" (Schön 19).

The STC program has also long aimed to graduate students who are aware of the challenges of international and multicultural communication and can respond sensitively and knowledgeably in these contexts, thus "functioning in situations of indeterminacy and value conflict" (Schön 17). A current colleague, Laurence José, then a graduate student, and I designed an assignment focusing on international and multicultural communication in an upper-division class that many STC and STEM students take (Brady and José). Recently, the program has required that students take an upper-division course in international technical communication and complete a year of modern language study. Majors are now thus introduced to concepts that prepare them for complex problem solving in international and multicultural contexts—comparative rhetorics, genres, cultures, and languages—before they graduate, but often not until they are advanced students. Leaving required coursework in international and multicultural communication to the later stages of students' programs suggests that it is specialized or advanced. It is indeed challenging since it foregrounds the relationship between the local and global, asking students to examine their own cultural identities and how those infuse their communication practices in broader contexts. But challenges like these require the kind of sustained reflection that might be built into the curriculum from the start, with students beginning such reflection in an introduction to the field and returning to it as they move through their course of study.

To be useful to beginning students, I thus wanted to design a HU 2600 assignment that gave students time to begin processing the concepts I've discussed. I focused on the communication needs of actual people, who could discuss the multi-faceted problems they faced, explain the benefits and challenges of addressing those problems, and offer feedback as students worked through the iterative stages of the problem-solving process. Since international and multicultural theories are central to technical communication, I also wanted an assignment that foregrounded these theories and demonstrated their practical applications. Finally, since communication projects such as this are open-ended, requiring a mix of skills and perspectives to define them, I wanted students to work in teams—and understand the difference between teamwork and group work—to produce the most usable solutions. To make a start on these goals, I piloted an extended international client project during the fall semester of 2013, which has served as a basis for subsequent international projects I've designed each year since then, partnering with international programs and their directors. The final deliverable, due at the end of the semester, was an informational brochure for international exchange students new to the United States and the Upper Peninsula (U.P.) of Michigan.

General Assignment Description

Because HU 2600 is an introduction to technical communication, the assignment instructions may appear different from those used in many writing classes. First, I used a memo for the instructions, not so much to model the format as to provide an opportunity to discuss the conventions and exigencies of a genre often used in the field. Chunking information—an organizational strategy typical in memos—allowed me to foreground the project's components, such as its purpose, objectives, goals, context, and parameters. Finally, I used the memo's descriptive headings to suggest, among other important details, audience complexity: the final brochures would be resources for at least two different groups, each of which had different needs and interests: clients—MTU's International Programs and Services (IPS)—and users—international exchange students.

Like most writing instructors, I distribute a calendar of the semester's work to students at the beginning of each term, but I also cut sections from this calendar that apply to particular assignments and paste them in with the instructions. Doing so gives students a project-by-project snapshot of important dates and deliverables, thus preparing them to manage their time in ways that reduce, as much as possible, late nights and last minute work. The complexity of this project in particular also called for regular discussions about setting goals, establishing deadlines, and monitoring progress, topics that were more easily taken up with a calendar as a reference point. Finally, our STC Advisory Board members have consistently emphasized the importance of project management skills for our graduates, and the calendar, included in the project, supported that experience for students.

Clients

In the spring semester of 2013, six months before the project launched in the fall, the assistant director of MTU's IPS contacted me, indicating that she and a colleague, the coordinator of IPS admissions, wanted to develop an informational brochure for international exchange students. If any STC instructors or students were interested in taking on the project and IPS used the resulting materials for advising or recruitment, students would be fully and publicly acknowledged.

Although former HU 2600 classes had successfully sharpened their communication and project management skills while working with a range of clients from the university and local communities, IPS administrators were ideal clients. Giving introductory students the opportunity to learn about the challenges and rewards that program administrators face as they develop programs for international students, and recruit and advise them, served as a platform for future instruction in international and multicultural communication. This, in turn, offered students a keener appreciation for the importance of thinking beyond demographics to consider an audience's cultural practices, attitudes, and values. Asking students in this introductory course to work on a project sponsored by international programs also indicated that global issues infuse the STC program and the MTU campus community, that these issues are taken up—and taken seriously—every day in academic and nonacademic workplaces, and that they are central to the field of technical communication. Finally, the assistant director and admissions coordinator played active roles in the project and thus became educational partners, as well as clients. In addition to coming to class to discuss their goals, hopes, and expectations for the project, they also provided demographic information about former international exchange student populations and arranged for current exchange students to come to our class to share their experiences as they had arrived and then adjusted to life at MTU. The assistant director and admissions coordinator also gave substantive feedback to all students about their work throughout the project, answered email queries, participated in usability testing, and attended the final client presentations.

Users

Exchange students from China, Finland, and Germany, then enrolled at MTU, came to class to discuss information they thought necessary to any international student considering studying abroad, thus offering potential content for the brochures. Since these students hailed from Asia and Europe, each described a unique set of experiences. All, however, highlighted important cultural differences between the U.S. and their home countries. Teaching and learning styles, classroom practices, and social interaction were often noted. One student, for instance, observed, "At Michigan Tech, there is a lot more homework and it's strange how students have to be present at classes all the time. At my home university, we don't need to be present as long as we do all the work on time." Another remarked, "Professors at Tech are much closer to the students. They make you feel welcome. You are not anonymous." Students agreed that Americans, in general, are friendly and helpful. One student commented, "The absolute best thing is the wonderful people I've met." In addition, when asked what three things exchange students missed most from their home countries, the consensus was "family, food, and public transportation." Students were also helpful in explaining the importance of preparing specifically for life in Michigan's U.P. Here winters stretch from October through May, the snowfall averages 218 inches, and temperatures often hover at below freezing for weeks. Weather like this, they pointed out, however, offers many opportunities for hockey, skating, broomball, snowboarding, downhill and cross-country skiing, and snowshoeing. Some of their advice for incoming exchange students was thus to "make the most of your time in the U.P. Do as much as you can outside. Studying is important, but the experience is once in a lifetime."

Combined, these comments indicated to all of us in HU 2600 that detailed information about what to expect and how to prepare for life in the U.S. and the U.P. was particularly relevant for international students coming from different climates and locales. We spent subsequent classes identifying major themes and concepts that emerged from our notes, returning to them throughout the remaining weeks of the semester as we took up rhetorical issues, such as audience complexity and accompanying content choices.

Student Teams

In addition to the fact that professional communicators often find themselves in teams with other writers, designers, and subject matter experts, this assignment was multi-layered, requiring proposals and reports, as well as the informational brochure. Its goals were also complex: to give students experience in rhetorical problem solving in international and multicultural contexts, in writing and design, usability testing, project management, and teamwork. To address this complexity, I decided to have students tackle the project in teams and built in several steps to support their work. While these steps did not completely eliminate conflicts or miscommunication, they did make the dynamics of teamwork more visible to students, and thus they were more mindful of their responsibilities in securing its benefits.

Scaffolding Activities

To prepare students for team work, I began the project by asking them to post to a discussion board brief descriptions and explanations of their least and most successful team experiences. In subsequent classes, we discussed these responses, identifying strategies for productive collaboration, as well as behaviors that undermined it. Students talked with each other about their skills, abilities, interests, experiences, and schedules. We looked at theories of team development—how successful teams establish goals and structure, coordinate workflow, encourage balanced participation, and give each other timely, honest feedback. And I introduced a team contract assignment, which asked students to do the following: name their teams; set a weekly face-to-face meeting time; write a list of expectations for meeting attendance and preparation; establish systematic ways to communicate between meetings; and establish a process for terminating members who repeatedly disregarded the terms of the agreement. At the end of these discussions, six self-selected teams formed, each comprised of three students, and each of which submitted client proposals, usability testing reports, and an informational brochure (see Client Proposal and Usability Testing Report assignments below). After collaboratively writing their own contracts, students signed them and submitted them to me. To reinforce the ongoing process of successful teaming, midway through the project, I set aside class time for students to identify two points of informative feedback for each team member and for themselves that they thought would improve their team's dynamics. At the end of the semester, I asked students to review their team contracts and rate how often they and their team members had met the expectations outlined there.

Once teams had formed, we turned our full attention to basic rhetorical concepts, which took on multiple meanings in this project. The audience for the brochure, for instance, consisted of two broad groups—IPS personnel and exchange students—each of which would read the brochures with different purposes and might thus expect a slightly different style, content, and tone. Facts about topics such as visas, travel to MTU, housing, insurance, health care, and expenses, would be important to both groups, but the first would use them to advise and recruit while the second would need to understand how to apply the facts in their preparation or upon their arrival. In other words, advising incoming students that they will need a visa to study at MTU calls for a style that is different from explaining how to apply for one: the first lends itself more to description, summarizing the required documentation and reasons for it; the second more to prescription, instructing users in how to acquire the documentation and what to do with it. In addition to questions of style, who would use the brochures and for what purposes brought up questions of content and tone. Both the IPS and student audiences needed thorough explanations of international and U.S. laws and regulations, as well as university requirements. But exchange students would also want to read about cultural and sports activities, student organizations, and travel opportunities. Adjusting to U.S. social customs, understanding classroom practices, and making American friends were also topics that seemed important to include. Grappling with what content to include in the brochures and in what detail led HU 2600 students back to discussions of audience: how could the overlapping yet distinct needs of the two audiences be addressed? How would these needs impact the ways in which the brochures were organized and what hierarchies of information might suit both equally well? Since IPS would use the brochures to represent its program, which in turn would represent MTU, students agreed that maintaining a professional tone was important, but what, they began to ask, constitutes such a tone and could it be infused with the kind of enthusiasm that might appeal to prospective and incoming international students?

To begin to answer these questions, teams reviewed the MTU IPS website to determine what information the program had made available and compare it to what current students had reported as important. They also reviewed informational brochures produced by other universities. While each team came up with its own analytic methods and approach, all focused on how study abroad programs were represented, both in design and writing. Teams asked, for instance, what visuals were used to highlight the benefits of studying at these campuses and of studying abroad generally. How did existing brochures integrate visuals and text? Was there a balance of the two, or was one featured in the page design? How effectively did they combine to make information easily accessible? How did the language of these brochures connect with students and make it clear that they would be welcome members of the university and local communities? How did they—or did they—talk about diversity in these communities? Did visuals suggest that diversity was valued? In addition to basic legal information about international students traveling and living abroad, did the brochures offer descriptions or action shots of university programs, student organizations, travel opportunities, or local activities and points of interest? How detailed was the practical information they included about, for instance, airport and shuttle information, academic calendars, resources, and expenses? How did the brochures convey excitement, enthusiasm, and professionalism?

Questions like these indicated that HU 2600 students had moved far beyond assuming that their brochures would be a list of quick tips on how to fit into U.S. culture, and I wanted to validate that thinking. I thus used the questions to build in opportunities for students to read about, experience, discuss, and reflect on what it means to communicate in international and multicultural contexts. One article we read focused on contrastive rhetoric and reported research findings on how cultural attitudes toward group orientation, individualism, consensus, competition, and authority affect communication practices. As students discussed the article, they applied it to their own lives and began to appreciate why, for instance, their experiences with faculty in U.S. classrooms—often informal and conversational—were different from those reported by some of their international peers—more formal and usually lecture-based. Articles like this were thus useful in helping HU 2600 students understand that many customs—their own included—are culturally situated. Important, too, was that while the author explained how contrastive rhetorics informed her "preliminary framework [...] through which communicators can better analyze culturally diverse audiences to make informed communication choices" (Thrush 416), she also highlighted a caveat—that such an approach, used uncritically, can lead to generalizing about cultures.

To work against this impulse, we discussed additional articles that took up global communication from perspectives similar to our two audiences. While the parallels between IPS and technical writing programs were not direct, reading calls for increased attention to educating STC students for careers in what will surely be a global workplace (St. Amant) gave us insights into the commitment of our IPS clients to strengthen their program's outreach to international communities. Reading about how cultural differences directly affect the ways in which students collaborate in classrooms (Bosley) offered compelling evidence for the importance of addressing such differences explicitly and sensitively as we worked to produce brochures that would be useful to international students. And hearing one instructor, who had taught abroad, comment that "educational practices and worldviews from each side of the exchange require significant compromise" (Dautermann 141) made it clear that whether we were students, faculty, administrators, from the U.S. or abroad, we could all learn something from the project.

Interactions with international students and IPS clients played a crucial role in helping HU 2600 students better understand cultural differences and answer the questions that they raised throughout the semester. During our initial discussion, exchange students and IPS clients shared their contact information, which HU 2600 students used to follow up with additional questions and requests for discussions throughout the semester. Midway through the term, the class was invited to a potluck hosted by international students. And as they finished drafts of their brochures, HU 2600 students arranged for extended meetings with clients and users to test the usability of what they had written and designed. Although similar to peer feedback in many writing courses, usability testing focuses on those who will use the documents—their interests and needs. Guiding them through a series of activities and questions, usability testing is intended to offer insights into how satisfied users are with the documents. In the case of this assignment, IPS and international students gave feedback on how successfully HU 2600 students had made the information accessible, how easy it was to remember, and how successfully it supported the tasks they wanted to complete, whether traveling to the U.P. or understanding its culture.

Client Proposal

To: Students: Introduction to the Field of Scientific and Technical Communication (HU 2600)
From: Ann Brady
Re: Project Proposal

Following is information about internal project proposals.
As a team, write a 2–3 page proposal, in memo format, in which you:
1. Indicate the purpose of your proposal (forecasting statement);
2. Introduce your proposal (the "history" of the project—that is, what you learned from our client and current international exchange students in terms of needs and goals);
3. Explain your proposed tasks (for example, reviewing needs and recommendation reports from SU 3120);
4. Describe your deliverable;
5. Indicate a schedule;
6. Describe each team member's experience (in design, writing, digital, marketing, international communication, employment, etc.);
7. Use APA style references—websites, pdfs, survey results, etc.—that you are using in your work.

Usability Testing Report

To: Students: Introduction to the Field of Scientific and Technical Communication (HU 2600)
From: Ann Brady
Re: Planning and Reporting Usability Testing

Here are instructions for planning your usability testing and for reporting your results.

Planning Usability Testing:
1. Decide on goals for your test. What do you need to know to make your document useful and usable? Accuracy? Accessibility? Style or tone?
2. You need 3–5 users to test your document to get robust results.
3. Decide on what kind of testing—or combinations of testing—you want to do:
    - Structured Observations
        A. You observe users engaging in the work your instructions are intended to explain while you take notes.
        B. You follow up with a debriefing in which you ask the users to discuss successes and problems with your instructions while you take notes.
    - Beta Testing
        A. You ask users to test your instructions in their own setting.
        B. You ask them to report their results in a questionnaire.
    - Low-Tech Testing
        A. You give users (1) your instructions, (2) index cards, (3) pens or pencils, and (4) the following observer instructions: Write down anything you want to record; Put only one idea per card; Leave your cards on the desk when you go.
        B. You schedule a de-briefing meeting where users meet with you. Here, you ask them to:
        (1) Organize their cards.
        (2) One possibility is to attach a piece of tape to each card, put them all in one place on a wall, and then have the users move them around into categories.
        (3) Once users have organized the cards, you prioritize the results.

Writing Usability Reports:

Once you've completed the testing, you'll need to write up the results, something that's generally done in usability work. For HU 2600, consider this an informal report, use descriptive headings and deductive organization, and follow these steps:

1. Begin with the goals of your test.
2. Explain how you recruited participants.
3. Describe the test design—what you asked participants to do.
4. Explain when, where, and how you conducted the tests.
5. Summarize the major problems you uncovered.
6. Summarize the minor problems you uncovered.
7. List "Verbatims"—direct quotes from participants that strikingly describe successes and shortfalls.
8. Recommend next steps for your revisions.

WORKS CITED

Bosley, Deborah S. "Cross-Cultural Collaboration: Whose Culture Is It, Anyway?" *Technical Communication Quarterly* 2.1 (1993): 51–62. Print.

Brady, Ann, and Laurence José. "Writing for an International Audience in a US Technical Communication Classroom: Developing Competences to Communicate Knowledge Across Cultures." *Nordic Journal of English Studies* 8.1 (2009): 41–60. Print.

Dautermann, Jennie. "Teaching Business and Technical Writing in China: Confronting Assumptions and Practices at Home and Abroad." *Technical Communication Quarterly* 14.2 (2005): 141–159. Print.

Mirel, Barbara. *Interaction Design for Complex Problem Solving: Developing Useful and Usable Software.* San Francisco: Morgan Kaufmann, 2004. Print.

Schön, Donald A. *The Reflective Practitioner.* New York: Basic Books, 1982. Print.

St. Amant, Kirk. "Thinking Globally, Teaching Locally: Understanding the Nature of Technical Communication in an Age of Globalization." *Teaching Intercultural Rhetoric and Technical Communication: Theories, Curriculum, Pedagogies, and Practices.* Eds. Barry Thatcher and Kirk St. Amant. Amityville: Baywood Publishing Company, 2011. 1–14. Print.

Thrush, Emily A. "Multi-Cultural Issues in Technical Communication." *Teaching Technical Communication: Critical Issues for the Classroom.* Ed. James M. Dubinsky. Boston: Bedford/St. Martin's, 2004. 414–427. Print.

Framing the Personal Narrative
Composition and Documentary Film

Jodie Childers

Supplemental Materials

- Rationale
- Pre-Writing Activities
- Student Writing Sample

Writing Assignment

    For this assignment, you will write either a cinematic memoir or a series of vignettes that reflect on a series of personal photographs. As you move through the writing process, you will be expected to think like a filmmaker and a photographer, engaging with the aesthetic strategies and vocabularies that both use as you create a compelling and consciously crafted final essay. You must complete all of the pre-writing exercises as they will help you think visually about your own project, but you are only expected to choose one of the options for your final paper. Feel free to include any of the pre-writing work in your final draft.

    For both options, you will write about your own life from the first person perspective. Option #1 asks you to think like a filmmaker as you construct a narrative sequence with a plot and an internal or external conflict. For Option #2, you will compose your story in and through snapshots, like a photographer, describing the physical composition of each image and reflecting on its emotional core.

As you work toward your final draft, you will be expected to complete all of the pre-writing activities (noted below) as well as a rough draft before the submission of your final paper.

- Pre-Writing Exercise 1: Storyboarding a Memory
- Pre-Writing Exercise 2: Outside the Frame
- Pre-Writing Exercise 3: Establishing Paragraph
- Pre-Writing Exercise 4: Photographic Memories
- Pre-Writing Exercise 5: Zoom In, Zoom Out
- Draft
- Final Paper

Option #1

For this assignment, you will become the director of your own life story as you create a narrative that employs the techniques of a filmmaker to construct an essay that comes alive in the reader's mind like a film. Filmmaking involves the manipulation of externals in a sensory experience that appeals to the eye and the ear simultaneously. When we think cinematically, we consider how visuals and sound work together to create narrative over a time sequence.

Before you begin, it is important to think about what makes a strong film. List your favorite movies. What about these movies engages you as a viewer? Be specific.

Now brainstorm a list of stories from your life that have a beginning, middle, and end. Which of the stories are the most visual? Also, remember that the story must have a conflict, whether external or internal. While internal struggles can make powerful films, it is important for you to think about how you would convey that internal struggle visually. For instance, would you use voice-over narration to explore the inner transformation of the narrator?

Now, take that story and think like a director. What is the setting? Who are the main characters? What is the central conflict? Brainstorm a shot list and possible dialogue. The final step is to turn the narrative into prose. See below for the shot list and the example of the opening paragraph of a cinematic memoir.

EXAMPLE: THE GREAT LEAP SHOT LIST

Shot Style	*Subject*	*Rationale*
Establishing shot	sky, river, train bridge	to establish the setting (time and place) and set up the context
Wide shot	the narrator and Brian on the bridge	to place the main characters in relation to the setting

Shot Style	Subject	Rationale
Medium shot	the narrator and Brian	to establish the relationship between the main characters
Close shot	bottle of whisky	to suggest risk, danger
Pan across	to power plants	to create ambience
Pan down	from sky to river	to capture the magnitude
Close shot	narrator's face	to convey fear and anticipation

It was after midnight. The sky and the river seemed to be made of the same substance: darkness. Brian and I stumbled along the train bridge, the whisky from the bottle we passed back and forth mostly spilling on the train tracks. The only light came from the power plant across the river. Tonight we were going to jump from the darkness above into the darkness below. We weren't suicidal. We just wanted to take a swim under the synthetic stars.

Create your shot list before you begin writing, and be sure to include a rationale or justification for each shot. You must ask yourself why it would be best to use a close shot, a medium shot, or a wide shot at any given moment in the story. Explain. Then as you write, attempt to recreate the movie in the mind of the writer. Notice how the above writer uses descriptive language that places the reader into a spatiotemporal scene. Like this writer, try your best to avoid telling us what is happening. Imagine the story as a montage: a sequence of shots that relate to each other to create a visual narrative. Remember to appeal to the reader's ear as well as the eye. You may even want to add a sound sequence to your chart so that you can capture not only the visual content but the auditory experience of the moment as well.

Option #2

In his essay "Understanding a Photograph," John Berger states that a photograph "bears witness" to the photographer's choice to preserve a moment in time (292). He differentiates between the distinctive temporalities of film and photography: "A movie director can manipulate time [...] not so the still photographer. The only decision he can take is as regards the moment he chooses to isolate. Yet this apparent limitation gives the photograph its unique power" (293). Although a photograph can capture only one moment in time, what is outside the frame is just as important as what is within it. According to Berger, "what is shown invokes what is not shown" (293). For this essay, you will write three to five short, poetic vignettes on a series of personal photographs, describing what is revealed and what is concealed.

First, choose a set of photographs from your life (these can be of you, your family members, or of places), and reflect on them, describing the moment that was captured and what was left out of the story. As you select your pictures, think about how you will use them to establish a tone. Choosing pictures of perfect, happy moments can create a superficial essay. Instead, look for pictures where there is something hidden underneath the surface, a smile that hides fear, sadness, or anger. As you choose your photographs and think about them, consider the words of Anne Lamott: "We write to expose the unexposed. If there is one door in the castle you have been told not to go through, you must. The writer's job is to turn the unspeakable into words—not just into any words, but if we can, into rhythm and blues" (198).

Like Sherman Alexie's piece "An Indian Education," organize your paper in lyrical moments and anecdotes rather than in a traditional essay form. Like his essay, which is organized around grades in school, there must be an organizational structure that you consciously choose for this piece. Whether connected chronologically or thematically, the pictures must be linked in some way, and your introductory paragraph should place us into the affective space of the essay and set the tone. For instance, a former student arranged her pictures around seasons; another arranged hers around family traditions, rituals, and celebrations, contrasting personal, emotional moments with the larger social relationships in the family. Feel free to be creative! Be sure to scan the photographs into the final body of the paper.

EXAMPLE: PHOTOGRAPH #1—CHILD BLOWING OUT CANDLES

It was my seventh birthday, the year of yellow, my favorite color. I remember yellow cake, yellow dress, the yellow bus I took to school every day. Then there were the bruises, the ones that turned from black and blue to brown and yellow, slowly healing. Why didn't my mother ask me about them when she tucked me in at night? Why didn't my teacher notice them when I helped her clean the chalkboards every day after class? Why didn't I speak up? I was too scared to tell anyone what happened every day on the bus.

Notice how the writer doesn't focus primarily on the picture, but instead uses it as an entry point into a reflection about her experience of being bullied in 2nd grade. Also notice that the writer provides both an exterior and interior description of the picture—it is not simply a physical description of the image but a thoughtful, poetic vignette that gets at the emotional core of the memory.

Rationale

In her address, "Composition in a New Key," Kathleen Yancey argues for the creation of a "new curriculum for the 21st century" and "a new vocabulary, a new set of practices" (308). The emphasis on inventing a language to understand, describe, and assess the composition of our time has been a recurring theme in her work, and she foregrounds this in another article,

"Looking for Sources of Coherence in a Fragmented World": "If we are to value this new composition—text that is created on the screen and that in 'finished' form is also mediated by the screen—we will need to invent a language that allows us to speak to these new values. Without a new language, we will be held hostage to the values informing print, values worth preserving for that medium, to be sure, but values incongruent with those informing the digital" (90).

While it is imperative to formulate a new language for what we are doing in the classroom and to articulate the terms of the discipline accurately, it can also be valuable to pull from the lexicons of other fields to construct a polyglot vocabulary that can inform the ways we talk not only about writing for new media but also about the traditional writing process. Framing the Personal Narrative is an assignment I designed to encourage students to think about the writing process from the outside in as they take on perspectives from film and photography.

Many scholars like Yancey and Jody Shipka have revised our conceptions of the text and of the traditional academic essay, opening up the composition classroom to include a variety of genres and multimodal texts. This has also led to a fascinating cross-pollination between fields. Borrowing vocabularies from these other disciplines and creative practices is a helpful way to get students to see the writing process from multiple perspectives and to understand language as one form of communication among many mediums of meaning making. As a documentary filmmaker and photographer, I have found it especially helpful to use analogies from my own creative practice to address the abstract ideas about writing that are often difficult to explain without concrete examples.

This practice began organically as I started unintentionally peppering metaphors from my own experience into classroom conversations. I often found myself asking students to think about establishing shots as they were writing about places or to consider zooming in and zooming out on objects or people as they wrote descriptive pieces. These suggestions worked, often producing better results than the standard comments I had repeated for years such as "add sensory details" or "use vivid language." Elizabeth Daley argues that "the multimedia language of the screen has become the current vernacular" (33). She points out that "metaphors from the screen have become common in every aspect of conversation" (34). While Daley is more interested in arguing for what she calls a "literacy of the screen," her ideas can be applied to how we can reimagine and reinvigorate the writing process from the perspective of other disciplines and discourses. Pulling from this "language of the screen" that many students are already fluent in serves a dual purpose, to both familiarize and defamiliarize the writing process.

Because 21st century students are inundated with visual media, many come into the classroom with perceptive eyes, and even those who are not yet adept at critically thinking about the media they take in understand the power of the image, oftentimes more so than the power of the word. Their eyes have been trained to comprehend the semiotics of film and television and to read sequences by filling in visual gaps, and, most importantly, they have opinions about what does or does not work in a movie, an advertisement, or a photograph. This assignment encourages students to hone that perceptive and confident eye and to also turn it inward as they imagine themselves as the directors of their own writing tasks, looking at their memories from new perspectives, vantage points, and angles.

As they work towards their final projects, students perform close readings of photographs and fiction and non-fiction film sequences to become "directors" of their own writing tasks and to appreciate the writing process as both an intuitive mode of communication and a series of consciously constructed choices. Using John Berger's essay, "Understanding a Photograph," the students discuss time, space, and composition in photography and read a single snapshot closely to examine presence and absence: what is both in and outside of the frame. They also engage in a series of informal writing prompts that emphasize perspective—they "zoom in" and "zoom out" on objects and spaces and describe what they see; they analyze foreground and background in photographs, and they think about visual transitions like hard cuts, dissolves, and fades.

As they work through these pre-writing exercises, students analyze how images work to create meaning, and they practice writing their own pieces informed by film and photography. Storyboarding provides an effective way to get students to think about writing as invention in a tactile and creative way as they map out stories and sequences visually. We also closely read cinematography to discuss how shots, like words, communicate on multiple levels while editing is particularly valuable when discussing transitions in writing. To build these connections, I ask students to write a descriptive piece that provides a close shot and a wide shot of a particular location. I also ask them to pan around a place and describe it—this helps students think about the way in which the writer, like the cinematographer, controls what the audience sees. If the cinematographer zooms in on a teacup on a shelf, we know that this teacup may be important in the future. I encourage students to do the same thing—to use their description strategically to push narrative forward, not simply to cloak their prose in dense description without purpose.

Photography is also a helpful tool to get students to think about how we make choices as writers. A photographer captures a moment in time and space and preserves it because she finds it valuable or meaningful in some way. Yet a photograph has limits and boundaries—only so much can be captured in a single still shot. Much is left out. I ask students to think about their lives as a series of snapshots, to think about both the literal pictures that the family has captured but also the mental snapshots they have preserved in their memories. Then, I encourage them to dig deeper into the real and the imagined pictures, to analyze what is inside and what is outside the frame, what is revealed and what is concealed. This need not be a dark family secret, but it can be. It can simply be the hidden fears that the camera cannot capture, the thoughts and feelings during the picture or the moments in time preceding or following the snapshot. One student, for instance, wrote about her secret feelings of jealousy directed towards her sister during a seemingly ordinary birthday photograph; another student, whose excerpt is included below, wrote about the tensions between her personal, private thoughts and her family's social universe during important rituals and celebrations. The final draft gives students the opportunity to apply these visual techniques in their own writing as they create traditional or multimodal projects that include text, images, and, in some cases, video. Since film and photography emphasize perspective taking, this assignment is also especially effective in a diverse environment because it encourages both the writer and the audience to think about grounding, perspective, and positionality.

Borrowing from other aesthetic practices provides a way to break open the writing process for our students and for ourselves, providing us with new lexicons to talk about both the intuitive aspects and the academic conventions of writing. As the field of rhetoric and composition pedagogy broadens our conceptions of textuality, it makes sense for instructors to also import the metaphors and vocabularies from other practices of meaning making into the composition classroom. Yet one of the challenges I've encountered is addressing gaps; sometimes, there is simply not an accurate metaphor from film or photography to correspond with a particular issue in writing. This is why I also focus on the limitations of mediums, asking them to reflect upon what they can and cannot do with language, film, and photography. What I am most interested in is not a direct match between writing and cinematography, for instance, but instead, a means to get students to think about their writing from a different angle and to ultimately get excited about the prospect of using language to make something meaningful.

In *The Making of Meaning: Metaphors, Models, and Maxims for Writing Teachers*, Ann E. Berthoff states, "I believe we can best teach the composing process by conceiving of it as a continuum of making meaning, by seeing writing as analogous to all those processes by which we make sense of the world" (69). By having students think about writing the memories and moments of their lives as snapshots and film sequences, I hope to facilitate a writing process that encourages them to "make sense" of their own lives: to get them to see their writing and their lives from the outside in, rather than from the inside out, and to create lively and dynamic prose, while understanding more fully the strengths and limitations of the word and the image. As one student noted, when discussing the relationship between writing and photography, "Art (literature & photography) connects human beings to each other in that it allows us to share each other's perceptions, emotions, and experiences. Each of the two mediums has limitations. In photography we can see things but with writing we can actually feel what someone was feeling because their emotions were conveyed in writing."

Pre-Writing Exercises

Pre-Writing Exercise 1: Storyboarding a Memory

Storyboards are used in filmmaking to visually map out a sequence. For this exercise, you will create a short storyboard of between five to ten frames for a particular narrative in your own life. You do not need to be an expert in film or a great artist to storyboard a scene. Instead, proceed intuitively, thinking about ways to use the visual nature of the medium to tell a story and convey emotion.

- Choose a short and compelling narrative from your own life. There should be a beginning, middle, and end to the narrative, though it doesn't have to wrap up perfectly.
- Now you can begin drawing. On the paper provided, fill in the boxes with sketches that flesh out the most significant moments in the narrative. You do not have to draw perfectly. Instead, you are simply looking to convey visually the key scenes of your narrative.
- Now transcribe the storyboard into text, writing the narrative from beginning to end in one or two paragraphs.
- Questions: Which was more effective at capturing your narrative: the storyboard or the written account? Why? Which medium is more natural for you: the visual or the written? Did you encounter any limitations as you drew your story or as you wrote it? Explain.

Pre-Writing Exercise 2: Outside the Frame

- In "Understanding a Photograph," John Berger argues that a photograph "bears witness to human choice." What do you think he means by this?
- He also states that what is significant about a photograph is not only what is recorded, but what is not contained within the frame. How do you interpret this statement?

- Choose one of the photographs from the course blog and discuss the choices the artist has made. What is included? What is left out? Based on this, how do you interpret the photograph's meaning? Now choose one of your own photographs, and analyze what is revealed and what is concealed.

Pre-Writing Exercise 3: Establishing Paragraph

In many films, physical space and time are communicated to the viewer through establishing shots that convey the setting and its context in relation to the narrative. For this piece, you will write an establishing paragraph that puts the reader in a particular setting from your memory.

- Watch the short clips from the movies posted on the blog. Describe how each establishes the space and time and how the setting sets the context for the narrative of the film.
- Now write a paragraph that functions in the same way, establishing both the space and time. Think not only in terms of year, but also about time of day, season, etc. Be sure to appeal to both the eye and the ear of the audience. Oftentimes, a setting makes itself visible through sound, for instance, a rooster crowing at dawn.

Pre-Writing Exercise 4: Photographic Memories

- What are the most iconic photographs from your childhood? List three or four of these photographs and describe each one in three to four sentences. Try to be as accurate as possible.
- Now think back in your memory, and create a list of particularly vivid memories that are like snapshots in your mind.
- Question: Which was easier to write, the description of the real photograph or the mental snapshot? Why?

Pre-Writing Exercise 5: Zoom In, Zoom Out

For this activity, you will play with perspective, examining an object, person, or place from various positions. Imagine that you are a photographer with a zoom lens. You will be creating two descriptions from two vantage points: a close shot, zooming in on the subject and a wide shot, zooming out. The close shot description will capture the fine details of your subject, whereas the wide shot description will place the subject in the setting.

- Zoom In: Description #1

Zoom in on the subject of your choice and describe it in minute detail. Feel free to add your own imaginative spin or to even editorialize on the act of describing. Think, for instance, of Margaret Atwood's poem "Cell."

- Zoom Out: Description #2

Now zoom out and describe the scene that surrounds your subject. You can make your "shot" as wide as you'd like. You may even want to try to write from an aerial perspective or to create a panorama of your surroundings.

Student Writing Sample

In this excerpt from a longer essay, the student writer describes and reflects upon two pictures that capture moments from her life. The first is a picture of the student and her brother in front of a mandir, and the second is a picture of the student with her family at a wedding. Both vignettes explore the divide between her social self and her private self.

Sunday Morning Prayers

Early morning before sunrise, my uncle convinced us to accompany him to gather flowers from the surrounding neighbors. He was working with the government and only came home on the weekends. It was his usual routine, and he wanted us to spend time together. I still remember how grumpy and tired I was until I took a nap that day. We went to the neighbors nearby, but ended up going to three streets in the village because my uncle wanted a variety of flowers for prayers.

When we returned home, my uncle told me to gather some flowers from our flower garden. At this time, the sun had risen, but it was still dim. I proceeded to a hibiscus plant. Brightly colored red petals stood out from the plant gaining my attention. Therefore, I rushed over; when I stretched out my hand to break the flower from the stem I was inattentive of the two beady eyes that were staring at me from below the other stem. I heard a hiss. When I looked, it stuck its tongue out.

"Snake!" I yelled.

I ran frantically from the plant towards my uncle. As my uncle walked next to the plant, the snake, which was a beautiful lime green, fell on the ground, and slithered away. I was very terrified. That snake could have bitten me, I thought to myself. After that incident, we continued gathering the remaining flowers and decorating the mandir. As we performed worship, I could not stop thinking about the snake and where it wandered to.

A Family Affair

It was a time for celebration. Our cousin, the eldest amongst the girls, was getting married. The first night of our visit brought laughter, dance, and excitement. The majority of my extended family was present. Rarely did we have such an opportunity. My grandmother[,] seated in the brown chair at the far back[,] was very happy to have her grandchildren and great grandchildren all together. The father of the bride[,] along with some other men[,] was in the backyard cooking various foods. At the back of the house, the sapodilla trees were blossoming. The pungent smell of the flowers filled the atmosphere. It was truly a magical night.

The next day, my brother and father went home to care for our pets while my mother and I stayed behind to help with the preparations. We had a few pets, and among them was a pet goat named Ramoo. He was black and white with solid brown horns. He was old, but always managed to chase me from his pen. When they came back, my dad told me that Ramoo had died. I was devastated. I went in the bathroom and closed the door. My pets were a part of my family and I loved them dearly. After a while, I opened the door, tried to recollect my thoughts, and continued to take part in the celebration.

Works Cited

Berger, John. "Understanding a Photograph." *Classic Essays on Photography*. Ed. Alan Trachtenberg. New Haven: Leete's Island Books, 1980. 291–294. Print.

Berthoff, Ann E. *The Making of Meaning: Metaphors, Models, and Maxims for Writing Teachers*. Montclair, NJ: Boynton/Cook, 1981. Print.

Daley, Elizabeth. "Expanding the Concept of Literacy." *Educause Review* 38.2 (2003): 33–40. Web. 1 August 2014.

Lamott, Anne. *Bird by Bird: Some Instructions on Writing and Life*. New York: Anchor, 1995. Print.

Shipka, Jody. *Toward a Composition Made Whole*. Pittsburgh: University of Pittsburgh Press, 2011. Print.

Yancey, Kathleen Blake. "Looking for Sources of Coherence in a Fragmented World: Notes toward a New Assessment Design." *Computers and Composition* 21.1 (2004): 89–102. Web.

_____. "Made Not Only in Words: Composition in a New Key." *College Composition and Communication* 56.2 (2004): 297–328. *JSTOR*. Web. 01 Aug. 2014.

Blogging Advanced Composition

Elisa Cogbill-Seiders,
Ed Nagelhout *and* Denise Tillery

Supplemental Materials

- Rationale
- Scaffolding Activities
- Sample Evaluation Sheet

Writing Assignment

Our writing assignment is a semester-long project, linked to our six course objectives:

• Writing, developing, revising, and editing multiple drafts of a text.

• Distinguishing, understanding, and producing different genres for particular readers in specific rhetorical situations.

• Practicing and refining rhetorical strategies for constructing texts.

• Giving and receiving thoughtful feedback on higher- and lower-order concerns.

• Performing effective research and incorporating source materials seamlessly into a text.

• Recognizing and employing emerging technologies for communication.

Assignment Materials

Since we conceive of all courses as works in progress, the numbered materials listed in this section are the most recent iterations from our Course Management System: typically, as shared resources, we expect each instructor to revise, edit, and update them prior to the start of the semester.

(1) The Set-Up

ACTIVITY 1—PLATFORM

There are many different blogging platforms on the Internet. They vary according to usability, purpose, and cost. Take a few moments to reflect on what you plan to do with your blog. Then look through each of the linked platforms to decide which best suits your needs. When you're done, write a short reflection of each blogging platform. Describe how you think it would or wouldn't help you design and maintain your blog. What are the advantages and limitations of each one? Post your reflection to the "Activity 1—Platform" discussion board and explain which platform you plan on using.

- Blogger—www.blogger.com
- Wordpress—www.wordpress.com
- Wix—www.wix.com
- Tumblr—www.tumblr.com
- Edublogs—www.edublogs.org
- Livejournal—www.livejournal.com

Activity 2—Set-Up

Congratulations! You have a blogging platform! Believe it or not, you've taken a major step already. Now we'll work on developing the basic set-up.

For this activity, you will need to decide how you want to present yourself and your blog to your particular community and the wider internet world. Find *three* blogs that write about your topic. What kinds of usernames, titles, and avatars do they utilize? Do they use their real names? Are the titles eye-catching? What kinds of pictures do they use for their avatars? Once you find this information, check the guidelines of your particular blogging platform to develop the following:

- Username
- Blog Title & URL
- Password
- Update Your Profile

- Upload Avatar
- Check Settings
- Blog Theme

Once you have completed these steps, you must post two things to the "Activity 2—Set Up" discussion board: (1) Links to the three blogs you researched and (2) Your username, title, avatar, and theme along with explanations detailing why you chose them.

Activity 3—Pages

In this activity, you will learn how to create "Home," "About," and "Contact Me" pages. The difference between a *blog post* and *blog page* is that pages are static rather than dynamic. Check the three blogs you researched for Activity 2. If you click on the "Home" link, it takes you to the main page. The "Home" link is an example of a *page* because, no matter how many times you click on it, it will always take you to the main page of your website. Having clear and organized pages improves the readability of your blog, but it also gives you an opportunity to address the rhetorical situation, namely how you present yourself to the intended audience of your blog. For this activity, you will need to check the support section of your blogging platform to create Home, About, and Contact Me pages by following these steps:

- *Create a Home page.* Put the link either in the top menu or the sidebar, according to what best suits your needs.
- *Create an About page.* Believe it or not, the About page of a blog usually gets the most internet traffic, so you must consider what to write here very carefully. A good place to start is to think about the purpose of your blog: are you trying to persuade, inform, or evaluate? You will need to optimize what you write in this About section to fit those needs. What do you think your audience needs to know about you? How can you best "sell yourself" to your community of readers? Once you've finished writing the About page, post the button next to your Home page.
- *Create a Contact Me page.* This is how your readers contact you. You can use an e-mail address, though you may wish to avoid using your personal address. If you don't want to include an e-mail address, you can develop a contact form (check your blogging platform support for information on how to make one) to protect your privacy. You should avoid giving out any personal phone numbers.

After you have completed each step, you need to offer a brief reflection on your experience and post it to the "Activity 3—Pages" discussion board along with a link to your blog. What did you do to complete the activity? Did you have any difficulty? How did it help you develop your blogspace more effectively (and/or more efficiently)? What did you learn about your blogging space and your (potential) blogging network?

Activity 4—Connecting—Comments, Tags and Publicizing

Successful blogs participate in the larger community by commenting, tagging, and publicizing their blog posts.

- *Commenting.* Bloggers must leave posts on other relevant blogs and also respond to comments left on their own blogs in a timely fashion. Commenting on other blogs is a way to participate actively in the larger blogging community, and it also draws attention to your own writing. Responding to comments left on your own posts shows your audience you consider their opinions and care about their needs.
- *Tags.* Tags help you organize your blog posts by grouping related posts together. For example, if you've written three posts about dessert recipes, you can add the tag "dessert recipes" to each post. Interested readers may then click on the "dessert recipes" tag, which will then bring up every post you've ever written on the topic. It's a useful way to get your audience to stay on your page; doing so helps develop a consistent readership.
- *Publicizing.* You may publicize your blog in many different ways. You can add a link to your Facebook or Twitter profile. Or you can e-mail your post to friends, who may then forward it to other people. Commenting actively is another (easy) way to publicize your blog—include your blog's web address in your e-mail signature; every time you leave a comment, the blogger and their audience will see the link.

For this assignment, you must include your blog on your e-mail signature and leave comments on the three blogs you researched for Activity 2. Post a link to your comments or upload images of your comment to the "Connecting—Comments, Tags, and Publicizing" discussion board.

Activity 5—Images

Carefully review your class notes regarding copyright and fair use of images in your blog posts before starting this assignment. Now, you can review the image-embedding instructions on your blogging platform's support page. Once you're done, take a look through the following image search engines.

- Wikimedia Commons
- Multicolr Search Lab

- Getty Search Gateway
- Pixabay
- Google Search (hint: you can limit your search results to open source images)

Each of the search engines finds images in different ways. Write a short reflection of each search engine in the "Activity 5—Images" discussion board. Explain how you might utilize each search engine, and for what purpose. Which search engine do you think you will use the most? Share links to pictures you find with each one—that's five links!

Activity 6—Videos

You can embed videos in your blog posts by uploading your own files or sharing links from YouTube. Each platform will have a different procedure for using videos. Check your blogging platform to learn how to embed videos. Once you're done, write and share a post on the "Activity 6—Videos" discussion board explaining how to embed videos on your blog and include three links to different videos you could use.

Activity 7—Widgets and Plugins

A *widget* is a tool you can embed in your blog, like a music player or a weather forecast. Widgets are made by your blogging platform, though you may need to upgrade your membership to utilize some widgets. There are many kinds of widgets compatible with different blogging platforms.

A *plugin* is a code you can add to existing software to increase its functionality. For example, you could install a flash player on your internet browser to watch an animation. Plugins are different from widgets because they change the way your blogging platform works by altering the code, and they are usually made by third-party providers. There are many different kinds of plugins, but usability is determined by your particular blogging platform.

For this activity, you must do a Google search for an article discussing widgets and plugins that work on your blogging platform. Share the links to both articles in the "Activity 7—Widgets and Plugins" discussion board. Next, you must pick two widgets and two plugins. Explain what they do and how you plan on using them. How will they enhance the content of your blog? Although widgets and plugins are not required for this assignment, they are useful tools. If you install either a widget or a plugin, share a link to your blog along with your reflection.

Activity—Publishing

Now you're ready to begin publishing your blog posts! But not yet. Let's begin by checking how to "add a new post" on your blog. Each platform has different guidelines, so you will need to check the support section first.

Now let's review some of the different parts of the typical blog post: title, date published, text, and comments. You might also see tags either at the top of the post or the bottom, depending on your style and theme.

- *Titles.* The title is what your audience will see first, so you must carefully develop one that best appeals to your audience and suits your purpose. Your task is to pique the readers' interest. An attention-grabbing title is important!
- *Date Published.* Every post displays the date (and sometimes the time) you published it. Blogs depend on consistent and reliable publishing to maintain their readership. Make sure to post on a timely basis.
- *Text.* There are many different ways to format the text of your blog, but they're mostly contingent upon the blog theme, your writing style, purpose, context, and audience. But here are a few things you should pay extra careful attention to: shorter paragraphs, using headings, linking, color and font options for text, and embedding images and multimedia.
- *Comments.* As you know by now, comments are an important feature of every blog post (check "Activity 4—Connecting—Comments, Tags, and Publicizing"). Make sure to develop a commenting system that is easy to check and manage.

For this assignment, you will focus on the textual aspect of your blog posts. Revisit the three blogs you found on "Activity 2—Set-Up." Pay special attention to the ways they format their paragraphs: are they short or long? What kinds of headings does the blogger use, if any? Do they use different colors and font styles? In what ways? What kinds of images or multimedia do they use? How many do they use per post? Answer these questions on the "Activity 8—Publishing" discussion board. Next, you will need to find two articles that deal specifically with formatting blog posts. Summarize each post on the same discussion board and report back on what the articles suggest. Make sure you explain how you will implement the techniques into your own blog. You must also discuss how you know the advice is credible.

Activity 9—Community (Audience) Analysis

To write an effective blog, you need to understand who your readers are and why they will want to read your posts. Please respond to the following questions to help you understand your readers more effectively:

- What is your topic area?
- What do you anticipate is the average age of your readers?
- Are they mostly women? men? or an equal mix?
- What is their educational background?
- What is their cultural background?
- What is their level of work experience?
- How much do they already know about the subject at hand?
- What is their primary goal for reading your blog?
- Are they motivated readers?
- What information and skill-sets will they need to understand your posts effectively?

Activity 10—Reflection

Now that you have completed all ten activities, you need to offer a brief reflection on your experience. What did you do to complete the different activities? Did you have difficulties? How did these steps help you develop your blogspace more effectively (and/or more efficiently)? What did you learn about your blogging space and/or your (potential) blogging network?

(2) The Writing Process

Laying the Groundwork

As a way to prepare you for ALL of the writing that you will be doing this semester, we want you to analyze your writing process and your rhetorical situation for your blogs:

Figure 1: The Writing Process

- What is your writing process?
- How much time will you write per week? Per day?
- When will you make the time for planning? For drafting? For revising? For editing?
- When will you make the time to reflect on your writing process?

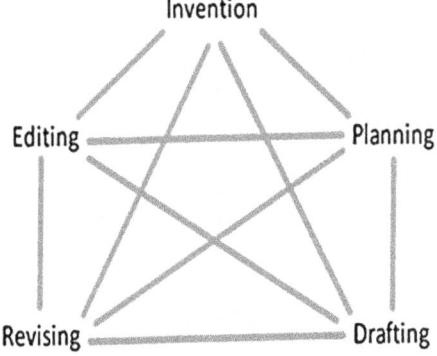

Figure 1. The Writing Process.

Figure 2: Rhetorical Situation

- Why are you writing this blog? What is your theme? What are possible topics?
- Who are you as a writer? Describe your expertise.
- Who are your readers? What do they hope to gain from reading your blog?
- What are the genre constraints? How will you deliver your text? Will you consider multimedia?

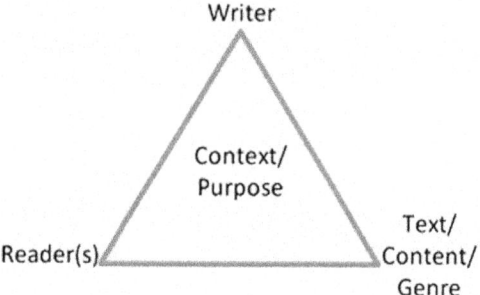

Figure 2. Rhetorical Triangle.

Answer these questions on the "Laying the Groundwork" discussion board. Then respond to at least two of your classmates in some way. We will continue to explore these questions throughout the semester.

Analyzing and Evaluating Other Blog Posts

Find and share an online article or blog post that will provide us with support for developing our skills as writers, such as advice on good writing, good blogging, or other helpful topics for improving writing skills. Or, more importantly for the goals of this course, you might share a piece on developing and/or maintaining a successful blog, such as the following examples:

- "Is Writing Torture?" by Avi Steinberg (www.newyorker.com/online/blogs/books/2013/02/elizabeth-gilbert-versus-philip-roth-is-writing-torture.html).
- "Editing vs. Proofreading: What's Most Important" by Richard Darell (www.bitrebels.com/social/editing-vs-proofreading-whats-most-important-infographic/).
- "How to Create a Blog—A Beginner's Guide" by Eric Griffith (www.pcmag.com/article2/0,2817,2416439,00.asp).

Introduce the article by summarizing the content and explain what you liked or didn't like about it. Talk about how you plan to use the article to help you create your blog.

(3) The Deliverables

The Blog Posts

Each of you must publish at least 8 well-considered blog posts. Each blog post must go through a full drafting process to receive full credit: plan, draft, peer review, revise, instructor response (optional), revise, edit, and submit for evaluation. We can negotiate any other requirements, but, as you can see on the Course Workload section of the Syllabus, you will get credit for posting a first draft and credit for responding to the drafts of your peers. Ideally, all of your blog posts will be connected in some way: by theme, by topic, by issues, etc.

Keep in mind that you will be working on multiple posts at different stages of completion. It's important that you prioritize your work so that you meet all of your deadlines as effectively and as efficiently as possible.

Sample Three-Week Workload (Hybrid Section)

9	In-Class	Plan Blog Post #5 Responding to Organization Peer Review Blog Post #4	
	Online Activity	Blog Post #3 Blog Post #4 Blog Post #5	Responses to Peer Blog Posts #4 Due by Oct 22 Blog Post #5 Draft Due for Peer Review by Oct 25 *Blog Post #3 Due for Evaluation by Oct 25* Blog Post #4 Draft for Teacher Response by Oct 25 (OPTIONAL)
10	In-Class	Plan Blog Post #6 Responding to Claims and Support Peer Review Blog Post #5	
	Online Activity	Blog Post #4 Blog Post #5 Blog Post #6	Responses to Peer Blog Posts #5 Due by Oct 29 Blog Post #6 Draft Due for Peer Review by Nov 1 *Blog Post #4 Due for Evaluation by Nov 1* Blog Post #5 Draft for Teacher Response by Nov 1 (OPTIONAL)
11	In-Class	Plan Blog Post #7 Responding to Lower-Order Concerns Peer Review Blog Post #6	
	Online Activity	Blog Post #5 Blog Post #6 Blog Post #7	Responses to Peer Blog Posts #6 Due by Nov 5 Blog Post #7 Draft Due for Peer Review by Nov 8

| Online Activity | *Blog Post #5 Due for Evaluation by Nov 8*
Blog Post #6 Draft for Teacher Response by Nov 8 (OPTIONAL) |

The Final Reflection

The Final Reflection asks you to analyze the work you performed during the semester and demonstrate how you achieved each course outcome. I expect you to exhibit skills for effective essay writing and *show* how you met each of the course outcomes. To do this, you should refer specifically to the work you did throughout the semester. It is a good idea to organize your essay in terms of the five course outcomes.

- Construct various texts based on audience, purpose, genre, and context.
- Show a complex understanding of the composing process.
- Articulate rhetorical choices.
- Evaluate claims of various arguments and determine their relative merit.
- Argue effectively by marshaling resources, analyzing and synthesizing information, and employing appropriate materials.

Survey all work that you've done throughout the term. Moving outcome by outcome, find evidence to illustrate how effectively you did (or did not) accomplish each of the course outcomes.

Plan your reflection, and then write a thesis-based essay (3–4 s/s pages): open with an introduction that establishes the context for your reflection. After the introduction, define each course outcome in your own words and indicate briefly how the work you have completed reflects achievement for each course outcome (and refer to specific work from the course that you completed). Conclude the essay with any comments about the course in general and what I might do to make the course better in the future.

The Final Reflection should be an example of your *best* writing.

Rationale

Our students are writing on social media platforms more than ever, which means the promotion of rhetorical and informational literacies in our composition pedagogies is increasingly important (Yancey, "Made Not Only in Words" 320). Advanced Composition at UNLV is a 400-level course that builds upon our students' existing digital literacies by making blogging the centerpiece of the course. We wanted this course to extend beyond traditional research-based essays, which too often are written in isolation or for an audience of one. By having students build and maintain their own blogs, we push them to understand audience and purpose in more complex ways. They define a community of interested readers through digital media, join conversations with an engaged community of writers, and participate purposefully on topics important to that community. For these reasons, despite serving mostly English education and English majors, our course is easily adaptable to a wide range of majors. The assignment described in this essay is the only "assignment" for the semester, achieving all course objectives (described below). As we are committed to digital literacy, we teach this course in a hybrid format and make all materials available digitally to students online from the beginning of the semester.

Computers and the Internet have influenced the way we produce, access, and store information, but we must also consider the ways they have changed how we read and write. Before the early 1990s, reading and composition were often solitary activities in the academic world. Students also depended heavily on the opinions of their professors, who were at the top of the information hierarchy. Even today many English literature courses still use the following model: the essay is the primary genre, and its composing process is often viewed as an individual one. But this model is increasingly divorced from our students' own personal experiences of textual production and reception (Clark 28). Our students have never known a time before Facebook, smartphones, or the Internet (Buck 10). They use social media sites regularly, send text messages, and spend several hours a day reading—on websites and mobile devices. Similarly, every post they make to Facebook or Twitter or Tumblr is read by multiple audiences. They are virtually *never* alone in their writing or reading lives, thanks to the ubiquity of networked devices.

As a result, we emphasize digital literacies and a student-centered pedagogy to prepare students for writing beyond the university. Writing assignments in college composition courses need to engage the multiple literacies of the contemporary college student; more importantly, students need to understand writing as part of active communities of discourse.

Blogs (a shortened version of "web log") emerged in the late 1990s when new programs such as Blogger, LiveJournal, and many others made it easier for people with little or no knowledge of HTML to write on the Internet (Garden 485). These tools democratized the Internet by opening it up to the general public. Eventually, the form developed into the multimedia structures we know today, combining links, images, audio, and text in myriad ways.

For our purposes, what differentiates a blog from other types of websites is the comment system and methods for archiving information. The comment system gives readers and writers an opportunity to engage. Employing a comment system diminishes the degrees of separation between author and audience, thereby opening a channel for communication, for creating community, that was previously difficult or impossible. A blog also archives entries using folksonomy, making older material readily available and searchable to the casual reader (Alexander 34). These factors force bloggers to consider the rhetorical situation of their posts in more complex ways, especially as issues of audience and genre. Students in our class are more conscious of their choices for writing and easily move beyond an "audience of one" so prevalent in teacher-centered classrooms.

The topic possibilities for blogs are infinite, growing and developing in response to the needs and interests of a discourse community: each a concrete example where a community and a discourse are shaped together. Many blogs are personal; therefore, it's possible to find a blog on almost any topic, but the key is engagement, connection with a larger group of thinkers. For example, historian Dr. Felicity Henderson at the University of Exeter maintains a blog written for specialists and non-specialists alike. *Robert Hooke's London* (hookeslondon.com/) catalogs Robert Hooke's involvement in the early Royal Society. Readers can access the blog for free, and it serves as an important way for individuals, groups, and professional associations to communicate, regardless of social conventions like race, gender, or social status.

Scaffolding Activities

In spite of their familiarity with digital writing, our students still have some misconceptions about the composing aspect of blogging. Many students are accustomed to approaching digital writing with an informal attitude and believe that bloggers just throw up some text and click "Publish" without drafting or revising. Our scaffolding activities are meant to force students to attend carefully to each step of the writing process, from invention through final proofreading. We share professional blogs with students and reinforce the lesson that the most popular, successful blogs are products of careful writers who attend to the needs of their readers and spend time and effort on crafting and revising readable, enjoyable entries.

The Set-Up activities we describe remind students that composing in a digital environment begins with the choice of tools. The ten activities guide students through the basics of blog formation. Our early versions of the course linked directly to Sue Waters' Edublog Teacher Challenges: Personal Blogging (teacherchallenge.edublogs.org/personal-blogging/). We revised her outline to better meet our needs. *The Set-Up* focuses primarily on the technical requirements for setting up an active blog site and for incorporating features that will make the blog more effective. The focus is always on how those tools and affordances play a role in meeting the reader's needs. The final two activities prepare students for determining a focus for the blog, connecting to other blogs, joining a broader discourse community, understanding the requirements for crafting a considered blog post, and reflecting on what these activities mean to them as developing writers. As a way to create our own classroom community, each of the activities requires students to share their experiences and the rhetorical choices they made in setting up their blog on a class discussion board.

The Writing Process asks students to interrogate and articulate their own writing processes. Their findings are the basis for small-group and whole-class discussions about the rhetorical nature of writing, and their own strategies for crafting and delivering successful writing. Then, students are asked to find, identify, and evaluate writing advice posted on the web. They share their findings, and the class participates in far-ranging discussions about good advice, bad advice, and how to incorporate strategies into their own writing processes. Next, students are asked to research the discourse communities they will be joining with their blogs. They find, analyze, and summarize content on published blogs relevant to their topic area. They follow a typical literature review strategy by mapping the current topics under discussion in the community, the most prominent and/or effective voices, the positions that writers are taking on these topics, the variety of styles writers use in arguing the topics, and the nature of the conversations among various groups of writers. Finally, they explain how they plan to join the conversations occurring in a specific, yet larger community.

The Deliverables require students to write and maintain their blogs through a process-driven approach. Students complete and post a first draft of their blog entry to a discussion board for peer review. Using a student- and instructor-negotiated rubric, they respond to each other both in writing and face-to-face. After revising, students may submit a revised draft for instructor response. Finally, students are expected to complete final revisions and edits on a third draft before submitting for evaluation. Students create eight total blog posts over the last half of the semester following this process, which means they are working on multiple posts at different stages of the process at the same time. Students must plan their time effectively and prioritize their workload to be successful.

The last deliverable is a *Final Reflection*, which asks students to describe their learning experience in the course, the ways that they did (or did not) meet the course objectives, and revisions that would make the course more effective in the future.

By building all these activities into our course, we offer students opportunities to develop traditional rhetorical skills, while also improving their digital and visual acuity in a connected and multimedia writing environment.

Sample Evaluation Sheet
(Negotiated with Students)

Score / Criteria		Excellent 5	Good 4	Average 3	Fair 2	Poor 1	SCORE
Content	Thesis/ Main Idea	\multicolumn{6}{l}{Does the post have a clear and specific thesis central to the argument? Does the post stick to a single topic? Are the connections to the blog's themes and main arguments clear for the readers?}	
	Development	\multicolumn{6}{l}{Is the post clearly organized? Does the post develop the thesis or main idea with clear major points? Does the post make an effort to link rather than stack ideas, and do most links support the overall premise?}	
		\multicolumn{6}{l}{Does the post seem complete, with a logical conclusion? Is the topic appropriate for the length of the entry? Does the narrative have a clear beginning and ending?}	
Audience/ Community	Audience Awareness	\multicolumn{6}{l}{Does the post reach the intended community of readers with appropriate content, links, and style? Does the post include appropriate links and direct readers to appropriate content that can further their interest in the topic?}	
	Citations	\multicolumn{6}{l}{Do the links/sources support the overall premise? Does the post include appropriate external evidence to support the primary argument? Does the post acknowledge and cite sources appropriately and make use of copyright permissions?}	
Visual Appeal	Visual Design	\multicolumn{6}{l}{Does the content accurately fit in with the blog's overall design? Is the post visually appealing? Is the post readable? Are paragraph breaks used effectively and appropriately?}	
	Graphics and Multimedia	\multicolumn{6}{l}{Does the post use high quality graphics and/or multimedia to enhance and support the content? Does the post always acknowledge sources with a caption?}	
Style/ Language	Style and Language Use	\multicolumn{6}{l}{Does the writer have a strong individual voice, using straightforward language?}	

Score / Criteria	Excellent 5	Good 4	Average 3	Fair 2	Poor 1	SCORE
Revising and Editing			Does the language and style accurately capture the rhetorical situation? Does the writer use sophisticated sentences for variety and emphasis? Do the word choices accurately reflect the language of the discourse community? Has the final post been revised effectively? Does the writer demonstrate a good grasp of grammar and usage conventions? Has the writer edited the post closely?			
					TOTAL	

Works Cited

Alexander, Bryan. "Web 2.0: A New Wave of Innovation for Teaching and Learning?" *Educause Review* 41.2 (2006): 33–44. Print.

Buck, Amber. "Examining Digital Literacy Practices on Social Network Sites." *Research in the Teaching of English* 47 (2012): 9–38. Print.

Clark, J. Elizabeth. "The Digital Imperative: Making the Case for a 21st-Century Pedagogy." *Computers and Composition* 27 (2010): 27–35. Print.

Garden, Mary. "Defining Blog: A Fool's Errand or a Necessary Undertaking." *Journalism* 13.4 (2012): 483–499. Print.

Griffith, Eric. "How to Create a Blog—A Beginner's Guide." *PC Magazine*. 12 March 2013. Web. 27 August 2014. www.pcmag.com/article2/0,2817,2416439,00.asp.

Heap, Tania, and Shailey Minocha. "An Empirically Grounded Framework to Guiding Blogging for Digital Scholarship." *Research in Learning Technology* 20 (2012): 176–188. Print.

Henderson, Felicity. *Robert Hooke's London*. Web. 27 August 2014. hookeslondon.com/.

Steinberg, Avi. "Is Writing Torture?" *The New Yorker*. 8 February 2013. Web. 27 August 2014. www.newyorker.com/books/page-turner/is-writing-torture.

Waters, Sue. "Personal Blogging." *Edublog Teacher Challenges*. Web. 27 August 2014. teacherchallenge.edublogs.org/personal-blogging/.

Yancey, Kathleen Blake. "Made Not Only in Words: Composition in a New Key." *College Composition and Communication* 56.2 (2004): 297–328. Print.

———. "Writing in the 21st Century." Rep. National Council of the Teachers of English, Feb 2009. Web. 27 August 2015. www.ncte.org/library/nctefiles/press/yancey_final.pdf.

Proposal Writing in Technical Communications

BARBARA J. D'ANGELO

Supplemental Materials

- Rationale
- Challenges
- Student Writing Sample

Proposal Writing Assignment

Congratulations! You have been hired as a staff proposal writer for BJD Proposal Preparation, Inc. BJD Proposal Prep recruits and works with clients to help them obtain grant funding. During your probation period over the next 15 weeks, you will complete a comprehensive and persuasive funding proposal. To orient you to the world of proposal writing, you will complete a series of tasks that will be reviewed and evaluated. You will identify a client, identify an appropriate funding source and analyze its requirements, complete research necessary to support the request for funding, and compose the proposal based on the requirements of the funding agency. As part of this process, you will collaborate with other staff proposal writers to share drafts and provide feedback.

Course note: The scenario requires you to role-play, and you will turn in your completed proposal as an assignment. However, if you choose to also work with an organization to actually submit the proposal you complete, please indicate that when you submit the selection email assignment.

Selection Email

During this course, you will complete a funding proposal for an organization of your choice. Before you begin working on more in-depth research, your selection must be approved.

You should choose an organization in which you have interest. If you are a volunteer, for example, you might consider whether that organization is in need of funding. Or perhaps there is a school, educational support organization, or other non-profit that you would like to work with.

Submission: Send your email to me. In your email, identify the organization on whose behalf you will compose a proposal and explain thoroughly but concisely why you have selected it.

Survey of the Organization

Proposal writing takes a significant amount of research. Successful proposals require an understanding of the organization for which you're writing and of the funding agency that the proposal will be submitted to. In addition, it requires an understanding of the problem or need that will be the subject of the proposal/request for funding. There is only one way to gain that knowledge: research. To get started, you will complete the survey of the organization worksheet to learn about the organization you've selected.

Submission: Respond to *all* of the questions in the Survey of the Organization Worksheet on page 27 of the text. These questions will guide your research so that you have a complete understanding of your organization. You will use this information for your organization analysis in your upcoming report.

Organization/Funder Identification/Analysis

In this assignment, you will compose a short report in memo format to:

- identify and analyze the organization on whose behalf you will compose a proposal.
- identify and analyze the funder.

In the introduction to your report, describe the research methods you used to find information on both the organization and funding agency.

In section one, your first task is to identify and analyze the organization (your client). At a minimum, this section should:

- identify the name and location of the organization.
- use the information from your Survey of the Organization worksheet

to analyze the organization: *summarize* what you found in narrative format.

- briefly describe the potential need for funding that will be the basis of your proposal. At this point, it does not need to be formulated into a problem statement; however, after researching the organization, you should have an idea about what it is the proposal will request funding for.
- place the funding need in the context of the organization's goals and mission using your analysis. In other words, *analyze* information to make it clear that the funding need has context and purpose based on the organization's mission/vision.

In section two, you should identify and analyze the funder. Identifying a source of funding can be one of the most time-consuming aspects of proposal writing. There are many resources available online to help you locate funding, your textbook lists several in Appendix B, and I have included a list in Blackboard. In addition, the organization you are writing for may have suggestions based on current or previous grants they have received. You should also consider other sources. Local businesses, for example, will often fund local non-profit organizations but don't advertise their funding opportunities. To find them, you will need to search their websites.

Be sure that you select a funding opportunity that *requires a written narrative*. A funding opportunity that only requires completing a template with check boxes and/or short answers will not meet the requirements of this course. If you're uncertain about whether the opportunity you've found fits the course, check with me in advance before submitting this portion of the assignment. *Also be sure that you have access to the requirements and forms without having to create or register for an account.*

In addition, please do NOT select:

- a funding opportunity from NIH, NSF, Dept. of Education or other government agencies. These grants require significant expertise and require more time than we have in a 7.5 week course.
- an opportunity that requires an initial letter of inquiry.
- a bid or contract.

Problem/Need Worksheet

That problem or need represents what funding will be requested for. To convince a funding agency to award a grant, they need to be persuaded that the problem or need is real. After all, anyone can say they need money to do something that sounds worthwhile. But funding agencies want proof. To provide that proof, you need evidence. To find evidence, you need to do research.

Submission: For this assignment, complete the Worksheet to Develop the Problems/Need Statement (posted on the course site). Keep in mind that, depending on the organization you have selected, some of the questions may not be relevant or you may need to adapt them. Or, you may find information that is relevant but doesn't quite fit the questions—if you do, simply add it at the end.

Draft Problem Statement and Goals and Peer Reviews

DRAFT

Although the funder you have selected may not use this terminology, the problem statement, goals, and objectives are key components of a proposal: they explain exactly what the organization will do with the funding to address the problem or need.

For this assignment, you will draft your problem statement and goals and objectives. You will submit your draft as a generic problem and goals/objectives statement; in a few weeks, you'll adapt it to the format required by the funder you're using.

Your problem statement should be accompanied by sufficient background information that you have gathered through the research you've completed. In other words, you must convince me as the proposal reader that there really is a problem significant enough (for the organization you represent and for its constituents) that I should agree to fund your project/program. Part of being persuasive is to be clear, focused, and specific.

Submit your draft to the course site for peer review.

PEER REVIEWS

In the world of proposal writing, peer review plays a significant role. As you have already learned, collaboration is a key feature of writing a proposal. Part of being collaborative is to give constructive feedback on drafts. As an employee of BJD Proposal Prep, you will work with your fellow proposal writers to review each other's drafts throughout the rest of the course.

Complete 2 peer reviews of your peers' draft problem statement, goals, and objectives using the peer review guide.

Budget Worksheet

Budgets are another component of funding proposals. The budget tells the funder how the money will be spent and whether it will be spent on items that they are willing to fund. As a result, you should read the funder's guidelines carefully to determine what you can and cannot include. Some agencies will not fund salaries, for example. If your budget requests salary information, not only will you not receive that amount but you risk having the funder question your entire proposal.

Budgets are also about ethos—demonstrating that the organization is responsible and professional, that it understands the project/program, that it understands the funder, and that it has taken the time to pay attention to the details.

Submission: Using the sample line item format in the text (p. 97), create a budget for your proposal. If the funding agency requires a different format, you may use that in place of the sample. Use your funder's guidelines to ensure you do not include items that are not allowable.

Draft Budget and Evaluation Plan/Peer Reviews

Budget and Evaluation Plan Draft

Include your budget (revised, if necessary, from feedback) *and* a justification for items listed. Use the format the funding agency requires; however, include a justification even if your funder does not require one.

Complete the 4 steps on pages 88–92 in Coley and Scheinberg for writing an evaluation plan. Then, write a narrative evaluation plan. Complete an evaluation plan even if your funder does not require one.

Post your draft to the course site for peer review.

Peer Reviews

Complete 2 peer reviews of your peers' drafts in your group using the peer review guide.

Full Draft and Peer Reviews

Compose a complete draft of your proposal in the format required by the funder. Use the feedback you've received on previous drafts to revise and pull your proposal together following the guidelines of your selected funding agency.

Post your draft *and* a copy of the funding agency guidelines/criteria to the course site for peer review.

Peer Review

Complete 2 peer reviews of your peers' drafts in your group.

Completed Proposal

Submit your completed proposal in the format required by your funder. If you have questions about what to include (or what may be left out), email me in advance.

Rationale

Proposal Writing is an undergraduate (senior-level) writing course in the Technical Communication (TC) Program at Arizona State University (ASU). The course is designed to help students learn how to research and compose effective funding proposals. The course is an elective for TC program majors; however, due to its pragmatic and real-world nature, it attracts students from a variety of other disciplines, including majors from nursing and health care, engineering, social sciences, and humanities.

As a genre, funding proposals can be one of the most difficult to learn and teach because they require a deep understanding of the rhetorical constructs of audience and purpose as well as flexibility to adapt to the specific conventions imposed by individual funding agencies. Proposals also present challenging research opportunities for students to find content related to the purpose of the proposal and the audience for it.

To address these challenges, the course is process-oriented and uses a role-playing scenario with sequenced assignments to step students through the stages of research and writing. The course also uses an approach to help students understand the intersections of the three communities that are key to effective proposal writing: the organization submitting the proposal, the funding agency, and the broader community to which the organization and funding agency belong. This approach is one that is advocated in the text for the course[1] and effectively aids students to understand and analyze the rhetorical context of proposal writing.

Course Structure

As a process-oriented course, the use of sequenced assignments is pragmatic and helps to reduce the anxiety associated with a complex project. Within the role-playing scenario, students act as employees of a fictitious proposal writing company with me (the instructor) as their supervisor. As a result, they are expected to approach each assignment as a professional and to address me in the same manner they would address their boss at work. Although students are required to submit their final proposals to me as a course assignment, I give them the option to work with the organization (or client) they select to submit the proposal once the course is over. Several students have chosen to do so; a few have been funded. While it is not a requirement of the course, the students who choose to work with an organization to submit their proposal "for real" gain the additional experience of learning the challenges associated with working and coordinating with organizations to pull together a successful proposal.

Selecting and Analyzing an Organization and Funding Agency

This portion of the course is divided into three assignments: a selection email, organization analysis worksheet, and a short report to identify and analyze both the organization and funding agency. The selection email gives students a way to begin thinking about and identifying the organization for which they will compose a proposal. It also gives me an opportunity to provide students with feedback to help them focus and overcome problems.

Next, students complete a survey of the organization worksheet from the course textbook. The worksheet provides guiding questions to help students conduct research on the organization they have selected. This portion of the research process encourages students to go beyond surface research to find additional information about the organization's mission and values, projects it is involved with, how it is organized and funded, etc. This information is critical to proposal writing for three reasons: (1) to understand the organization well enough to establish ethos in the proposal, (2) to identify a problem or need for funding that falls within the organization's mission, (3) to identify the context for the problem within the broader community of which the organization is a part.

Students then select a funding agency. For many, this is the most difficult and time-consuming portion of the course. First, they must select a funding agency that is appropriate for the context of their selected organization. Second, they must select a funding agency for which they have access to application requirements, criteria, and formatting guidelines so that they can compose their proposal to submit as part of the course. This second phase of research, in which students must learn to use grant databases or to identify relevant corporate foundations, is a critical component because it helps students to learn and recognize the importance of matching mission and values between an organization and funding agency. In addition, the time-consuming nature of researching funding agencies is a very real-world lesson for students to learn about being a proposal writer. Lastly, it leads students to learn the importance of recognizing and adhering to genre requirements and that funding agencies also exist within a broader community that influences their goals and mission.

To complete the analysis of their selected organization and funding agency, students submit a short report. This report goes beyond the initial selection email. Here, they bring together their research to summarize what they have found and analyze information in a way that makes it clear why the organization and funder are a good match. Students are urged to dig deeper in their analysis than a simple statement of purpose (for example, that the organization is a pet adoption agency; the funding agency provides funding to facilitate pet adoptions). Instead, they are urged to compare values and mission statements along with other criteria such as geography, community interests, and more so that they more fully establish a link between organization and funder. This analysis leads into the next portion of the course, in which they draft the content for the proposal.

Content Preparation: Drafts and Peer Reviews

Students draft content over the next several weeks and conduct peer reviews. Not only does this process allow students the opportunity to work through the development of complex persuasive content in stages, it also allows them to work together in groups in a collaborative fashion similar to real-world proposal writing. Similar to the first portion of the course, worksheets in the course text provide either guiding questions or templates for each component.

The first part of content development is finalizing a problem or need statement. In a third stage of research, students complete a worksheet and use traditional research practices they are familiar and comfortable with (searching Google, news items, library databases); however, it also builds on their previous research to connect what they find to what they have previously found about their organization and funding agency.

Students then apply their research and analysis of it to complete a draft problem statement, goals, and specific objectives. This is the persuasive heart of the proposal since it provides evidence and it articulates the specific and measurable goals/objectives that would be accomplished if funding were granted.

In the next phase of content development, students complete a budget worksheet to identify costs associated with their proposal. As a fourth stage of research, students must find or identify reasonable and realistic costs. Students then compose a draft budget and evaluation plan in which they articulate how goals would be evaluated to show success.

Both the draft problem/need statement and draft budget/evaluation plan are submitted for peer review using peer review guides with specific questions to help them provide relevant and constructive feedback.

The Final Step: The Proposal

In the final stage of the project, students complete one final draft of a complete proposal. Students revise and compile all previous writing into one cohesive whole, following the requirements of their funding agency. For peer reviews, students post the funding agency's guidelines so that part of the feedback they give and receive is whether or not their final draft meets both formatting guidelines and content criteria.

After revising their final drafts, students revise one last time and submit their final proposal for grading.

Challenges

As a pedagogical strategy, assignment sequencing has long been recognized as a way to facilitate completion of complex projects (see Bean[2], for example) and works well for this course. The role-playing scenario allows students to experience what it might be like to be a proposal writer "for real" and to learn the complexities of researching and writing a real proposal. In addition, the use of drafts-peer reviews for content development allows students to learn from one another through constructive reading and feedback.

A potential downfall for the instructor is the amount of feedback required, particularly at the beginning of the course when students are selecting organizations and funding agencies. Most students select local non-profit organizations; for example, animal rescue organizations, local youth groups or other non-profits. Some students, however, select large national (or international) organizations in the hopes of solving large cultural or social issues that are too big for one proposal. The email assignment allows me to help students get on track and overcome confusion.

While time-consuming, feedback helps students who are struggling and it gives all students a sense of reassurance that their work is important and valuable. In an online class this is particularly important. In course evaluations, students typically comment on how valuable assignment sequencing and feedback are.

- "All of the assignments leading up to the final project were relevant and worthwhile."
- "The instructor ... gave individual attention to assignments and took the time to provide detailed and personalized feedback on our assignments. It made it feel as if the work we were doing was important, to both her and us, which made me want to learn."
- "I have been trying to learn the intricacies of proposal writing for a while now. This course taught me more about proposal writing than I have ever learned."
- "It took the proposal writing process step by step, breaking down the various components. This made it much easier to understand and not so overwhelming."

Another challenge in the course is the tendency for students to confuse grant proposals with the soliciting of donations. For many students, the two initially seem to be the same; after all, they both raise money for an organization. In addition, creating a fundraising appeal appears to be simpler than the research required to write and support a grant proposal. Most students overcome this as they develop content; however, for those who persist in misunderstanding the differences, problems arise in problem or need statements that are more focused on the use of pathos for emotional appeal to solicit donations than on the use of logos to provide evidence for a problem and the establishment of goals that are fundable. To help address this problem, I've added additional reading resources that explain and highlight the differences along with a discussion board prompt[3] early on in the term so that students are able to reflect on and discuss the differences.

When I first taught the course, electronic submission systems were rare so finding funding agency criteria and submission guidelines (and formats) was not problematic. As time has gone on, more funding agencies have adopted systems that require organizations to register for an account prior to receiving guidelines. While this streamlines the process for the funding agency, it makes it more difficult to maintain this component of the course. As a result, this component of the course may change in the future.

Despite challenges, students consistently comment in evaluations (and later in email to me) that the structure of the course helped them to learn effectively. As an instructor, it is a rewarding course to teach and in which to watch students grow as professional writers.

NOTES

1. Soraya M. Coley and C. A. Scheinberg, *Proposal Writing. Effective Grantsmanship* (Los Angeles: Sage, 2014). Print.

2. John C. Bean, *Engaging Ideas* (San Francisco: Jossey-Bass, 2001). Print.

3. "Difference between donation and grant": differencebetween.net/business/finance-business-2/difference-between-donation-and-grant/); "What is the difference between a grant and a donation": grants.leeschools.net/pd/pdf/Grant%20or%20Donation.pdf.

Supplementary Materials: Student Proposal

The following proposal was composed by a student during Spring 2011 on behalf of the Phoenix Chapter of the Society for Technical Communication. The funding agency was Lockheed Martin. The proposal encompassed an application followed by the project narrative; only the narrative is included here. This proposal was submitted on behalf of the chapter after the course was over but was not funded. Used with the student's permission.

STC-Phoenix Writing Competition Proposal

PROJECT

The Phoenix Chapter of the Society for Technical Communication (STC-Phoenix) is seeking funds for the STC-Phoenix writing competition as a community program that encourages technical communication in over 1000 students in grades 5–12 in 15 counties in Arizona. A total of $910 is needed to support the annual STC-Phoenix writing competition that will be held in March 2011.

For nearly 50 years STC-Phoenix has hosted the STC-Phoenix writing competition as part of a community program that, in 2010, benefited over 1000 students in grades 5–12, in 15 counties in Arizona. The STC-Phoenix writing competition is held annually as a part of the Arizona Science and Engineering Fair (AzSEF). AzSEF and the STC-Phoenix writing competition provide life-long learning experiences that encourage students to seek careers in 16 fields of science from animal science, mechanical engineering, and physics. As part of AzSEF, the writing competition encourages technical communication as a tool for success in science careers.

Technical communication is a key tool to success in science careers ranging from research aides (who are at the beginning of their science careers) to program and society directors (who are advanced in their science careers). All scientists use technical communication on a daily basis to write research papers, reports, proposals, speeches, and research plans, etc. All of these types of technical communications are part of a cycle where technical communication leads to increased research, professional recognition, increased funding opportunities, and increased career opportunities.

It is not only the belief of scientists and STC-Phoenix that technical communication is important. Grade school students and science fair organizers also believe technical communication is important. A participant of the Southern Arizona Science and Engineering Fair said: "Remember, this is NOT a Science Fair Contest. This is a *communication* contest" (SARSEF). Science fair organizers have specific guidelines for the written portion of a student's research project. These guidelines are exact replicas of internationally-accepted, professional, scientific documentation standards—illustrating the fact that even science fair organizers recognize they are preparing students with technical communication skills for their science careers.

AzSEF gives students the chance to design, fund, implement, and present a project using scientific methods. However, the writing competition is the only part of AzSEF that gives students the opportunity to write about their project. When students are given the opportunity to write about their research, they learn many skills in technical communication such as writing abstracts, providing a bibliography, designing a project board, and writing problem statements. Students begin honing these skills in grade school and use them as tools throughout their careers.

To accomplish the goal of providing a writing competition for 2011, STC-Phoenix has recruited and trained a volunteer manager. Beginning January 2010, the volunteer manager will begin organizing the writing competition and the evaluation of the writing competition will conclude with awards being distributed by the end of March 2011.

PROBLEM STATEMENT

STC-Phoenix is requesting $910 to fund the STC-Phoenix writing competition for 1146 students in grades 5–12 in Arizona for 2011. STC-Phoenix is requesting these funds due to a decreased budget as a result of the 2008 recession.

Two factors contribute to STC-Phoenix's difficulty in funding the STC-Phoenix writing competition for 2011. Historically, STC-Phoenix funded the STC-Phoenix writing competition through membership dues or, intermittently, from company donations. Since 1997, STC-Phoenix has lost 236 of 309 members for two reasons; the chapter was split into two and the recession forced many to cancel their membership. Various $1000 donations from Honeywell and Lockheed Martin (2003) were received over the years. However, companies stopped donating, also due to the recession.

Goal: *To fund the STC-Phoenix writing competition as a community program that encourages technical communication in students in grades 51–2 in 15 counties in Arizona.*

Objective: *To obtain a total of $910 for the STC-Phoenix writing competition for 2011.*

IMPLEMENTATION PLAN, PREPARATORY ACTIVITIES

Organizing and implementing the STC-Phoenix writing competition [require]s much effort from the volunteer manager[,] who, starting in January of each year,

- revises flyers announcing the STC-Phoenix writing competition;
- maintains AzSEF email address;
- conducts writing workshops for students/teachers/parents;
- recruits and organizes volunteer judges;
- reviews and updates screening guidelines;
- trains volunteer judges;
- attends the AzSEF awards ceremony;
- submits winners to the international competition, if held;
- assists winners with report preparation for international competition;

- helps organize other science fair writing competitions; and
- prepares certificates and coordinates mailing checks.

Judging Activity

During the morning of judging day, all reports are screened for adherence to Intel's International Science and Engineering Fair content guidelines. These guidelines require each report to have:

- front matter (title page and table of contents);
- an introduction (purpose and hypothesis);
- materials and methods (detailed description of methods);
- results (data, analysis, results, statistics);
- discussion (explains how conclusions were reached);
- a conclusion (summarizes results);
- acknowledgements (credits any assistance); and
- references/bibliography (list of referenced documentation).

Reports are also judged on organization, clarity, relevance, accuracy, and appearance. All reports are scanned and each judge identifies up to three finalists. During the afternoon, all judges review the reports of the finalists and provide a score between 0 and 10, based on the above criteria. Scores are totaled[,] and the top three students win the three awards.

Within a week after the STC-Phoenix writing competition, the manager coordinates mailing the award checks. While recruiting volunteer judges, the manager informs judges of the minimum $15 for lunch and $10 for parking, and that receipts must be provided for reimbursement. At the end of the day, the manager collects and submits all receipts.

Evaluation Plan

STC-Phoenix's objective is to obtain $910 for the STC-Phoenix writing competition for 2011. The first expected outcome for this objective is that a maximum of $460 will be spent on monetary awards for nine winners. The second expected outcome is that up to $450 will be spent on administrative expenses. Evidence of meeting the expected outcomes includes distributing $460 in award amounts to nine students, reimbursing volunteer judges for up to $25 for parking and lunch, and covering up to $50 in office supplies. Data collection will occur by gathering receipts for all administrative costs and photocopying award certificates.

Budget

The $910 for the STC-Phoenix writing competition for 2011 is outlined in Table 1.

Award Amounts: For 2011 the total award amount of $460 for the nine awards will be spread amongst elementary, middle, and high school students.

The $460 award amount is average when compared to other science fairs. For the 2010 AzSEF, few sponsors awarded money. Intel gave $200 but that's the most. Most of the awards were certificates, although local sponsors give money and/or little trophies. Donors awarded other similar science fairs amounts that varied from certificates to awards up to $8000. At the Southern

Category	FTE	Salary Range (per month; US dollars)	Total
Personnel			
AzSEF Volunteer Committee Manager	0.065	$0	$0
Volunteers	0.004	$0	$0
Financial Officer	<0.005	$0	$0
Total Amount for Personnel		$0	$0
Total Percent of Budget		$0	$0
Awards			
Senior Division (Grades 9-12)			
First Place			$100
Second Place			$75
Third Place			$50
Junior Division (Grades 7-8)			
First Place			$75
Second Place			$50
Third Place			$25
Elementary Division (Grades 5-6)			
First Place			$50
Second Place			$25
Third Place			$10
Total Award Amount			$460
Total Percent of Budget			51%
Operating Expenses			
Volunteer Costs			
Lunch for 16 judges ($15/judge)			$240
Parking for 16 judges ($10/judge)			$160
Office Supplies			$50
Total Operating Expenses			$450
Total Percent of Budget			49%
Total Budget Request			$910

Figure 1. Budget composed by student.

Arizona Regional Science and Engineering Fair (SARSEF), awards were certificates, medals, or monetary awards between $25 and $1000. Although the $460 is small compared to $1000 and $8000, it is in keeping with awards for science fairs within the Phoenix region.

Personnel: The STC-Phoenix Writing Competition manager position has always been a volunteer position and will remain so for 2011. There is no salary.

Operating Expenses: Operating expenses for the 2011 STC-Phoenix Writing Competition are basic and include parking and lunch for volunteer judges and minor office expenses. Since 2006 STC-Phoenix has averaged 16 judges each year. Lunches at the venue average $15 and parking $10. Thus, for 16 judges and minor office expenses, the total is $400.

Since 2008 STC-Phoenix has not been able to provide money for lunch and parking, but would like to cover these costs in 2011 due to the recession. Judges typically spend an entire day evaluating science projects. Up until 2008 employers in the Phoenix area supported the STC-Phoenix writing competition by providing a regular salary for volunteer judges. Since 2008 all employers have eliminated this benefit

For 2011 STC-Phoenix plans to devise a method for on-line judging. This method would allow students to submit their science project documentation on-line and for judging to occur on-line. Thus, administrative costs would be further reduced for 2012 and [would give] judges the opportunity to participate without missing work.

Works Cited

AzSEF. *AzSEF.* 10 April 2010. zsef.asu.edu/documents/2008_AzSEF_Report.pdf.

Southern Arizona Regional Science and Engineering Fair. www.sarsef.org. 8 March 2010. 6 April 2010. www.sarsef.org/.

Past Meets Present
Exploring the University Archives to Compose and Connect

Christine Denecker

Supplemental Materials

- Rationale
- Pre-Composing Activity
- Pre-Storyboarding Graphic Organizer
- Peer Feedback Worksheet
- Grading Rubric
- Self-reflection Worksheet
- Student Sample

Past Meets Present

Your second assignment, entitled "Past Meets Present," challenges you to compose a digital essay tracing students, places, and events at the University of Findlay (UF) across time. More specifically, you will focus on one topic, one idea, one event, or one area of interest on which to do research and then see how that topic, idea, event, or area of interest has been shared and experienced across generations of UF students.

For example, you might choose to trace the evolution of the dining hall or of "Old Main,"[1] throughout the years. You could trace the growth of a particular sports team or club. You could also look at sorority life, homecoming, marching band, or a particular major across the University's history. Fashion, trends, and traditions are also good possibilities for this assignment.

The research you do for this assignment will be conducted in the Shafer

Library archives. Here you can look through UF yearbooks, newspapers, memorabilia, and photos. UF's head archivist will also share stories from the past including folklore, traditions, and little-known facts about your University's history.

As you focus your research, first consider these questions/prompts.

- What organizations, groups, or teams are you already a part of or might be a part of?
- What do you find curious about campus life and the way things are done at UF?
- Is there an area of campus or a building you'd like to know more about? That might be a great place to begin the work for your assignment.
- Do you have a relative, friend, or neighbor who attended UF? What memories do they have of the University?
- Use one of our class readings on the millennial generation[2] as a starting point. For example, at least one of our readings compares millennials to "the Greatest Generation" in terms of values and commitment to service. Does this comparison hold true at UF?

The topic possibilities are endless, and you might not be completely sure until you begin doing some research. We will take our first trip to the archives together; bring some initial ideas with you to that class session, and we'll go from there!

Additional Important Information

- Before beginning your actual digital work, you will need to clear your topic with me. Then you will need to storyboard your essay before creating it.
- Since you will be using visuals from the archives for this assignment, please follow carefully the rules to scanning and checking out archived materials. This information is available at the library and will be shared during our class visit to the archives.
- Keep in mind that you do not have to be an expert to create a digital essay. Your assignment can be completed in PowerPoint, MovieMaker, iMovie, etc. Choose the medium you feel most comfortable using. You will be graded on your rhetorical choices as a writer, not your technological expertise!

Audience: Your classmates, your instructor, UF alum; we will be submitting these to OilerNation[3] to run as part of UF's "Traditions" page!

Approach:

1. The following elements need to be included in your essay:
   a. A clear claim/thesis/message

    b. Examples/evidence
        i. Your evidence can be visual, auditory, and textual. You'll need to use at least *two* of these mediums in your digital essay.
        ii. You will probably need to scan archival materials.
        iii. Be sure to keep track of where you get your evidence; you'll need to cite this evidence at the end of your digital essay.

2. While you will have some words in your essay, consider how you might use other "available means" to help get your message across. In other words, there should be a balance of words, images, etc., in your digital essay.

3. Come up with an appropriate title. This provides a good opportunity to build audience interest.

4. Your essay will end with a "Works Cited" frame(s) or slide(s) listing sources used (including pictures, music, outside resources, etc.).

5. Don't forget to proofread your work for errors.

6. If you need extra help, contact me or schedule an appointment with someone at the Student Technology Center (STC) here on campus. There are student coaches there available to help you with your digital questions.

Length: 3–5 minutes in length
Grading: A grading rubric will be provided.

Rationale

Students entering a university often lack connections to the institution and to one another. As Patrick O'Keefe notes, "For first-year students, their entry to university may coincide with a period of instability in their lives, which can disrupt the capacity of students to persist with their studies" (606). As a result, "developing a 'sense of belonging' is critical to the success of college students" (O'Keefe 607). That sense of "belonging" includes both academic and social elements—from crafting one's identity as a scholar to locating and entering supportive social circles. Simply put, first-year persistence "is directly influenced by the level of social and academic integration of the student into the institutional environment" (Spady qtd. in Turner and Thompson 103). That academic and social integration can come in many forms from first-year seminar programs to cohort learning experiences; however, research suggests that curriculum designed with the specific needs of first-year students in mind is a "primary way to engage students both academically and socially" (Crosling, Heagney, and Thomas 12).

    Academic and social integration are integral components of the "Past Meets Present" writing assignment designed for a College Writing I class at UF. The assignment challenges students academically in that they conduct primary research into a specific place, organization, or phenomena that their generation of college students shares with a previous generation or generations. And since the assignment is a digital composition, students must also make rhetorical choices using a variety of mediums for expression, including visuals, music, and traditional alphabetic text. The critical thought that goes into these decisions along with the technological elements of the assignment help to build students' scholarly identities. Social integration occurs in tandem with the primary research and digital composing, since students utilize the university's library archives to make generational connections. Similarly, students' collective perusing and researching of the university's past allows them to become familiar with one another as they become familiar with the traditions, lore, and identity of the learning community they have joined.

If, as Patrick Turner and Elizabeth Thompson argue, "this generation requires a vital integration of technology use and communicative strategies" (94) and "ownership of academic work and campus participation are crucial to creating a sense of community" (Marsee and Davies-Wilson 83), then a first-year composition project that marries the digital with social assimilation to the campus should result in the type of engaged curriculum likely to foster a sense of belonging and of commitment to an institution. The "Past Meets Present" digital essay assignment begins with the students' exploration into their own generation as a means for building community within the classroom. Guiding questions include: what do they, as incoming freshmen, have in common as a generation? And how do their life experiences as Millennials compare to those of previous generations? At the beginning of the semester, students explore these questions through a series of readings and videos that juxtapose Millennials with the Greatest Generation, Baby Boomers, and Generation X. The ensuing class discussions allow for students to make personal connections and links between their generation and those that have come before them. The first assignment completed for the course, an analysis of one characteristic of the Millennial generation (as discussed in *Millennials Go to College* by Neil Howe and William Strauss), lays the groundwork for the "Past Meets Present" assignment and primes students to make connections via technology across the generational landscape of the institution.

As the second major assignment in the course, "Past Meets Present," also directly plays off one of the seven characteristics Howe and Strauss attribute to the Millennial generation: a tendency to be team-oriented. In a preparatory activity to the assignment, students collaborate in class brainstorming sessions about the topics, events, and elements of current college life that they find to be relevant and interesting. These discussions serve as the genesis of the primary research that students conduct into the university's past. For example, a female student on the swim team may wonder about the history of the sport at the university and when women were first permitted to participate. Another student, interested in architecture, may want to know more about the archway that adorns the campus entrance and its accompanying myths, which have been passed down by generations of students. Still others may want to know about the fraternity they are pledging or why certain rules exist on campus. Others may be curious about homecoming traditions, the fashion of previous eras, or how specific majors were added or developed.

Howe and Strauss argue that "teaching techniques that combine teamwork and technology [...] may yield spectacular results" (102); thus, the brainstorming sessions that begin the assignment give way to group exploration at the university archives. In this space, students conduct primary research by examining yearbooks, newspapers, photos, and other artifacts to explore connections between elements they currently value in their university experience with how previous generations perceived those same elements in times past. The goals here are threefold: one, students will find topics to pursue for the digital essays; two, students will locate artifacts to use as evidence in their essays; three, students will become better connected to one another and find their own unique connections to the university.

The "technology" portion of the "teamwork and technology" curricular design advocated by Howe and Strauss is evidenced in the assignment's multimodal approach, which "integrates different modes of communication, blending word and image, for example, with music" (Connors and Sullivan 222). While all multimodal texts need not be digital, the "Past Meets Present" assignment requires students to compose using PowerPoint, iMovie, MovieMaker, or a similar platform. Pamela Takayoshi and Cynthia Selfe argue the value of multimodal composing, stating, "students become so engaged in their [multimodal] compositions that they push themselves beyond the boundaries of the assignments and demonstrate learning that goes well beyond teachers' expectations" (4). Due to the multimodal nature of the assignment, students are challenged to use "*all available means* to communicate in productive ways" (Takayoshi and Selfe 8) when crafting their "Past Meets Present" compositions.

The notion of "all available means" is central to discussion of the assignment and to its implementation. Photos, news clippings, beanies worn by the 1920s football team—these become the "available means" students use to craft their multimodal arguments about characteristics, values, or interests shared across generations of students at The University of Findlay. In addition, the university archivist also serves as a "means" or resource, providing stories of traditions, explaining the importance of the archival collection, and answering students' questions as they explore UF's rich history. Mickey Marsee and Dennis Davies-Wilson contend that "collaboration with a faculty member or a librarian on a research project, even just one time during a student's college experience, could be a life-altering experience leading to success" (81). Additional collaboration occurs as coaches from the Student Technology Center (STC) assist students as needed in the technological aspects of their compositions. Similarly, students in class often provide technological assistance to one another. Thus, "all available means" extends to not just material resources but to relational ones as students craft their digital compositions.

Pre-composing activities, such as a free-writing assignment and additional readings into the university's past as found in *Findlay College: The First Hundred Years*, serve to help students gain focus for their projects following their initial class brainstorming session and archive trip. Additional independent trips to the archives are generally necessary as students begin to compose their essays. Once students have chosen topics, the combing through of archive materials continues with increased intention: students scan images to use as evidence, work on drafts of their thesis statements, and begin contemplating how best to use visuals, music, and alphabetic text to communicate their intended messages. A storyboarding activity helps students organize information and illuminates areas where additional research may be needed. Likewise, a "screening" session where students share their digital essays in progress allows for peer feedback and much needed revision during the composing process. To borrow the words of Turner and Thompson, this "collaborative learning environment […] motivates millennial students to be self-reflective and active participants in constructing knowledge" (95). While the exchange of ideas on improving content and message is certainly an integral part of these screening sessions, a rich technological exchange often occurs as well, with students sharing tips on best practices for layout and design, sound integration, and more.

Upon completion, each assignment is screened in class a final time in its entirety. Here students can witness how research, analysis, and synthesis can culminate in thesis-driven compositions that utilize visual, audio, and alphabetic text to depict life past and present at the university. From sports teams to Greek life, to fashion, to music, to housing—the list is endless. The class then votes on the top three submissions, and these projects have the potential to be posted on the university's intranet "Traditions" webpage in collaboration with work hosted by The University of Findlay's Spirit Initiative Committee. The promise of possible internal publication raises the stakes on the "Past Meets Present" assignment and provides yet another mechanism to integrate students within the university community.

To bring the project to a close, students respond to prompts found on the Self-Reflection worksheet, and then grades for the projects are determined by the instructor using a rubric shared with the students during the composing stages of the assignment. Of important note is the fact that students are not graded on their technological expertise or prowess; they are scored on the rhetorical effectiveness of their compositions. At the course's end, many students cite the "Past Meets Present" assignment as among their favorites in the course.

With that said, instructors who want to implement the "Past Meets Present" assignment in their own classrooms should consider their students' technological needs as well as the support available at their particular institution. Selfe's *Multimodal Composition: Resources for Teachers* includes a "Student Expertise Grid," which aids instructors in assessing students' technological capabilities prior to assigning a digital essay. Similarly, instructors must be aware of the tendency of some students to focus on the technological and not the rhetorical aspects of the composition. These issues often rectify themselves during the peer feedback screening process, when students have the opportunity to see how their work is "read" by an audience beyond themselves.

Instructors who implement the "Past Meets Present" assignment might also encounter the tendency for students to approach the work from a simplistic comparison-contrast angle. Granted, the assignment *does* ask students to compare one aspect of current college life with that same aspect from an earlier generation (or generations); however, pushing students beyond a surface comparison rests on the shoulders of the instructor, just as it would if students were analyzing one aspect of the past through the lens of the present in a traditional alphabetic essay. Conversation, one-on-one conferencing, pre-composing activities, and storyboarding exercises can help move students beyond one-dimensional comparisons to deeper synthesis and analysis of material.

Citation of sources may stand as yet an additional challenge of this assignment, since students must cite photos, music, archived materials, and other resources contributing to the overall finished product. As a result, instructors should discuss and model citation requirements when the assignment is first given to students. In addition, instructors who take a proactive approach by devoting a class session solely to documentation (early in the process) or those who require students to "cite as they go" will experience fewer issues with missing, incomplete, or inaccurate documentation in their students' work upon submission of final projects.

Since successful assimilation into a college community hinges on the early relationships students build with their peers and with their postsecondary institution, assignments for first-year college students that combine academic challenge with opportunities to link students' present lives with an institution's past might serve to achieve a number of goals. "Past Meets Present" strives to do just that—uniting rhetoric, digital literacy, academics, and socialization all in one space with an emphasis on connecting students with their new university community.

Pre-Composing Activity

Assignment #2 Past Meets Present

To prepare for Monday's class, respond to at least *two* of the following prompts. You'll need to *write for at least 20 minutes on each*—that should be enough to get the "writing is thinking" element going.

You can write your responses by hand or put them in a Word document. Either way, *bring your responses with you to class*. The responses will be used in producing the storyboarding phase of your assignment. Storyboarding will begin during our next class session.

I've divided the prompts into two categories: one for those of you who have a good idea of the topic you want to pursue for this assignment, and one for those of you who are still trying to figure that out.

I don't know my topic prompts:
- Spend some time writing about what you viewed/read while working in the library archives. What struck you as you were looking over the generations of UF students? What images and/or words struck you? Be specific and descriptive. What emotions, ideas, or questions did these images and words evoke? In other words, what understanding are you beginning to form about the topic(s) you are interested in? And what is still unclear to you about this topic and its history at UF? Can you begin to pinpoint what significance this topic might hold? Why or why not? What further research might you need to do?
- After reading Chapter One of *Findlay College: The First Hundred Years*, spend some time writing about what interests you or surprises you about the beginnings of UF. What did you learn? How does this information change or increase your understanding of your new "home" or even of the assignment that you're now working on? This is now your history, too, after all!

I'm pretty sure I know my topic prompts:
- Take some time do an internet search of the particular generations you were studying in the archives. What was going on in the world during some of the decades that you found most interesting? What were some of the major stories, trends, influences, fears, successes, etc. of the time periods you were focusing on? How were elements from those time periods reflected (or not) in the materials you reviewed in the archives? Finally, discuss how this web search helped (or didn't!) your approach to this assignment.
- Every good digital essay (like its movie counterparts) needs a soundtrack. What specific song(s) should or could accompany your digital

essay? (This may require some internet research). What song(s) would help tell the story or give readers insight into the eras, people, and values touched upon in your potential work? Explain.
- It's time to compare. How does the topic you've been focusing on (and its relationship to previous generations) compare to the UF you know today? For instance, if you are exploring a student group, do the students across generations seem to share any similar values, interests, or goals? What did that value, interest, or goal "look" like during the past? What does it "look" like today? Explain.

Pre-Storyboarding Graphic Organizer

Topic	Generations/time periods to be covered	Comparison points to today's UF students/campus
Message/Focus of essay	Images you've located to use	"Soundtrack"

Peer Feedback Worksheet

Assignment #2: Past Meets Present

Now that you have a rough draft of your Assignment #2 prepared, it's time to get some feedback from me and from your classmates. As you share your essay in draft form, we'll provide feedback using the grid below (adapted from Selfe's *Multimodal Composition: Resources for Teachers*, 2007). Just mark the appropriate spot on the continuum and leave a comment as explanation.

| 1 | 2 | 3 | 4 | 5 | 6 |

Unclear messageClear message and focus
Comment:

| 1 | 2 | 3 | 4 | 5 | 6 |

No comparison across generationsStrong comparison across generations
Comment:

| 1 | 2 | 3 | 4 | 5 | 6 |

Weak use of "available means"Strong use of "available means"
Comment:

| 1 | 2 | 3 | 4 | 5 | 6 |

Ineffective organizationEffective organization
Comment:

| 1 | 2 | 3 | 4 | 5 | 6 |

Little attention to framingCareful attention to framing
Comment:

| 1 | 2 | 3 | 4 | 5 | 6 |

No documentationCorrect documentation
Comment:

| 1 | 2 | 3 | 4 | 5 | 6 |

Weak overall effectStrong overall effect
Comment:

| 1 | 2 | 3 | 4 | 5 | 6 |

Little evidence of careful planningMuch evidence of careful planning
Comment:

This final note is to help you prioritize your work. The person giving you feedback finds the following to be strong attributes of your essay at this point.

_____

_____

_____

Your reviewer also suggests that your essay could be strengthened with additional attention given to the following three elements. (If you're the person giving feedback, be specific, please!)

1)

2)

3)

Grading Rubric

Assignment #2: Past Meets Present Digital Essay

Student:_____

Semester:_____

    College Writing I students will compose a Digital Essay to be graded with the following criteria based on the standards listed below. *This essay is worth 150 points or 15 percent* of the student's overall grade for the course.

T = Target Level (10)	There is clear evidence demonstrated in this area.
A = Acceptable Level (7.5–9)	There is an average amount of evidence demonstrated in this area.
U = Unacceptable Level (0–7)	There is little or no evidence demonstrated in this area.

Standards	Score and Comments
Message/Thesis The essay includes a clear message that an audience (beyond the composer) will find compelling and/or relevant. The composer utilizes key words to develop and sustain the message throughout the essay. The message underscores a shared element (or elements) held across generations at UF. X3	
Development The essay includes a comparison between past and present UF generations.	
Development The thesis is developed effectively; in other words, thorough and persuasive information is used to support the thesis. "All available means" were considered and utilized in crafting the assignment. X2	

Standards	Score and Comments
Organization The essay has logical organization and flows effectively from one idea to the next.	
Introduction and Conclusion The introduction and conclusion provide a frame for the essay and help create cohesion regarding the essay's message. X2	
Documentation The essay includes appropriate documentation internally and on the Works Cited slide(s). This includes documentation of pictures, text information, and sound/music.	
Style The writer's choice of words, visuals, and/or music is appropriate to the essay and demonstrates a sense of the composer's voice.	
Formatting and Essay Length The essay meets the assignment requirements in terms of length and formatting (movie or Power Point).	
Grammar and Mechanics The essay is free of grammar and spelling errors, and/or errors in mechanics.	
Overall Effectiveness The essay is presented professionally and according to directions. This standard measures how well the writer meets the requirements of the assignment as a whole. X2	

Comments:

Overall Score:_____/150

Self-Reflection Worksheet

Assignment #2: Past Meets Present

Name_____

Please respond to the following questions as you reflect upon Assignment #2.

    1. Describe the strengths of your digital essay. What did you do well as a writer? How did you employ "all available means" in constructing your essay?

    2. If you had more time to work on this essay, what would you do and why?

    3. Explain *at least two* of the rhetorical decisions you made for this essay. For example, why did you choose a particular layout? Or color scheme? Or font? Or use of artifacts as evidence?

    4. As you look back over the assignment, how have you grown or changed as a writer? What are you aware of now that you weren't aware of before in terms of your own composing process? What are your "successes" as a writer for this assignment?

Student Writing Sample

Since it is difficult to represent the entirety of a digital student essay in a traditional print venue, selected slides are included here to demonstrate the types of essays produced in response to the "Past Meets Present" assignment. The samples chosen are of student Korinne Magnuson's work completed in PowerPoint.[4] She opens her digital essay with a faded newsreel counting down to her production. In the background, Elvis Presley sings, "One for the money; two for the show" from "Blue Suede Shoes."

Next, Korinne has her essay fade into a title screen, which gives the audience an idea of the connection she has made between past and present generations at UF. She then follows with a series of slides that underscore her thesis: despite the sixty year divide, pop-culture of the 1950s continues to have a marked impact on the fashion, music, and celebrity enjoyed by contemporary UF college students. She intersperses slides containing traditional alphabetic text with slides that provide evidence (via photographs from UF yearbooks and archival collections) for her argument. For example, she includes the following slide (Figure 1) regarding 1950s pop-culture fashion.

88 Twenty Writing Assignments in Context

Figure 1. This figure represents clothing worn by students at UF in the 1950s (courtesy of the University of Findlay, University Archives).

The rhetorical structure of Korinne's essay demonstrates a pattern of alphabetic text supported by visuals as evidence. Music, first from the 1950s and then from the 2000s (Pitbull using a riff from the 1950s) accompanies the text and provides a nostalgic background tying together past and present. Korinne continues her work with an overview of 1950s clothing trends, including men's fashion and eyewear (Figures 2 and 3) along with women's shoe trends (Figure 4), then shifts to a comparison of fashion in the 1950s and that of today.

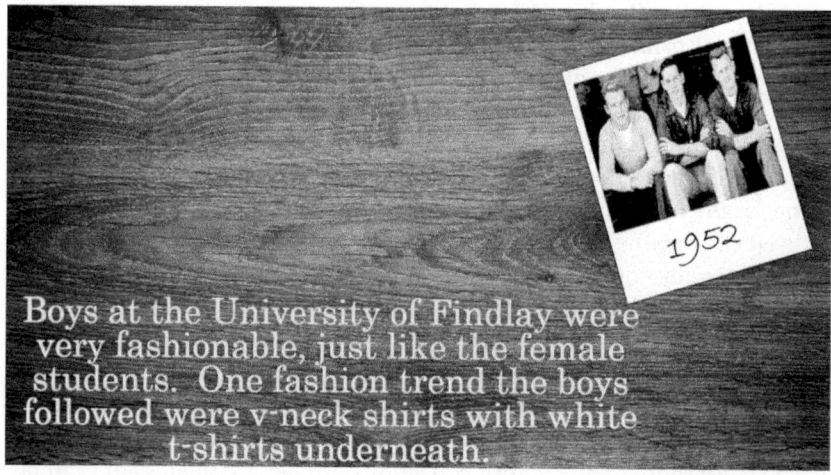

Figure 2. Depicted in this figure is male fashion at the University of Findlay, circa 1952 (courtesy of the University of Findlay, University Archives).

Past Meets Present (Denecker) 89

Figure 3. Featured in this figure are depictions of eye-wear and clothing worn by UF student in the 1950s (courtesy of the University of Findlay, University Archives).

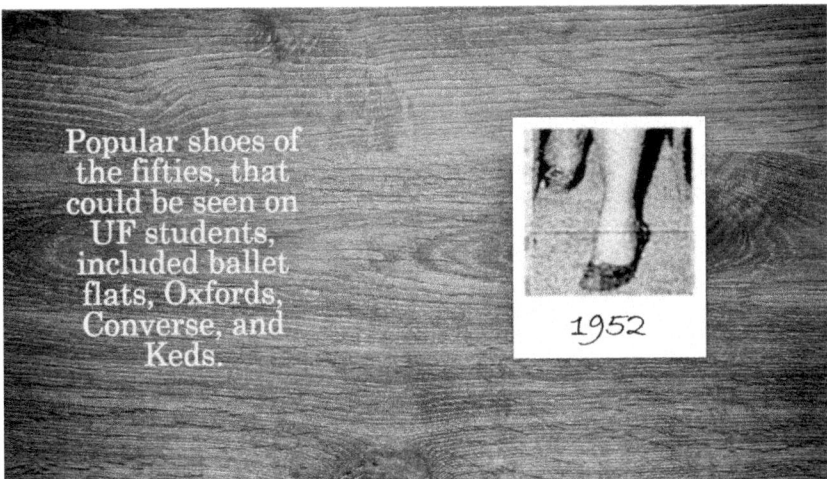

Figure 4. Highlighted here is an explanation as well as a photograph of footwear worn by female students at UF during the 1950s (courtesy of the University of Findlay, University Archives).

Her argument continues with additional back and forth visual evidence that 1950s pop-culture trends in eyewear and clothing remain evident a half-century later among UF students (Figure 5).

Eventually, Korinne synthesizes the 1950s pop-culture trends she has identified as having an impact on the current generation and concludes

Figure 5. This figure depicts recent UF students wearing fashion reminiscent of 1950s-era students at the University of Findlay (courtesy of Korinne Magnuson, personal collection).

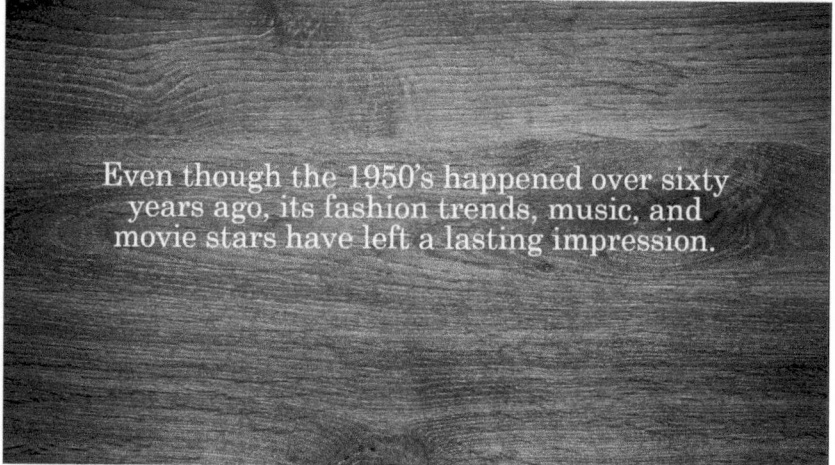

Figure 6. Here a claim is made about the impact the 1950s continues to have on present-day college students.

with a textual wrap-up of her argument (Figure 6). Undergirding her thesis (and difficult to depict in this limited space) is the message that one generation cannot deny or escape the influence of previous generations. In other words, each generation's story contributes to a larger, on-going, shared narrative.

Notes

1. "Old Main" is the University of Findlay's flagship building.
2. Class readings included excerpts from *The Greatest Generation* by Tom Brokaw, *Millennials Go to College* by Neil Howe and William Strauss, and *Findlay College: The First Hundred Years* by Richard Kerns. Students also read the following articles: "Expanding the Concept of Literacy" by Elizabeth Daley; "The Millennial Muddle" by Eric Hoover; "The Millennial Student: A New Generation of Learners" by Michele Monaco and Malissa Martin; "Millennials: A Portrait of Generation Next," Pew Research Center; and "Reinventing Library Buildings and Services for the Millennial Generation" by Richard T. Sweeny.
3. OilerNation is the internal website for The University of Findlay.
4. Korinne's finished essay consists of 56 slides.

Works Cited

Connors, Sean P., and Racheal Sullivan. "'It's that Easy': Designing Assignments that Blend Old and New Literacies." *The Clearing House* 85.6 (2012): 221–225. Print.

Crosling, Glenda, Margaret Heagney, and Liz Thomas. "Improving Student Retention in Higher Education: Improving Teaching and Learning." *Australian Universities' Review* 51.2 (2009): 9–18. Print.

Howe, Neil, and William Strauss. *Millennials Go To College*. Great Falls, VA: Life-Course Associates, 2003. Print.

Marsee, Mickey, and Dennis Davies-Wilson. "Student-Curated Exhibits: A Vehicle Towards Student Engagement, Retention, and Success." *Research and Teaching in Developmental Education* 30.2 (2014): 80–90. Print.

O'Keefe, Patrick. "A Sense of Belonging: Improving Student Retention." *College Student Journal* 7.14 (2013): 605–613. Print.

Takayoshi, Pamela, and Cynthia L. Selfe. "Thinking about Multimodality" *Multimodal Composition: Resources for Teachers*. Ed. Cynthia L. Selfe. Cresskill, NJ: Hampton Press, Inc. 2007. 1–13. Print.

Turner, Patrick, and Elizabeth Thompson. "College Retention Initiatives Meeting the Needs of Millennial Freshman Students." *College Student Journal* 48.1 (2014): 94–104.

Writing the Brain
A Multimodal Assignment Sequence
JASON W. ELLIS

Supplemental Materials

- Rationale
- Pitfalls and Avoidance Strategies
- Student Writing Sample

Figure 1. Photograph of Brinsley Tyrrell's "Behind the Brain Plaza" at Kent State University in Kent, Ohio (photograph by Jason W. Ellis).

Major Project 1: Writing the Brain

The primary purpose of project one, "Writing My Brain for Success at Georgia Tech," is to give students an opportunity to experiment with WOVEN (written, oral, visual, electronic, and nonverbal) multimodal communication using overlapping media: Twitter, the poster, and the written essay.[1] Its secondary purpose is to reinforce proven methods of learning success: learning over time (process) and learning through practice evaluation (reflection).

I designed this assignment for ENGL1101, because there is a body of evidence that conscious reflection enforced through writing can cause subtle shifts in a person's thinking over time. In a sense, we can each "write" our brains through this practice over time. In this assignment, we are taking this a step further by expanding the project to include other modes of expression.

The goal of this project is for you to explore what you want to get out of your learning and life experiences at Georgia Tech. This project should serve as a guide for writing your brain for the success that you want at Georgia Tech. Your overall project should address some or all of these questions: Why am I here at Georgia Tech? What led to my being here? What do I want to achieve? What do I have to do to meet my goals? Whom can I turn to for advice and support? How can I supplement and improve my experience here with other activities, new friendships, and professional connections?

The three primary media that you will use in this project are Twitter, Storify, and a poster. Twitter is a form of social media that supports text up to 140 characters, tags, links, and images. You will curate your tweets with Storify. The poster is a primarily visual medium for condensing information in visually communicative ways with a special emphasis on design. The essay form supports textual argumentation and elaboration. Your essay will follow MLA formatting. It is important for you to consider who your audiences are and the way your audiences will interpret the information you attempt to communicate. As a communicator, you must reflect on your choices, intention, and possible revisions to turn your project into an even stronger set of artifacts using the revision process.

Audience is an important and necessary consideration for any communication and composition that you undertake. You should imagine your audience to be your peers—other beginning college students. However, you also need to consider the genre conventions of each medium. Twitter is a new communicative medium, and it is far more social and casual than the essay. The poster is visual and it has its own issues of design and style. The essay is formal and designed using particular conventions.

The multimodal elements of communication can be summarized as WOVEN, or written, oral, visual, electronic, and nonverbal. Your work in this project will incorporate all of the WOVEN components of communicative composition. Think about how your project (and the process of making it) achieves multimodal synergy.

To receive credit for this project, you must complete it in its entirety and meet the process-driven deadlines.

Part 1: Twitter and Storify

Take one day this week to tweet as often as possible about your thoughts relating to your experience at Georgia Tech, your thoughts about college success, and your thoughts about your future. Use your tweets as a place for making observations about yourself and others, reflections on yourself and others, and planning your path through the day, semester, and years. Think about things that you are doing, could be doing, should be doing, want to be doing, etc. What are things others are doing that you would like to emulate and what things would you not want to emulate? What are your dreams and are you doing what it takes to achieve those goals? Are your dreams changing? All of these things are fair game for this assignment.

In addition to writing your thoughts in your tweet, each tweet should include an attached photo that you take with your smartphone or laptop's webcam. The photo should always show your surroundings or point-of-view. Your photos can be selfies. All of the photos must be taken by you and not pulled from the web.

Always be mindful of audience and the public nature of Twitter when recording your thoughts.

You should tweet a minimum of 32 times for this assignment (based on the likelihood that you are awake for 16 hours and tweet twice an hour). Of course, you can tweet more often than that and I would encourage you to do so. Think of your tweets as evidence and material that will inform the remainder of your project.

Now, go to storify.com, signup for an account, and create a new Story. Title your Story and write a description of your Story. Search for your tweets using Storify's right sidebar (e.g., I would search for @dynamicsubspace under Twitter and User). This will reveal all of your tweets. Drag and drop your tweets from your "day of tweeting" into your Story on the left. Click in the space between your tweets on your Story to type. For this part of the assignment, I would like you to write at least one sentence reflecting on each tweet and its corresponding image. Some questions to consider include: Why did I think that thought at that particular time? What is the context of my thinking that? Has my thinking changed since I tweeted that thought? With these thoughts recorded for reflection, how might I build on these thoughts now or in the future? If you blog, you can include links to relevant information from your blog. You might link to class websites or other web sources if they are relevant to what you have to say in reference to your tweets. After you have finished "curating" your tweets with your meta-thoughts, publish your Story, view your published Story, expand it completely (keep clicking "Read next page" until you can see your whole Story in your web browser window), and then choose to print and save as a PDF (Mac users have this functionality built-in, but PC users might need to install software such as CutePDF or use a Mac in the Library Computing Cluster).

Name your PDF as gtid#.storify.pdf and upload to T-Square under Assignments.

Part 2: Poster

Read your Storify Story and choose your favorite 5–6 tweets that you would like to represent in photographs. Using any camera that you have available (the library's front desk can check out a camera to you for short periods of time if you do not have access to a camera, webcam, phone with a camera, friend with a camera, etc.), take new photos (do not use your previously impromptu photos attached to your tweets) that visually communicate the essence of your selected tweets.

Using a graphics program such as Paint.net (www.getpaint.net), the GIMP (www.gimp.org/downloads/), ComicLife (plasq.com/apps/comiclife/macwin/), Adobe Photoshop, or other software, create a U.S. letter sized poster (8.5" × 11"—it can be oriented as portrait or landscape) that tells your audience of peers what you want to get out of your learning and life experiences at Georgia Tech. Arrange, resize, crop, and edit your 5–6 photos to create a visual collage of your photos.

Your poster may not include any words, but it should communicate something about you and the message of your tweets.

Save your draft poster as gtid#.poster.first.jpg (make sure it has the correct physical dimensions and is saved using high quality settings) and upload it to T-Square under Assignments. Email a copy to your team members for peer review. Based on your team's feedback, you will revise your poster, name it gtid#.poster.final.jpg and include with your final Project 1 files.

Part 3: 5-Page Essay

Finally, citing your tweets, Storify story writing, and poster, write an MLA-formatted, five page, double-spaced essay with the theme of "Writing My Brain for Success at Georgia Tech." It should accomplish these three things: (1) identify what you're thinking about your situation and what your goals at Tech are in the present, (2) propose goals or a direction for yourself that cover the next few years, and (3) reflect on your use of different media to explore, plan, and shape your thinking for success at Tech. In your first paragraph, you should introduce yourself to an audience of your peers and set out a thesis statement (your argument) for your essay. The remainder of the essay should always connect back to your thesis statement.

How you approach the topic and meet the requirements for this essay will be up to each student. However, you will want to carefully plan your overall structure (strategic thinking) with an outline before writing your essay.

You should quote your tweets, Storify story writing, and poster at least once each in your essay. For these quotes, you will use MLA formatting to create parenthetical citations and a Works Cited page (this would be your essay's sixth page). We will discuss this in class, and you can learn more in WOVENtext and in the Purdue OWL website (owl.english.purdue.edu/owl/resource/747/01/).

Save your draft essay as gtid#.essay.first.docx and upload it to T-Square under Assignments. Email copies to your team for peer review. After you revise your essay based on this feedback, you will name your final version gtid#.essay.final.docx and include it in your final project files.

Deliverables

Before arriving to class on the Project 1 due date, attach all of your Project 1 files to T-Square under the Assignment section of our class site. This is a checklist of the files that you should upload (you will want to re-upload your drafts when you turn in your completed project):

- gtid#.storify.pdf
- gtid#.poster.first.jpg
- gtid#.poster.final.jpg
- gtid#.essay.first.docx
- gtid#.essay.final.docx
- gtid#.anyothersupportingdocumentslikeoutlines.docx

Holistic Grading

I grade your work holistically. First, this means that your work must be complete, on time, and done using the writing process. If these components are not met, you will likely lose points. Second, I evaluate your work using the attached grading rubric. I will include constructive criticism and advice with your grade. This feedback will be useful for your final portfolio. Third, your grade will likely be higher if you can develop more revisions of each part, because each revision is like a mathematical iteration bringing you closer to being a very effective communicator. However, this process only works when your revisions are substantial—going back to the foundations of your writing, composing, and ideas. Simply copyediting or proofreading in the revision process will help with the Conventions section of the rubric but not likely the other parts of the rubric. Carefully consider how you use the revision process to improve your work and communications.

A Word of Advice

No matter where you might find yourself, you can always find new opportunities for growth, improvement, and success. Instead of simply saying, "I'll make the best of things," seek out adventures, experiences, and opportunities wherever you are. If you do, you will find yourself in an unanticipated future with unforeseen rewards. The trick is to remain dynamic, flexible, and enthusiastic.

Schedule

Week 1	Introduce Project 1, Writing the Brain Sign up for Twitter. Follow professor on Twitter @dynamicsubspace. Select a day for your day of tweets during the following week.
Week 2	Record your thoughts throughout a full day on Twitter. Due at the beginning of Week 3: Submit a PDF of your archived day of tweets as a Storify story on T-Square.
Week 3	Take photos that represent highlights or themes in your day of tweets. Transform your day of tweets into a visual poster using your photos. Due at the beginning of Week 4: Submit a PDF or JPG of your single page poster on T-Square.
Week 4	Transform your day of tweets, Storify story, photos, and poster into an essay. Due at the beginning of Week 5: Bring three, stapled copies of your essay draft to class for peer review within a team of four students.
Week 5	Peer review and revise your essay before the final due date for the project. Due at the beginning of Week 6: Submit your essay, poster, Storify story, and any other supporting documents on T-Square.

Rationale

I designed the "Writing the Brain" assignment after I began teaching at the Georgia Institute of Technology as a Marion L. Brittain Postdoctoral Fellow in the School of Literature, Media, and Communication. I wanted the assignment to introduce students to the major emphases of the Writing and Communication Program, namely rhetoric, multimodality, and process-driven composition. Also, I wanted the project to integrate into the "Writing the Brain: Composition and Neuroscience" theme that I developed for my English Composition I syllabus. Following this syllabus, students learn about the human brain's abilities, limitations, and possibilities—with a specific focus on those topics that feature in the learning outcomes of English Composition I: communication, interpersonal collaboration, and problem solving. We discuss how each student makes choices that shape her or his experiences and "wire the brain," or, put in our composition terminology, "write the brain." Combining these two threads resulted in this multi-part assignment that enables students to compose in different media, see how their communications are shaped by the media being used, and experience how they can leverage new and old media communication tools for their own purposes—personal and professional.

I introduce students to the assignment during the second week of class after I have completed my lectures on rhetoric (logos, ethos, pathos, kairos, and telos) and multimodality (using Georgia Tech Writing Program's WOVEN—written, oral, visual, electronic, and nonverbal—approach), because it serves as a sandbox for students to explore those lessons within the scope of their own exploration of what it means to be a successful college student. Additionally, I connect these ideas to the way our brains work specifically in regard to language, literacy, and memory.

Simultaneously, students read John Medina's neuroscience popularization *Brain Rules*, which teaches them how to be better students and communicators with neuroscientific insights. Through these readings, students pick up threads connecting their experiences to scientific discoveries relating to the brain. For example, they might observe, "I have a terrible memory when it comes to the periodic table." Then, after reading the chapters on short-term and long-term memory in *Brain Rules*, they see how these systems work and learn strategies for improving their memory. Finally, these realizations filter back into the assignment. We discuss issues of audience and integrating research into their writing. In this project, their research derives from their tweets, Storify story, and poster.

During the early stages of the composition process of the assignment, I introduce students to the grading and feedback rubric that I use on their assignments (Burnett et al. 57). The rubric is adaptable to different kinds of assignments, because it emphasizes students' rhetorical decisions and their execution of those decisions in the assigned multimodal media. The rubric helps students think about their decision-making processes, and it provides me with an easy to read tool for providing an overview of my assessment of each student's work. To do this, I create a Word document with a copy of the rubric on each page, and the document has as many pages as I have students. At the top of each page, I type the student's name, and I shade the boxes that capture where I see the students' work. Then, I write a letter to the student at the bottom of the page that discusses the project's strengths and weaknesses, invites the student to meet with me during office hours, and states the project grade at the very end. I save the grade for the end of the letter in the hope that the student scans and processes some of the feedback before focusing on the grade. To assign the grade, I scan through all the projects and create lists of projects that correspond to each letter grade bracket. Then, I read through each project carefully to fill out the rubric, write the letter, and assign a grade that captures the overall effectiveness of the project as a whole.

Another strategy for using this rubric is to assign points to the scales for each category, or adapt the rubric in part or whole for particular purposes. One of the challenges to grading a multi-module project composed across different media is the uneven execution on the part of students. However, this challenge gives the instructor a lot of things to comment on that can actually help students make better rhetorical choices by leveraging their successes in one medium against those they are less successful with in another medium. For example, one student might write a highly effective poster and tweets, but a less effective essay. The instructor can explain how the student might adapt some of Twitter's and the poster's affordances to compose a more effective essay. Put another way, the instructor can describe one or two strategies observed in the student's successful communications and how those things can be employed by the student as a heuristic of general communication effectiveness. Then, the instructor has to balance the strengths and weaknesses of each student's work in each medium and how that should figure into their overall project grade. Some students will show a remarkable ability in all project media while other students will create better compositions in some but not all of the project media.

I spend time with the class helping them think about each medium's affordances and how those affordances are different and overlap in various ways with the other project media. Each component focuses on different modalities, which I outline on the assignment sheet and discuss with the students. In the first part, I introduce how they will use Twitter as a tool for personal reflection, using its multimodal affordances. I encourage them to follow William Gibson's observation that "the street finds its own use for things" (Gibson 199). I place no restrictions on how they use Twitter, but I ask them to be deliberate with their choices and consider why they are making those choices. We discuss how Twitter supports writing (up to 140 characters), mentioning (connecting to others), metadata (hashtags), referencing (hyperlinks), and multimedia (animated gifs, static images, and embedded video and audio). They use the affordances of Twitter to give as complete a record as possible of their thinking and their surroundings when they think certain thoughts, which slows down the rapid pace of their day, so that through observation, they become more deliberate in their thinking and, potentially, decision making. Recording their thoughts on Twitter problematizes the private activity of thought and the public activity of social media sharing. We discuss what this means and how it relates to various audiences—self versus others.

Students curate their day-of-tweets on Storify.com, an online curating tool for social media. In addition to collecting their tweets and accompanying images, they add context with additional writing, hyperlinks, and embedded online content. This reflective exercise has the added benefit of having them think about how their words can be collected with different new media tools and how their words can be arranged among others' writing and creative works. Students share their tweets and Storify stories with one another in peer review teams of four to five students. They do not review one another's tweets or Storify stories in the more rigorous and formalized way employed with the poster and essay. Instead, I ask them to learn from one another's work, comment on what they think works or not, and remember these as elements of the on-going emergence of their team member's projects. This last point helps them see how their projects and the projects of others emerge over time.

Next, each student selects a common theme or idea uncovered in her or his tweets and Storify story that is worth exploring using the visual medium of the poster. Using only images of their own creation (taking photos, creating images in graphic design software, rendering 3D images, etc.), they are tasked with expressing this theme in a visual poster. Originally, I had students use ComicLife (see Student Writing Sample) as a composition tool to help them arrange their images, apply filters, and add text. Since then, I have relaxed the assignment to include other tools that the students might find useful or already have some familiarity with. The poster phase enables students who are more visual in their thinking and expression to leverage those abilities to produce compositions that they might not otherwise have an opportunity to do. For those students who are not yet as developed in their visual expression, it gives them an opportunity to develop this ability in a relatively low-stakes phase of this larger project. For both groups of students, they learn how messages are shaped by the medium of composition and how layering information in complementary modes can result in multimodal synergy. During class, we discuss the broader implications of this, including H. Marshall McLuhan's lesson that "the personal and social consequences of any medium—that is, of any extension of ourselves—result from the new scale that is introduced into our affairs by each extension of ourselves, or by any new technology" (McLuhan 7). Thus, the medium shapes the message and the medium shapes us.

When a poster draft is completed, the students share their work in their peer review teams. This peer review session primes them for the peer review work that we will be doing in the final phase of the project and throughout the semester. Each team member shows her or his poster to the others. That person's teammates take turns interpreting the poster (meaning) and identifying one effective element and one less effective element (criticism). Then, the sharing member can respond to these comments. All team members type up their comments, share them amongst themselves, and post them on a learning management system (T-Square) for the instructor to read and respond to as needed. Before this exercise, it helps to show students a selection of posters in various genres to discuss what makes an effective poster. To generate discussion and tap into the knowledge our students already possess, I show students a selection of ineffective and poorly designed posters from a variety of genres (e.g., movie posters, advertisements, infographics, public service, science/engineering, etc.). This helps students articulate the visual literacy that they already know but might not know how to describe yet.

Finally, I assign the essay for a number of important reasons. First, many students have reported to me that they have not written a long-form essay before. In fact, students often ask if they may have more than five paragraphs in their essays! Therefore, this essay is a way of introducing them to formal writing without the exam-based constraints many of them have been indoctrinated with before attending college. Second, students learn how important it is for them to learn professional style. We discuss where MLA and other professional styles come from and how they will be important to their future writing in academia and beyond. We talk about the visual design of the document and how writing can be a visual medium, too. We discuss issues of plagiarism and self-plagiarism and how citation respects the intellectual property rights of others and situates the ideas of others and self within the argument that the student wants to construct in this essay. Furthermore, the students are only tasked with using their own collected data (Twitter, Storify, and the poster) for citation in the essay. This enables them to learn citation methods for new media in a lower-stakes assignment before encountering their final research-based Pecha Kucha presentation project at the end of the semester.[2] Finally, the essay gives them an outlet to say and explain the things that they found challenging to express on Twitter, Storify, and the poster. While I encourage them to experiment with using the earlier phases of the assignment and associated media to express themselves, many of the students find it difficult to do. I tell my students that this is to be expected and desired. If these assignments were easy, there would not be much purpose in doing them. As they learn from reading John Medina's *Brain Rules*, the human brain thrives on challenges. Those cognitive activities that require more thought, imagination, and inventiveness are those that lead to new, long-lasting cognitive skills, heuristics, and memories.

Throughout the project, I enforce timeliness with respect to due dates and a file naming convention for all files. These are meant to help students professionalize their behavior in a team environment and improve their organizational abilities.

Pitfalls and Avoidance Strategies

In my experience at Georgia Tech, most students impressed me with their projects. Besides the dedication of the students and the technical background of many, their work was supported by the material conditions of the students (required laptop ownership, easy access to cameras—personal or loaned from the library) and our institutional culture (Georgia Tech engineering students are expected to figure things out with minimal guidance).

At institutions with different material support, student expectations, and student needs, this assignment likely needs reconfiguration. Nevertheless, its different parts can be replicated in old media easily. For example, in the first phase, you can ask students to keep a notebook of their thoughts over a 24-hour period. Each note can be no longer than two lines (approximating the brevity of Twitter). Beneath the note, students sketch what is seen from their perspective (approximating the context of perspective in the attached Twitter image). Then, in the second phase, you can have students create a collage of their notes—clustering cutout notes and sketches around common themes or recurring ideas. In the third phase, students could use markers or other physical art media to create a poster expressing an important thread uncovered in the journal and collage. Finally, the essay phase would cite these earlier artifacts.

Regardless of how you might deploy this assignment, it's important to remind students throughout of the rhetorical, multimodal, and composition processes at the core of the assignment. On the one hand, some students focus on the technical aspects of one phase (particularly the photography/poster phase) to the detriment of their overall assignment and its process. On the other hand, some students become enmeshed in the theme of the assignment and the class without reflecting on their rhetorical choices. In both cases, I recommend repeating in digest form the assignment's primary purpose at the beginning of class and monitoring student progress through one-on-one chats during time set aside for working on the project during class.

The most often heard criticism from students is the desire for more time. If possible, introduce the assignment as early as possible and build in milestone due dates for drafts of each component. This serves two purposes. First, it helps the instructor follow the development of each student's progress on the assignment and intervene with those students who might need the most help but are unwilling to ask for it. Second, it reminds students that the project is a process that takes place over time and it is not something that can be completed in any satisfactory way at the eleventh hour. Framing the milestone due dates as drafts helps keep students moving forward on the overall project, but it can be helpful to them to recognize how these earlier drafts can be changed at any point along the path to project completion as their overall project develops. In this way, the composition process of planning, drafting, revising, and reflecting is emphasized for all of the project's modules, and it is a process that can be invoked by the writer as needed to shape her message based on sound rhetorical decisions.

Student Writing Sample

This excerpted example comes from Jinming Hu, an exemplary student in my English Composition I class at Georgia Tech. This excerpt of his project illustrates the process flow of the assignment: Twitter, Storify, the poster, and the essay. It is included to show how a single thread can connect all four phases and give students an opportunity to return to their thinking on multiple occasions and encourage reflective practice.

Twitter Excerpt

- Jinming Hu (@jmh51193): Mad hyped for my first physics recitation. Haha but not really.
- Jinming Hu (@jmh51193): Once again, I find myself like a deer in the headlights understanding absolutely nothing that is going on.

Storify Excerpt

- "I was going into my first recitation in physics II […] I added sarcasm to the thought because some humor makes unpleasant upcoming situations easier to digest a little" (Hu par. 13).
- "This tweet validates what I said before. I didn't really know how to do the problems and my groupmates helped me out while I sat [amidst] confusion" (Hu par. 15).

Poster Excerpt

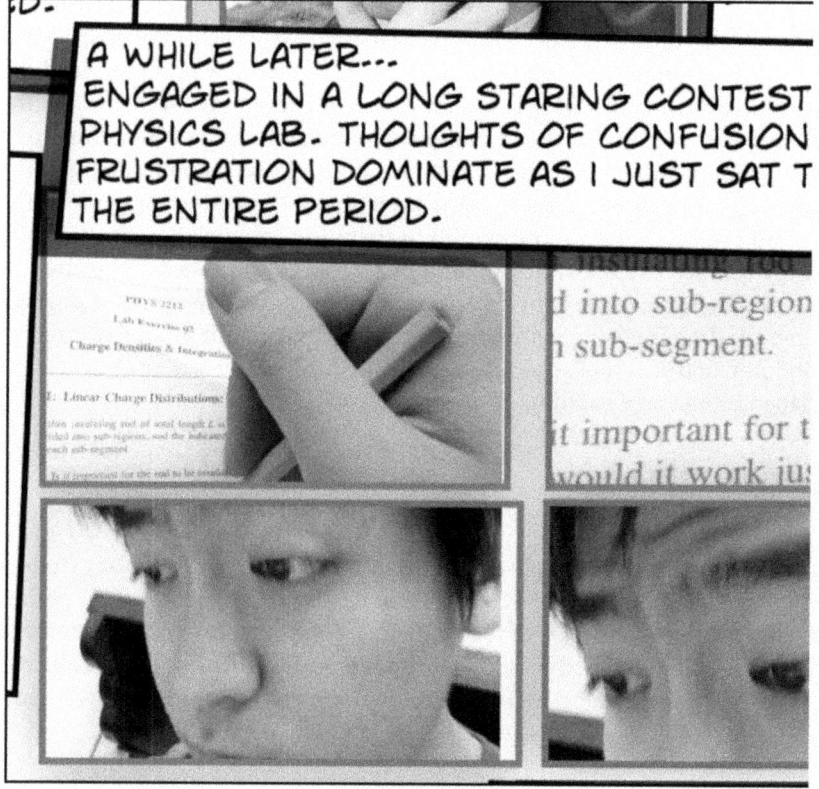

Figure 2. Excerpt from "Writing the Brain" poster by Jinming Hu.

Essay Excerpt

"It appears from this analysis of my thought (and thus in analyzing my analysis), I take negative events of my past and try to create negative perceptions of what will happen. The sarcastic undertone in the tweet downplays this pessimism, but overall brings about a fairly cynical perspective on things" (Hu 2).

NOTES

1. Learn more about the Writing and Communications Program's WOVEN approach to composition here: wcprogram.lmc.gatech.edu.
2. Pecha Kucha is a presentation style that foregrounds images, orality, and non-verbal communication over the typically text-laden PowerPoint-based presentation.

Created by architects Astrid Klein and Mark Dytham, Pecha Kucha presentations contain twenty slides, which automatically advance from one to the next every twenty seconds. As the slides advance, the presenter speaks to the audience unencumbered by the need to interact with a computer or inadvertently go over the 6 minute 40 seconds allowed in this compressed presentation format. Pecha Kucha presentation style is useful for helping students learn how to maximize the multimodal aspects of their presentations and develop professionsl skills including adhering to presentation time limits. Learn more about Pecha Kucha and see examples presentations here: www.pechakucha.org/. Even without a Pecha Kucha assignment, it can be useful to mention this presentation style as an alternative to what Don McMillan calls "Live After Death by PowerPoint" in one of his popularYouTube videos: www.youtube.com/watch?v=KbSPPFYxx3o.

Works Cited

Burnett, Rebecca E., Andy Frazee, Kathleen Hanggi, and Amanda Madden. "A Programmatic Ecology of Assessment: Using a Common Rubric to Evaluate Multimodal Processes and Artifacts." *Computers and Composition* 31 (2014): 53–66. Web. 30 Aug. 2014.
Gibson, William. "Burning Chrome." *Burning Chrome*. New York: EOS, 2003. 179–204. Print.
Hu, Jinming. *A Very Average Day*. Storify, 18 Jan. 2013. Web. 29 Aug. 2014. https://storify.com/jmh51193/a-very-average-day.
Hu, Jinming (@jmh51193). "Mad hyped for my first physics recitation. Haha but not really." 17 Jan. 2013, 1:15 p.m. Tweet.
Hu, Jinming (@jmh51193). "Once again, I find myself like a deer in the headlights understanding absolutely nothing that is going on." 17 Jan. 2013, 3:30 PM. Tweet.
McLuhan, H. Marshall. *Understanding Media: The Extensions of Man*. New York: McGraw-Hill, 1964. Print.
Medina, John. *Brain Rules: 12 Principles for Surviving and Thriving at Work, Home, and School*. Seattle: Pear Press, 2008. Print.

Making Financial Contracts User-Friendly
Conducting Research, Redesigning Documents and Proposing Changes in the Workplace

Sarah K. Gunning

Supplemental Materials

- Rationale
- Rubric
- Classroom discussions
  - How to illustrate financial concepts
  - Conducting research
  - Writing in teams

Assignment

In groups of three, you will identify a financial contract and assess its usability with the document's target audience. Some examples might include credit card applications, student loans, mortgage applications, gym memberships, "payday" loans, rent-to-own agreements, or other business practices that make most of their money from long-term interest accumulation or pay-to-play services. Your team will identify areas of the contract that are confusing to users and will propose suggestions to redesign the contract in the form of a proposal and contract redesign.

The purpose of this assignment set has three major areas of focus:

- to develop a written proposal to convince an audience to take an action based on your persuasive skills and qualifications;

- to conduct primary and secondary research to enhance your argument; and
- to present information in a clear, attractive, and ethical manner so the customer feels confident about making an informed financial decision.

Leverage the knowledge you learn in class about developing convincing proposals through the current situation, the buyers' interests, and the benefits that the redesign will bring the company. Companies need to protect themselves in legal terms, while ensuring growth and return on investment. However, your company would not exist without your customers.

How can you, as a future business leader, ensure that the objectives of your company's process/product are transparent to its users? Keep in mind that you will have a college education, whereas many of your customers may not. Particularly for services such as student loans, mortgages, payday loans, we already know that the user population in question does not have the capital to pay up front, and therefore is a vulnerable population. Companies handling these services should seek to make the terms and conditions of these loans transparent and easy to understand.

This assignment asks you to assume you are employed at the company that develops your financial contract. You work for the company, yet your paycheck comes from your customers. How do you balance the utilitarian needs of your company while maintaining ethics of care principles needed to maintain good relationships with your customers?

Proposal Content

The Cover Letter includes a 1-page, professionally-formatted cover letter, written to the company's CEO and signed by the project manager, forecasting the importance of the proposal and why it is needed.

The Proposal will contain six major sections, plus an Executive Summary. Your proposal will be between 10–12 single-spaced pages.

The Executive Summary provides a concise overview of the entire proposal, using the thesis statement from each major section (write this section last).

The Introduction establishes background information about the product in question and the surrounding industry; provides current landscape of the political and judiciary context; includes characteristics of intended users and why the financial contracts are needed; and provides a "map" for the reader, forecasting the sections to come (Current Situation, Method, etc.).

The Current Situation discusses the pre-testing procedures for the original contract and how the team recruited participants to serve as usability testers; provides an overview of the pre-testing usability results; establishes five major areas that can benefit from a redesign, specifying exactly what is unclear/difficult to understand and any suggestions your users provide to make it more clear, finishing talking about each major area before moving onto the next; and provides a "road map" for your reader to help guide them through your argument.

The Method provides a detailed walkthrough of the changes your team proposes to the contract to improve the usability testing. I suggest you include before-and-after images to provide a quick reference point and to help paint a picture in the reader's mind.

Qualifications shows that you have improved the usability of the contract based on the post-test results, and that consumers feel more confident about making an informed decision about your product.

Costs & Benefits connects the short-term costs and benefits to the long-term costs and benefits of your proposed redesign. For example, a short-term benefit may include additional customers by word-of-mouth, while a long-term benefit would be financial gain or decreased litigation expenses.

The Conclusion ties all of the main points of your proposal together and reiterates the main points of your argument, in order, encouraging your readers to *act* on the proposal.

Proposal Timeline

The assignment will take place over four weeks, with two 75-minute in-class meetings per week. While you will have a majority of in-class meetings to work with your group members, use this time to provide updates to your group members and determine strategies for completing the next steps on your task sheet. Use Agendas and update the Task Sheet at each meeting (Wolfe).

WEEK 1: THE INTRODUCTION AND THE CURRENT SITUATION

- Visit a place of business or find an online application to evaluate for the first day of the project. Bring the contract to class. Scan it and store it in Google Drive. Ensure your team members can access the stored documents.
- Complete the Group Work Preferences worksheet[1] (Wolfe) and compare notes with your group members.
- Develop a Team Charter.
- Create a Task Sheet and divide tasks based on group preferences and time requirements.
- Conduct *secondary research*, or "library" research to gain a broad picture of your industry (credit card, mortgage, payday loan, cell phone, etc.) and any recent federal or state guidelines sanctioned. Collect 10 sources, and cite appropriately.

- Use the secondary research to identify characteristics of the product's users. *Primary research* is research you conduct with actual users, gathering information about their experiences. Identify five individuals who are willing to test the contract and evaluate it for their understanding.
  - Conduct Think Aloud Protocol (Nielsen) and take detailed notes with your users to identify areas on the contract that need clarification. Ask your users how the information might be clearer. Note their suggestions for the redesign.
- Interview a financial expert (loan officer, phone sales representative, credit counselor) about their industry's typical consumer behavior. What do most customers ask questions about? Are there topics with frequent misunderstandings? Determine among your group members which questions will provide the most support for your argument.
- Begin brainstorming about the changes your team can make to improve the contract usability based on your research findings.

WEEK 2: THE CURRENT SITUATION AND THE METHOD

- Develop your primary and secondary research findings into a well-built, organized argument in your Current Situation. Note: you don't have to redesign the *whole* contract; simply select the most important five areas to redesign/clarify from the primary research. Your Current Situation will illustrate the five major *problems* in the original contract.
- Use *document design principles* (Black, Stiff, and Waller) and *visual design principles* (Usability.gov) and examples to improve the confusing parts of the contract.
- Write the narrative of your Method section by discussing all of the changes you have made and the reasoning behind your design choices. Your Method will introduce the *solutions* to the five problems you introduced in the Current Situation.
- Integrate before-and-after screenshots of your redesign in the Method narrative. Label them appropriately as Tables or Graphics.

WEEK 3: QUALIFICATIONS, COSTS & BENEFITS AND CONCLUSION

- Conduct a post-test Think Aloud Protocol (Nielsen) of your new design with the contract's intended users.
- Use the results of your post-test to write the Qualifications section. Hopefully, your post-test results support the redesign efforts. If not, go back to the drawing board and re-design until you have your users' approval.
- Connect the short-term costs and benefits to long-term corporate goals in your Costs & Benefits section.

WEEK 4: CONCLUSION, EXECUTIVE SUMMARY AND EDITING
- Now that your proposal draft is complete, summarize the thesis of each major section in an Executive Summary.
- Spend two days editing your work. Edit the proposal first for content, then at the sentence level, and finally check for proofreading/grammatical errors.
- One group member should ensure the proposal is in "one voice" and transitions smoothly from one section to the next.

Proportion of Course Grade

The proposal contract redesign is 20 percent of a student's course grade. The breakdown of the assignment includes the written proposal, the contract redesign, and distribution of tasks among team members.

Rationale

By now, it is likely that your students have applied for a credit card, purchased a cell phone plan, investigated student loan options, or signed an apartment lease. How many students within your classroom have had the time and energy to read through all of the fine print associated with one or more of these contracts before signing? Have any been a "victim" of fine print? The purpose of this project is to help students incorporate a variety of research methods and document design skills to test the usability of a legal contract and to use sound reasoning strategies to propose changes to make the information easier to understand. In a few short years, students may be working for businesses that incorporate similar contract-based practices. At the very least, students will encounter these documents in daily life when buying a house or financing a car loan. It is essential for students to gain experience making ethical, well-informed, decisions about contracts. One way to gain practical experience in this area is to work with "everyday" business documents that have the potential to promote financial literacy.

Financial literacy is the ability to make informed decisions about incurring and managing debt and being financially secure (usability.gov). Recent studies indicate that education about financial decisions is more effective when it starts early in life, but needs to be revisited often and put into practice to work (Thaler; Supiano).

Where do students get the information they need to make financial decisions? Online calculators such as Bankrate.com (Bankrate) or BigFuture's online calculator for comparing financial aid awards (College) can be helpful for making short-term decisions, but borrowers should also have a good idea about the long-term consequences. How much salary will a person need to earn per month to pay off a $40,000 student loan, plus rent, credit cards, groceries, and other monthly expenses? These calculations are where current loan education processes fail borrowers.

In an informal survey with undergraduate students enrolled at a midsize, urban comprehensive university (n = 30), parents and family members were the most-cited source of financial education for the students (53.3 percent), and friends (7.3 percent). Ten percent of students said they were "completely on their own" when it came to financial decisions and could not ask their family members for good advice. Next, I asked students how comfortable they were when talking to their parents about making financial decisions. The results were mixed: 43.3 percent reported feeling "very comfortable," 30 percent were "somewhat comfortable," and 23.3 percent felt "not very comfortable" talking to their parents about finances. While some students trusted their parents' advice completely ("My parents are my best friends"), others noted, "[I don't talk to my parents] because they themselves are not good at financial planning" and "My mother does not know much about financing her own money, so she is usually the one turning to me for advice."

I created this project because my students were already attempting to navigate the financial literacy process on their own. The Internet is a major resource for educating themselves, particularly when "my family isn't too good when it comes to handling money, so I try to do my own research and make smart decisions now in order to become financially stable later." While students mentioned the student loan process can be "a little terrifying" and that it "makes [them] nervous," students are proactive and aware that they need to inform themselves *now*. If only about half of the students surveyed cited their parents and family members as their go-to resource for financial advice, why not educate each other through document design principles? Students can educate themselves and their peers about the intricacies of contracts and consequences in a classroom setting.

In 2009, the *New York Times* published an opinion article about how credit card information could be clearer for consumers based on the Nutrition Education and Labeling Act of 1990—the act that put nutrition labels on food packages (Gibson, Hall, and Harris). This project goes one step beyond the labeling act suggestion and asks students to provide contextual examples for the audience: what does a typical monthly payment look like on a $40,000 student loan? What is the difference between a subsidized and unsubsidized loan? What is the difference between a 6.0 percent interest rate and a 7.5 percent rate? Students care about this information because they are navigating these waters in real life, and they are worried about repercussions of not understanding the information, even with a college education. We can hold a conversation about this type of information in an English or Writing classroom, while providing applications in real life—particularly for students who have few places to turn for advice.

Rubric

Proposal	Wt (Weight)	0 Missing	1 Subpar	2 Marginal	3 Good	4 Excellent
Genre	2	Does not look like proposal genre	Missing 3+ components of proposal genre	Missing 2+ components of genre	Missing 1+ components of proposal genre	All proposal genre components are present
Executive Summary	5	Executive summary is missing	Provides a poor overview of proposal, misses sections	Provides a vague overview of whole proposal	Provides a good overview of whole proposal	Provides a very clear overview of whole proposal's argument
Introduction	5	Introduction is missing	Reader is unsure of document's purpose	Missing several components of intro or intro doesn't match body paragraph content	Missing 1–2 components of intro	All components are present and logically presented
Current Situation		Issue is missing	Issue lacks research or issue is hard to identify	Issue backed up with some research	Good research but needs 1 round of revision	Strong research, argued clearly, memorable
Issue 1	1					
Issue 2	1					
Issue 3	1					
Issue 4	1					
Issue 5	1					
Method		Solution/design is missing	Solution/design lacks research	Solution/design is backed up with some research	Solution uses good research but needs 1 round of revision for clarity	Strong thesis, organized, solution is clear
Solution 1	1					
Solution 2	1					
Solution 3	1					

Criterion	Points	F	D	C	B	A
Solution 4	1					
Solution 5	1					
Qualifications	3	Qualifications are missing	Qualifications are dubious	Qualifications are thin	Qualifications need 1 more round of argument revision	The section enhances the argument
Costs & Benefits (C&Bs)	3	C & Bs are missing	C & Bs do not illustrate argument very well	C & Bs illustrate argument fairly well	C & Bs illustrate argument (above average)	C & Bs illustrate argument (excellent)
Conclusion	5	Conclusion is missing	Conclusion leaves off several important items	Conclusion covers most important items	Conclusion includes 80% of items	Conclusion has all components
References	3	No references	Some references but no in-text citations	Some in-text citations	References are complete but in poor format	References and in-text citations present and in good format
Cover Letter	5	Missing	Is missing 25% or more of genre components	Is generic/boilerplate, not tailored to audience	Establishes connections to audience's interests in most areas	Establishes strong connections with audience's interests and needs
Overall reasoning	5	Lots of holes in argument	Several large holes in argument	Argument needs more research	Argument is well-supported in most regards but may need to develop a stronger conclusion	Argument is strong and leads reader to a specific conclusion
Transitions, Voice	3	Document's overall "voice" is inconsistent	Areas of the document may have an inconsistent voice	Transitions are choppy between topics	Document has a uniform voice in most areas	Document has a uniform, professional voice
General Readability	3	Impossible to follow	Most is hard to follow	Parts are hard to follow	Mostly easy to follow	Very easy to follow
Overall	52	F	D	C	B	A
Points Range		0–123	124–145	146–165	166–186	187–208

Classroom Topics

Discussing Personal Experience with Financial Contracts

How many students have signed a contract for a lease, new cell phone plan, or car note? Describe your experiences during the process. Did you have a good idea what you were signing up for? Have any of you had bad experiences with cell phone contracts, lease agreements, or gym memberships? What happened? How did you resolve it? What will you do differently the next time you have to sign a contract?

Illustrating Financial Concepts

The financial decisions you make now can impact your life for years. Consider student loans: the difference between obtaining a *subsidized* loan versus an *unsubsidized* loan can equal thousands of dollars between now and graduation, and even more money by the time the loans are paid in full.

Let's look at the table below. Example A is a subsidized loan, meaning no interest accrues while the student is enrolled in college. However, in Example B, the *unsubsidized* loan for the same amount costs the student over $8,000 more by the time the borrower is out of school. Right away, the student in Example B owes 25 percent more than when he or she began school (Table 1).

Table 1: Subsidized versus Unsubsidized Loans and the Effect of Interest Rates

Student Loan Interest Accrual During College

Example A. A loan of $40,000 with a subsidized interest rate of 7.5%

Year in school	Borrowed	Principle	Rate	Interest $	LOAN TOTAL	Interest paid per day during school
Freshman	$10,000.00	$10,000.00	0	$0.00	$10,000.00	$0.00
Sophomore	$10,000.00	$20,000.00	0	$0.00	$20,000.00	$0.00
Junior	$10,000.00	$30,000.00	0	$0.00	$30,000.00	$0.00
Senior	$10,000.00	$40,000.00	0	$0.00	**$40,000.00**	$0.00

*Interest begins accruing upon graduation, or when loan terms specify.

Example B. A loan of $40,000 with an unsubsidized interest rate of 7.5%

Year in school	Borrowed	Principle	Rate	Interest $	LOAN TOTAL	Interest paid per day during school
Freshman	$10,000.00	$10,000.00	0.075	$750.00	$10,750.00	$2.05
Sophomore	$10,000.00	$20,750.00	0.075	$1,556.25	$22,306.25	$4.26
Junior	$10,000.00	$32,306.25	0.075	$2,422.97	$34,729.22	$6.64
Senior	$10,000.00	$44,729.22	0.075	$3,354.69	**$48,083.91**	$9.19

Example C. A loan of $40,000 with an unsubsidized interest rate of 6.0%

Year in school	Borrowed	Principle	Rate	Interest $	LOAN TOTAL	Interest paid per day during school
Freshman	$10,000.00	$10,000.00	0.06	$600.00	$10,600.00	$1.64
Sophomore	$10,000.00	$20,600.00	0.06	$1,236.00	$21,836.00	$3.39
Junior	$10,000.00	$31,836.00	0.06	$1,910.16	$33,746.16	$5.23
Senior	$10,000.00	$43,746.16	0.06	$2,624.77	**$46,370.93**	$7.19

Example B and C show the difference between a 7.5 percent interest rate and a 6.0 percent interest rate. That small difference can add up to thousands of dollars over the years, particularly if this student has a lengthy loan term of ten to twenty years.

Lenders do not typically show tables such as these to users when they make a financial decision. This is where our project comes into play. We have the ability to translate vague information, such as "subsidized versus unsubsidized loans" into a visual display of information that the reader can relate to and make an educated decision about. Perhaps this reader is inspired to keep shopping for a subsidized loan after seeing this table. Another customer might wish to determine the amount of take-home pay he or she would need to earn upon graduation. This is where a graphic or image can replace a thousand words. Conduct your primary research and use calculators such as Bankrate.com to help educate your reader.

Conducting Research

This project incorporates both secondary ("library") research and primary ("data collection") research to develop a strong proposal. Combining the two types of research helps triangulate the proposal's argument, incorporating both statistics and qualitative narrative to illustrate the main points.

Getting Started with Secondary Research

Some of the first places you should look for research on your topic include the company's own website, national news providers such as the *New York Times*, *Washington Post*, *Boston Globe*, CNN, ABC, and other news providers, and YouTube, which often has customer testimonials that have been features on newscasts or investigations. You might also want to Google "[Company Name] customer reviews" to see what customers say about the company in user forums or in reviews. Be sure to cite the web pages where you get your information, and use quotations appropriately.

Getting Started with Primary Research

Your peers are an excellent population to ask about contracts. Make a list of desired characteristics of your users. You might want an equal number of males and females, a variety of age ranges and education levels, and background information on how they perceive the industry in question. Make a photocopy of the contract and provide your user with a pencil to circle areas that need further clarification. Resist the attempt to explain what content means, but ask your user what would help make the information more clear. Would an example help? A visual depiction of the price over time? A calculation of the total monthly payment? Make a list as you talk with your users.

Writing in Teams

Joanna Wolfe's book *Team Writing: A guide to working in groups* is an excellent resource for presenting and resolving conflict in collaborative writing projects. Several of the worksheets that are most helpful to this project include the following:

- Team Charter
- Team Preferences
- Communication Style Quiz
- Meeting Agenda
- Task Sheet

NOTE
1. All worksheets are found in Joanna Wolfe's *Team Writing: A Guide to Working in Groups.*

WORKS CITED

Bankrate. Bankratewww. 2014. 31 August 2014. www.bankrate.com.
Black, Alison, Paul Stiff, and Robert Waller. *Designing Business Documents.* Ed. Chris Burke. 1992. 30 April 2013. w ww.textmatters.com/resources/pdfs/businessdocs.pdf.
College Board. *Compare Your Aid Awards.* 2014. 31 August 2014. https://bigfuture.collegeboard.org/pay-for-college/financial-aid-awards/compare-aid-calculator.
Gibson, David, Carla Hall and Sylvia Harris. *Healthy Credit.* 23 May 2009. 25 May 2009. www.nytimes.com/2009/005/24/opinion/24gibson.html?module=Search&mabReward=relbias%3As%2C{%221%22%3A%22RI%3A5%22.
Nielsen, Jakob. *Thinking Aloud: The #1 Usability Tool.* 16 January 2012. 20 August 2014. www.nngroup.com/articles/thinking-aloud-the-1-usability-tool/.
Supino, Becky. *Teaching Financial Literacy is a Challenge, Both on Campus and Beyond.* 27 February 2013. 5 May 2013. chronicle.com/blogs/headcount/teaching-financial-literacy-a-challenge-on-campus-and-beyond/34083.
Thaler, Richard. *Financial Literacy, Beyond the Classroom.* 5 October 2013. Online news article. 31 October 2013. www.nytimes.com/2013/10/06/business/financial-literacy-beyond-the-classroom.html?ref=mortgages.
Usability.gov. *Visual Design Basics.* 31 August 2014. 6 June 2012. www.usability.gov/what-and-why/visual-design.html. Wisconsin Educational Communications Board. *Financial Literacy: Teach It!* November 2009. Website. 1 January 2014. wimedialab.org/finance/CK4Kentop.html.
Wolfe, Joanna. *Team Writing: A Guide to Working in Groups.* Boston: Bedford/St. Martin, 2010.

Geobiographies
A Place-Based Assignment Sequence
JIM HENRY

Supplemental Materials

- Rationale
- Other Pedagogical Considerations
- Pre-Writing Activities
- First Drafts
- Pitfalls and Avoidance Strategies
- Response, Class Themes and Revision
- Grading Rubric
- "Final" Revisions
- Subsequent Course Activities
- Full Online Syllabus with Student E-portfolios

Writing Assignment: Geobiography

This writing assignment will take the form of an essay, a genre with some established conventions (discussed below). Yet the specific genre of "geobiography" is an invented one; hence, we will all be exploring its forms and meanings as we proceed through the assignment's activities.

To get started, think of a geobiography as an autobiography that focuses on the way your life to date has been shaped by the geographies you have lived in or visited. Give details from your earliest memories up to the present day, including where you were born and grew up, any family stories that you would like to share, stories from school life (good and bad!), etc.

As part of this geobiography, focus in particular on places that have played a role in making you the person you are. These places can be as intimate as your desk at home, your kitchen table, or your favorite place to meditate. Try not to restrict your thoughts to these places alone, though. Include references to public places that have shaped you, too. If your family moved during your childhood, be sure to talk about that. (If you can get details on places that influenced your parents, their parents, etc., in an attempt to tell a little bit about family history that is situated in specific places, please do so.) As part of telling your geobiography, you are required to discover (or uncover) at least one fact about the history, geography, or social make-up of the places that have shaped you.

The simplest way to organize this essay is to begin at the earliest stage and take your reader up to the present, using a *chronological* order. Once you begin drafting, however, you may discover that a *topical order*—where you present your geobiography place by place regardless of when you spent time there—makes more sense. No matter which order you choose, your geobiography should have a clear *beginning*, *middle*, and *end*, and we will discuss what makes each of these parts of an essay effective as we go. Because the *title* of your geobiography is its very beginning, we will talk about how to come up with effective titles as our work on this assignment progresses. (If you have trouble coming up with a title for your first draft, don't fret; we will work as a class to help everyone engage with such challenges successfully.)

We will use this assignment to continue building a learning community and to position all of you as *intellectual teammates*, peers who can help one another progress. Your first draft should be approximately two pages, single-spaced, with a break between paragraphs. It must include meta-commentary on your intentions as an author, your aim, and the ways in which you are addressing your immediate audience of peers. (We will discuss the concept of meta-commentary in class, but for starters, consider this: How do you want to come across, and where in your essay do you think you achieve this self-representation?) The draft must be posted to the Resources folder in Laulima by Monday, September 7, at midnight. On Wednesday, please bring two printed copies of your meta-commentary and draft to class for peer review. We will use your reviews and the class discussion that follows to determine our grading rubric for the assignment and to ground the revising process that will follow.

Rationale

Place-based writing theorists have argued for focusing student writing on place since at least the appearance of Marilyn Cooper's "The Ecology of Writing." The argument she makes for understanding writing as "one of the activities by which we locate ourselves in the enmeshed systems that make up the social world" (373) has prompted instructors to teach writing "in *situ*" (Owens, "Teaching"), often connecting with issues of sustainability (Dobrin and Weisser; Owens, *Composition*; Weisser and Dobrin), cultural differences (Reynolds), student engagement with campuses (Mauk), and probing the histories of places of instruction (Brooke and McIntosh), to name but a few. Barbara J. Blakely and Susan B. Pagnac have described an ambitious Communications Foundation course for all entering first-year students at Iowa State University, in which eighty sections of the course focus heavily on the campus as a place, both to help students transition into the campus and to make use of the many opportunities for teaching and learning that it offers.

The first-year writing course in which this "geobiography" assignment is used at the University of Hawai'i at Mānoa is an English 100 section entitled "Composing in the Anthropocene Epoch." Like the course at Iowa State, it requires students to interact strongly with the campus, yet, as the title suggests, it also requires students to interact strongly with the surrounding environment and includes a research project focused on sustainability. At UH Mānoa, the content of first-year writing courses is left up to instructors who are also tasked with targeting common student learning outcomes, so this assignment does not carry the benefit of being enacted across multiple sections. (However, several PhD students who have taken a graduate course with me entitled Theory and Practice of Teaching Composition and who are also interested in place-based writing have made this assignment a part of their English 100 course.) The assignment enables me to teach the course from a perspective informed by my research, my teaching in other courses, and my campus service focused on place, the environment, and sustainability. Like the course at Iowa State, this very first assignment for the course parlays a common first-year writing assignment focused on individual students' past experiences, to set the scaffolding for assignments to come and to lay the foundation for the learning community I seek to foster in this course.

Other Pedagogical Considerations

I use no textbook for the course because I agree with Claude Hurlbert that composition textbooks "offer a no-geography. A no-place set out to take the place of place" (353). With the place-based focus of the course, I rely instead on sources available on the Internet, in our library, and elsewhere on our campus. This assignment occurs while students are establishing the shells of their e-portfolios, which will include drafts, revisions, and metacommentary for each assignment during the semester. Because the course seeks to establish and nurture a learning community, this first assignment also includes carefully sequenced activities in which students respond to one another as peer reviewers, post their responses to the course virtual environment, compare their performances as reviewers with those of peers, and state plans to revise based on response from peers, instructor, and course mentor. This sequencing, sample writing and response, and the advantages it offers for teaching peer review practices in this introductory FYW course are described in detail in "Teaching Intellectual Teamwork in WAC Courses through Peer Review" (Henry and Ledbetter).

My syllabus is entirely online, enabling me to update details and links regularly as students' oral and written performances suggest. The online version of this assignment carries a recapitulation of course work to date, including students' work with their writing mentor, an English graduate student who attends all classes and meets regularly with students individually and in groups—a version of classroom-based tutoring (Henry, Bruland, and Sano-Franchini; Spiegelman and Grobman). The online syllabus also includes a link to the e-portfolios of students who took an earlier version of this course in 2013, thus providing students with examples of how the 2013 cohort completed this assignment while also positioning current students as part of a course-specific writing and research tradition. When I show students the e-portfolios from the 2013 class, I stress that these virtual creations are enduring entities that students might extend beyond this course. I also stress that even after a "final" draft for an assignment has been submitted for a grade, students may continue to improve on the assignment and get credit for it. This geobiography assignment establishes scaffolding for later assignments in several ways, as described below.

Pre-Writing Activities

Campus demographics are such that incoming first-year cohorts consist of approximately 50 percent in-state and 50 percent out-of-state students, and class demographics regularly reflect this split. Because of the strong First Nation presence of Native Hawaiians in the state, even those local students of no Hawaiian ancestry are familiar with a number of Hawaiian terms and cultural practices that permeate everyday life. The status of "local" is fraught with issues of ancestry and provenance, too, given the state's history as a colonized land that brought migrant workers whose progeny have been born into citizenship (and, depending upon their national ancestry, now occupy varying socio-economic strata—see Okamura), alongside many other students whose parents or guardians might have come to Hawai'i for various reasons.

The social complexity of this classroom scenario is compounded further by the fact that English department faculty are predominantly Caucasian, in contrast to the student demographics campus-wide that show Caucasians as comprising only 21 percent of total students on campus, in comparison with 40 percent Asian, 17 percent Hawaiian or Pacific Islander, and 14 percent who have indicated two or more races on official records. The local students are aware of this complexity even before classes begin; those from out of state have most likely been learning daily lessons inflected by local demographic dynamics since arrival. And although this kind of demographic complexity is quite evident in Hawai'i, other complexities dependent upon place of instruction are certain to reveal themselves in other geographical contexts.

At the first class meeting, I ask students to interview the person sitting next to them about where she or he comes from to find out at least one memorable thing about that place of origin as it has shaped them as a person. I stress that they will be reporting to the class on their interviews, and one goal is to enable everyone to learn everyone else's first name quickly because we will be forming a learning community that needs to work together productively and critically to help everyone progress. They have only four minutes to confer—two minutes each as interviewer—and then we go around the room for presentations. During those presentations, lots of ad-hoc teaching from student to student takes place, as a student from Colorado, for example, explains hiking in the Rockies, or as a local student uses a term from 'ōlelo Hawai'i (Native Hawaiian, an official state language) or Pidgin (the lingua franca spawned by plantation labor practices and which now endures as a marker of being local—see Nordstrom) that an out-of-state student does not know. By the end of these brief discussions, place as written into one's everyday existence is evidenced through talk and teaching. Students follow up with a one-paragraph elaboration posted to our virtual discussion forum hosted on the University's course management server. The server's logo includes its name—Laulima—along with translations of this term from 'ōlelo Hawai'i: "Cooperation, joint action; group of people working together; community food patch; to work together, cooperate. *Lit., many hands*" (Laulima), so attentive students already notice a connection between officially expressed University values and course activities.

The next few class sessions are devoted to studying the rhetorical triangle and the concept of meta-commentary (cover commentary to essays that sets forth the author's aim, intended audience, and desired representation as an author) as it can help sharpen writing and enhance reviewing processes. As noted above, students are also setting up their e-portfolio shells, establishing place-holders for content to come while also nurturing a greater sense of assignment sequencing and scaffolding. In 2015, a student from the 2013 cohort came to class to show her e-portfolio and how she has extended it, thus demonstrating its usefulness beyond this class while alerting students to eventual WWW audiences. For the sixth class meeting, students' homework is two short readings—one from Dennis Kawaharada's *Local Geography: Essays on Multicultural Hawai'i* and the Introduction to Mathieu et al.'s *Writing Places*: "Where Are We From?" In the following class, we do a short whole-class activity on invention, using the Purdue OWL and these readings, then students are placed in groups of three to review their virtual postings on their place-based backgrounds from the previous week and brainstorm ideas on how each author can complete the first draft for the geobiography assignment.

First Drafts

For the following class session, students must arrive with a two-page single-spaced printed draft of their geobiography, accompanied by the three-paragraph meta-commentary. These drafts are expectedly rough yet ripe with possibilities. A representative first paragraph might look something like Jamie Wong's in the fall of 2013:

> My home since September 10, 1995 has always and hopefully will continue to reside in Kaneohe, Hawaii. I was born into a Chinese family where my father refuged away from Vietnam and my mother journeyed away from Taiwan. I have an older brother and a younger sister, making me the middle child. The house I've been living in is the house my maternal grandparents worked hard for since their arrival in Hawaii. I have lived with all their five children, with my mother being the eldest, at some point. The house started out being a cramped one story house where my mother, uncles and aunts had to sleep in one room growing up. After a few years of owning a successful Chinese restaurant, my grandparents expanded the first story and added another story above. My grandfather built a basement later to make more room for his first grandchildren (my siblings and I). Up until I was 10 years old, my siblings and I all slept on two queen size mattresses with our parents in that very basement.

Jamie's meta-commentary addressed her intended persona (or authorship), audience (her peers, professor, and class mentor), and aim (or purpose), which she summarized as follows: "My purpose in writing this paper is to show my life growing up as a first generation American. I really want to express that no matter what we are born into, whether it is a financially stable family or a hard-working family, we can find several reasons why we are lucky to be in the place we are at today. I also wanted to show the life of a middle child because I've been told that I behave extremely different from my siblings."

In class, each peer reviewer responds to one or two drafts (depending upon class time) with two primary goals: (1) provide at least one sentence per category on the meta-commentary sheet to show the author your impressions of how the writing met her or his intentions, and (2) fill the margins with comments and questions to help the author expand this draft to four pages. (The class mentor and I have also completed the assignment and responded to one another to model responding as "intellectual teammates," and I present our comment-filled pages to the class using a document cam projector. On campuses with no classroom-based tutors, instructors might solicit collaboration with a representative from the writing center to play the role of respondent and thus provide some modeling of response.)

Pitfalls and Avoidance Strategies

A recurrent pitfall in student drafts is focusing too much on the "bio" part of the assignment and not enough on the "geo." As the syllabus demonstrates (see below), the interconnections between people and places—and more specifically geographical places—form a theme that undergirds the course theme, composing in the Anthropocene epoch. Many students bring exposure to expressive first-person writing with them from high school, and they often have experience in writing biographical texts. Yet few have been asked to write geographical texts, and fewer still have been positioned to theorize biographical experiences with respect to geographies. This first assignment initiates such theorizing by focusing responses to drafts (by students and by me) on places that emerge in them and the potential of those places to prompt insights as a writer. I urge students to make sure that "geographical places" are addressed in their meta-commentary, a part of the assignment that naturally lends itself to theorizing, as in Travis Weaver's 2013 excerpt: "When you are used to a certain way things are done, or always go about your life the same way, you kind of shut your eyes to things that go on outside of that pattern. Going somewhere where you don't know anyone, where you're unsure of how to act, where you are a little on edge, is what reveals to us everything that's going on." In my response to individuals, I also repeatedly stress that s/he should be using writing not just to *report* but to *learn*, and that one way to learn is to identify some themes that have emerged and develop them, as explained below.

As one of the requirements of the geobiography is to discover (or uncover) at least one fact about their places' histories, geographies, or social makeup, another part of this "writing to learn" is built in. Quite expectedly, many facts will come from Wikipedia, and our response procedures position students to avoid the potential pitfall of relying exclusively on *Wikipedia* by reviewing students' facts as a whole class, discussing various *Wikipedia* pages for what they do and do not provide in the way of facts. These discussions early in the course thus provide scaffolding for much more in-depth discussions of sources when the research unit arrives.

Response, Class Themes and Revision

The next few classes are devoted to response and revision to help students expand their initial two-page draft to four single-spaced pages. The expanded page-length has two goals: (1) positioning student reviewers to elicit more development from peers rather than "correcting"; and (2) subtly leading students to complete an equivalent of an eight-page double-spaced essay. (Students often share with their writing mentor that they have never written a paper beyond two or three pages, and their big research project near the end of the semester calls for eight to ten pages. This assignment thus provides some scaffolding in the domain of sheer length, a point I will recall later when we begin the research project.)

Because I want students to value (and use) responses from peers in addition to mine, I respond to the first drafts only after the first round of peer response. Some of my responses recur across the group of students (e.g., how to think about titling an essay), and I project excerpts from student drafts onto the screen and invite brainstorming as a class to help individual authors, e.g., "What might Jamie develop as a title based on what you see in this first paragraph?" Mostly, I ask questions of students using the comment function of my word processor, all the while identifying themes that seem ripe for development. To Jamie's paragraph above, for example, I inserted some questions about how she thought the Chinese-ness of her household took special characteristics in the locale she discusses. I also noted that she had begun a theme of place as "earned" and also "sharing a place," and I asked her if she could possibly develop these themes in more detail.

I also do not want students to feel "locked in" to initial themes, just as I want them to appreciate how many more potential themes surface when the entire class production is reviewed. I distribute a table I have compiled that lists all the themes that have surfaced (I include students' names in each cell so that they can see where they "fit" so far and also so that they can consult other students' writing), and we use this table as a central part of the next class session. At the end of that session, students must freewrite for four minutes to augment their initial plans for revision in the light of the collective performance. The table in fall of 2013 was as follows:

Table 1. Initial Themes in Geobiographies: Place …

as "earned"	as "respected"	as a scene of confrontation	as shared	as it enables education
as it enables specific skills and views of nature	to practice and cultural/ gender coding	to exercise and independence	to transgress and travel	to be carefree, "at home" and festival or party

and consumer consumption	and pride	and community	and ancestry	and previous occupants or their remains
of education as it can augment sense of "home"	and security	and danger or safety	and socializing	and responsibility
and progress	and urban development	and official positions	and expectations	and subsistence
and survival	as in flux	and smells	and food	and amenities
offering excitement/ terror simultaneously	and water	and back and forth	and ethnicity	and the economies associated with it
and a better life	and religion	and sports	and memory or "amnesia"	as it shapes judgment
and leisure, including camping	and the outdoors	and dancing	and the beach	future places

Grading Rubric

After their initial drafting and before revising, the class collectively determines our grading rubric, a practice that prompts student ownership while subtly tapping the geobio dynamics enabled by who they are in this specific place, and how writing should respond accordingly. We begin by discussing what students deem most important to an effective geobiography, an activity that is aided by the fact that the geobiography is a fabricated genre and hence does not carry any pre-conceived ideas of what it "must" or "must not" include. In the fall of 2013, the final rubric was as shown on the following page.

"Final" Revisions

Students revise their drafts in the light of peer review, our reviews of it, my review, and our established grading rubric. As mentioned earlier, students have been informed at the first class meeting that they may revise any assignment during the semester to improve their grade and to enhance their e-portfolio. For this final submission (and for any subsequent revisions), they must submit the following: meta-commentary, detailing the evolution of their authorship, aim, and audience appeal; an effort chart that states explicitly how much time they spent doing what (I often respond to the chart to suggest ways to adjust efforts); their current self-editing checklist, with a note that they have both read the final submission aloud and applied it to this version; and the "final" draft. Readers can see the final version of Jamie's geobiography, along

English 100: Composing in the Anthropocene Epoch   Author:
Grading Criteria for Geo-biography Assignment

%	Criterion	Evaluation	#
10%	**Meta-commentary,** discussing your writing aim, audience, and authorship Tip: Show how your authorship has evolved by retracing the steps you took and decisions you made, citing others' influence. Goal: Make it easy for Jim to compare your intentions with the result. Include the mandatory "I certify I have read aloud."		
10%	**Effort.** Document the amount of work you put in. Talk about pre-writing, drafting, revising, reading, researching, meeting with Jamaica or me, or anything else. Compose a table that presents these various components with time spent. If you spend time on the CC grammar site, document the specific activities and time spent. If you read it aloud to a captive audience, document it.		
25%	**Content (Message or Point).** Does the content develop a specific theme or themes that relate **place** to who you are/have become/are becoming? Does your content go beyond just relating events and attempt to dig a bit deeper? (Travis's excerpt!) Have you carefully connected the dots across paragraphs so that the theme is omnipresent? Have you excised any information that does not fit this theme?		
20%	**Organization & Structure.** Does the essay have a **beginning, middle, and end** — in which the beginning paragraph forecasts the middle and the concluding paragraph makes sense of the whole essay? Does each paragraph develop one and only one principle topic? (**Tip**: print it out and in the margin next to each paragraph, write down what that topic is. If you have more than one, cut material or create more paragraphs.) Above all, **avoid the "and another thing" effect**, in which you give readers a lot of information but no guiding theme that pulls it all together. Finally, **use transitions** to forecast upcoming content.		
10%	**Development — Details & Support.** If you make a **claim** or state an **assertion**, provide a **concrete example** to illustrate. Keep in mind the idea to "**show**" (providing scenes in which readers live the event along with you) in addition to "telling" (merely stating that such and such took place).		
10%	**Style (Good Description, Creativity, Vocabulary, Sentence Variety).** Use **strong verbs** (Evan's example), **concrete nouns** ("loud, heavy steamrollers" rather than "trucks"), imaginative **imagery or metaphor** (Alema's "tree"). When reading aloud, be alert for the same word repeated in close quarters (use an **online Thesaurus!**). Vary short and long sentences for effect. (If you have time, take a paragraph and put a hard return at the end of each sentence. If all your sentences are the same length, look for a place to insert a short one, or fuse two sentences together.)		
15%	**Strong Grammar and Usage**, enabling your audience to read without distractions. *Tip:* Read aloud for this one, too. Using your editing checklist, proofread several times looking for specific problems. Use our online source to develop your expertise. **Strong Punctuation,** using punctuation for effect and demonstrating care *Tip:* Add those problems that have plagued you over the years to your editing checklist and make a point of mastering them. Commas and semicolons are the most troublesome, so focus in particular on them.		
Extra Credit			
Timely	One letter grade deducted for each day after deadline.		

Grading Scale

A+	A	A-	B+	B	B-	C+	C	C-	D+	D	F
97-100	93-96	90-92	87-89	83-86	80-82	77-79	73-76	70-72	67-69	60-66	0-59

Figure 1. Geobiography Grading Rubric.

with a host of other course materials, by visiting the web syllabus in "Writing and Designing Informational Booklets for International Exchange Students."

Subsequent Course Activities

The next assignment broadens from the focus on personal geobiographies to require a short essay on some place in Hawai'i. Their designated audiences are their classmates, their writing mentor, and me. The assignment seeks to build upon ad-hoc discussions of style that occurred during the geobiography by requiring part of this essay to reflect a visit to some place in Hawai'i and a recounting of what that experience was like, drawing on the five senses and striving for concrete nouns and active verbs. Juxtaposed with this personal experience must appear some archival research on that place. The campus library includes a rich Hawaiian Collection, and the class visits it for an orientation by a librarian. There students encounter sources such as Sterling and Summers's *Sites of O'ahu*, Pukui, Ebert, and Mookini's *Place Names of Hawai'i*, and other texts (including facsimiles of old newspapers in 'ōlelo Hawai'i for those who speak the language) that recount histories of different places on the island. Though libraries in other locales may not include such geographically focused collections, they may well include collections that do shed light on local geographies and that can support such a subsequent assignment.

This assignment is followed by a unit entitled "Mapping Our UH Places," inspired partly by an assignment in Reynolds's *Geographies of Writing: Inhabiting Places and Encountering Difference*. In this unit, students are positioned as fieldworkers studying the campus and reporting to one another on it. Writing from field observations and interviews is a new experience for many, and we devote class time to prepping these activities and to troubleshooting results. As a part of the desired reflexivity that good fieldwork requires, we revisit the personae of the geobiographies to discuss how writers might need to adjust their cultural filters as observers and interviewers.

A research paper on some topic in sustainability is the next assignment. To the issues of geobiographical influences on writing and cultural sustainability that have emerged during the previous units, students can now add biological and environmental sustainability as possible approaches. Students are urged to research a sustainability topic that might figure in their intended major. An advantage to scheduling this research component before the end of the semester is that students are not yet feeling the semester burnout and/or strong demands of other courses preparing for exams, and they accomplish the most ambitious writing with a few weeks yet to go in the semester. During this unit, we are all also analyzing our consumption patterns and carbon footprints, at times making connections with our geobiographical themes.

The course concludes with three options: a fictional piece with the Anthropocene epoch figuring somehow in it, a nonfiction report on possible employment opportunities in industries developing sustainability, or a report on a field trip to some site on O'ahu devoted explicitly or implicitly to biocultural sustainability.

During the last two weeks, students work with their mentor to finalize their e-portfolios and present them to me formally while I play the role of potential collaborator, scholarship committee, graduate school entrance committee, or possible employer—of the student's choosing. Our discussions return once again to our work with the rhetorical triangle, helping students adjust their writing for an internet audience while writing in the academic register. Many have augmented their writing with chosen visuals and explored in more depth and from different perspectives several of the themes that surfaced in their first drafts of the geobiography. During the debriefing after their e-portfolio presentation to me, students often comment that so much has transpired since they wrote that first geobiography draft, making it a valuable artifact in documenting their growth as writers.

Full Online Syllabus with Student E-Portfolios

Readers can find the full syllabus, with links to the e-portfolios of all students in the course, at the following URL: https://geobiographies.word press.com. The syllabus includes complete assignment details for all units and class-by-class activities. The e-portfolios enable readers to perceive how the foundational assignment of a geobiography influences directly and indirectly students' written performances and their representations of them across an entire semester, testimony to the potential of place-based writing to help first-year students engage with, as 2013 student Travis put it, "everything that's going on."

WORKS CITED

Blakely, Barbara J., and Susan B. Pagnac. "Pausing in the Whirlwind: A Campus Place-Based Curriculum in a Multimodal Foundation Communication Course." *Writing Program Administration* 35.2 (2012): 11–37. Web. 5 August 2014.

Brooke, Robert, and Jason McIntosh. "Deep Maps: Teaching Rhetorical Engagement through Place-conscious Education." *The Locations of Composition*. Ed. Christopher J. Keller and Christian R. Weisser. Albany: SUNY, 2007. 131–150. Print.

Cooper, Marilyn. "The Ecology of Writing." *College English* 48 (1986): 364–375. Print.

Dobrin, Sidney, and Christian R. Weisser. *Natural Discourse: Toward Ecocomposition*. Albany: State University of New York Press, 2002. Print.

Henry, Jim, and Lehua Ledbetter. "Teaching Intellectual Teamwork in WAC Courses through Peer Review." *Currents in Teaching and Learning* 3.2 (2011): 4–18. Web. 5 August 2014.

Henry, Jim, Holly Huff Bruland, and Jennifer Sano-Franchini. "Course-Embedded Mentoring for First-Year Students: Melding Academic Subject Support with Role Modeling, Psycho-Social Support, and Goal Setting." *International Journal for the Scholarship of Teaching and Learning* 5.2 (2011): 1–22. Web. 5 August 2014.

Howes, Craig, and Jonathan Kamakawiwo'ole Osorio, eds. *The Value of Hawai'i*. Honolulu: University of Hawai'i Press, 2010. Print.

Hurlbert, Claude. "A Place on Which to Stand." *Relations, Locations, Positions: Com-

position Theory for Writing Teachers. Ed. Peter Vandenberg and Sue Hum. Urbana: National Council of Teachers of English, 2006. 353–357. Print.

Kawaharada, Dennis. *Local Geography: Essays on Multicultural Hawai'i*. Honolulu: Kalamakū Press, 2004. Print.

Laulima. University of Hawai'i. Web. 27 November 2015.

Mathieu, Paula, George Grattan, Tim Lindgren, and Stacy Shultz. "Where Are We From?" *Writing Places*, 2d ed. Ed. Paula Mathieu, George Grattan, Tim Lindgren, and Stacy Shultz. New York: Longman, 2012. 1–4. Print.

Mauk, Johnathon. "Location, Location, Location: The 'Real' (E)states of Being, Thinking, and Writing in Composition." *Relations, Locations, Positions: Composition Theory for Writing Teachers*. Ed. Peter Vandenberg and Sue Hum. Urbana: National Council of Teachers of English, 2006. 181–197. Print.

Nordstrom, Georganne. "Pidgin as Rhetorical Sovereignty: Articulating Indigenous and Minority Rhetorical Practices with the Language Politics of Place." *College English*, forthcoming.

Okamura, Jonathan Y. *Ethnicity and Inequality in Hawai'i*. Philadelphia: Temple University Press, 2008. Print.

Owens, Derek. *Composition and Sustainability: Teaching for a Threatened Generation*. Urbana,: National Council of Teachers of English, 2001. Print.

———. "Teaching *in Situ*." *Relations, Locations, Positions: Composition Theory for Writing Teachers*. Ed. Peter Vandenberg and Sue Hum. Urbana: National Council of Teachers of English, 2006. 363–370. Print.

Pukui, Mary Kawena, Samuel H. Ebert, and Esther T. Mookini. *Place Names of Hawai'i*. Honolulu: University of Hawai'i Press, 1974. Print.

Reynolds, Nedra. *Geographies of Writing: Inhabiting Places and Encountering Difference*. Carbondale,: Southern Illinois University Press, 2005. Print.

Spigelman, Candace and Laurie Grobman. *On Location: Theory and Practice in Classroom-Based Tutoring*. Logan: Utah State University Press, 2005.

Sterling, Elspeth P., and Catherine C. Summers. *Sites of O'ahu*. Bishop Museum Press, 1973. Print.

Weisser, Christian R., and Sidney I. Dobrin. *Ecocomposition: Theoretical and Pedagogical Approaches*. Albany: State University of New York Press, 2001. Print

The Discipline Resource Guide Website

Dalyn Luedtke

Supplemental Materials

- Rationale
- Scaffolding Activities
- Pre-Writing Activities
- Pitfalls and Avoidance Strategies

Assignment

Every discipline has its own culture and practices. Negotiating and becoming part of that culture is an ongoing process that takes years; indeed, much of that process begins here at university as you learn the foundational knowledge that defines your chosen field. Specifically, you learn the conventions that define disciplinary communication, particularly how to read, write, and think as a practitioner. But you also discover where to make contacts and find jobs, where scholars publish, the future directions research and jobs may take, and how to interact with your colleagues, among many other details. Focusing on a wide variety of research methods and composing practices, the Discipline Resource Guide will help you become more professionalized within and across your chosen discipline. Because of the scope of the project, it comprises 50 percent of your final grade and you will work on it throughout the course of the entire semester.

Overview

As with much of the work you will eventually do, you will undertake the Discipline Resource Guide in small groups (3–4 people). You must work with colleagues whose majors are the same or nearly the same as your own. Together you will design a website, which will host all the materials you gather and produce for this project: (1) two interviews with practitioners in your field; (2) a homepage/introduction; (3) an APA-style annotated bibliography; (4) an ethics case study; (5) an infographic; (6) a short promotional video; (7) an "About" page with biographies for each contributor. You will then present your work to the rest of the class.

For our purposes, the *audience* for your website will be people who are seriously interested in pursuing a career in your discipline or those who have recently begun to do so. The *purpose* of the website is to compile what you would consider the most important resources to get started (hint: think about what you would have liked to have known or what you would still like to know) and to generate enthusiasm for your chosen career path.

The Process

First, as a group, you must decide which website builder you'd like to use (please DO NOT choose one that you have to pay for as there are plenty of effective, free options) and decide on a name for your *website*. One person will then create an account and register for the site. That person needs to grant access to the remaining members of the group, so that everyone may have access to the site (or, if your website builder allows it, add all your group members as contributors). You'll all be responsible for designing a website that is professional and reinforces the values of your field, as well as the content of your resource guide. You do not need to know how to code, though you may do so if you possess those skills.

Your website also needs an *introduction/homepage* that makes the purpose and audience of your website immediately clear to potential visitors. Because of the nature of your audience, the introduction should also provide an historical overview, acknowledgment of subdisciplines, and any information you think those with limited experience might need to understand the resources contained on your website.

Then, you will compile an APA-style, *digital annotated bibliography*, which should document some details of your discipline: job prospects and earning potential, education requirements, areas of sub-specialization, industry resources, and other important data for researchers and/or practitioners. Specifically, you must include 15 resources with annotations (you must have *at least 5 scholarly sources*).

You must also choose two people who are actively working in your field (not professors) as subjects for *interviews* about their background, the field in general, the expectations for those working in the field, the types of communication practices that they engage in or that define the field in general, how they learned those practices over time, common issues that students or new employees have with writing and communication, what the future looks like for those in your discipline, why they do what they do, and so forth. The goal here is to make connections in your field *and* provide your audience with an insider's perspective.

One page of your website must introduce the importance of ethics in your discipline through an *ethics case study*. You will research ethics case studies relevant to your field and pick one that you believe represents a significant ethical issue that your audience should be aware of. This page should include an introduction that discusses the importance of ethics in your discipline. Then, summarize the case study and provide a short analysis of the ethical issues demonstrated by the case and the possible solutions with justifications. This is just an introduction to one case, which is meant to raise awareness.

The *infographic* introduces visual components to your website. Infographics are visual and textual representations of information or data intended to inform specific audiences about a topic in a way that illuminates trends or patterns while also telling a story. They are, in essence, a visual representation of your research. Your job is to put together an infographic that represents some significant aspects of your discipline in an attractive, informative, and engaging manner. You could, for example, include employment numbers, demographic data, definitions of key terms, important discoveries, top schools, quotes, pictures of tools, places, people, or moments, explanations of processes, or any number of other discipline-related information.

You will also compose a *short promotional video* that acts as an advertisement for your discipline. The video may be composed of original footage or clips you glean elsewhere (as long as you adhere to fair use and copyright guidelines, which we will discuss). The video can explain an issue or concept in your field, show why it's exciting, discuss future prospects for workers, or cover anything that you think might be of interest to your audience that you haven't covered elsewhere in the project.

Finally, you will present all of your materials to the rest of the class. You must consider the best way to present that material and design a presentation/slideshow that is engaging, detailed, and audience aware. The presentation should be 20–25 minutes long.

The website and presentation will be graded holistically, focusing on audience awareness, visual appeal, level of detail, critical engagement, and effective design, formatting, and composition, but I've compiled a list of goals for each of your website's main elements:

- *Interview Material*: Specific, personalized questions; detailed responses with examples; an insider's perspective that complements and expands generally available information; attention to communication practices; a short bio that gives a clear picture of who your interviewee is and why you've chosen him/her; effective formatting/use of interview material.
- *Annotated Bibliography*: Evidence of thorough research; citations/annotations documented and designed effectively (APA); attention to detail; succinct, accurate annotations; annotations that clarify the strengths of each resource; variety (professional, scholarly, popular); at least 15 resources; attention to usability; audience awareness; clear, effective grammar and diction.
- *Homepage/Introduction*: Eye-catching visuals; clarity of purpose; short history/introduction to your discipline; clear navigation.
- *Ethics Case Study*: Introduction contextualizes the ethics case study on the website; discussion of the importance of ethics in your field; succinct summary of case study; analysis of the ethical issues involved; 1–2 possible solutions; engaging delivery for non-professional; cited in APA style.
- *Infographic*: Covers topic in-depth with details and examples; graphics illuminate the topic, making it easier to understand; use of design elements to enhance presentation (aesthetics); at least 6 sources (APA style); effective, correct grammar and diction.
- *Video*: Creative content or approach to assignment; purpose and audience are clear from the introduction; smooth transitions and clear audio; graphics and images show evidence of thoughtful selection; images and audio either created by user or documented appropriately.
- *Presentation*: Slides are concise; speakers reference slides; effective delivery (media, tone, eye contact, projection); evidence of planning; clear attempts to keep audience engaged; collaboration; smooth transitions between speakers and media/content; meets time requirements.

I will provide more detailed guidelines and instructions for each element as we proceed, but this prompt should give you a clear idea of where we're headed and what you'll be working on throughout the semester. Remember, the goal of this project is ultimately to learn more about your chosen field while refining your communication and composition skills.

Please keep in mind that most of you will be developing a lot of new technical skills throughout the course of this project, so it is vital that you uphold your team contract and meet your deadlines. Your group is counting on you.

Rationale

Founded in 1819, Norwich University is the oldest, private military college in the United States, and it was the first private college to teach engineering. Though there is a clear focus on the military and scientific traditions in our history, there is also a strong commitment to the literary tradition, which continues to inform our curriculum. Students at Norwich pick one of two "lifestyles" when they come to Norwich: Corps of Cadets or civilian. Between the two, there are about 2300 undergraduate students on campus. Within this context, several sections of EN 204 Professional and Technical Writing are offered every semester. The course is required for students in the following majors: Computer Science and Information Assurance, Civil Engineering, Construction Management, Accounting, and Management.

This context directly informs the design of the course as a whole and the particular assignment detailed in this essay. The students who take EN 203 come almost exclusively from the majors listed above, but each major recommends taking the course at different times. So, even though it is a lower-division course, it is common to have first semester sophomores and graduating seniors in the same class. My goal is to design assignments that *guide* all students, regardless of major or class, toward both professional and scholarly goals, make sense within our cultural context, and encourage students to play with new composing strategies in ways that complement the learning that occurs within their disciplines.

One of the strengths of the Discipline Resource Guide is the assumption that underlies its design—that students are capable of learning about their disciplines and the communication practices that define it with guidance from the professor rather than direction. While I do some lecturing and provide many detailed handouts that focus on rhetoric, the content of the project is gathered entirely by students through research, interviews, past and current experiences, and collaboration. Essentially, they are both the student, in that they have to learn a lot about their discipline as a whole, and the expert, in that they have to determine what is most important for new or prospective students to know and explain it in a way that is engaging and useful. In other words, students become more professionalized by reflecting carefully on what they have already learned and connecting to professionals who are active in their discipline.

The length and scope of the project are also rooted in practical considerations. When I began developing this project, it was the culminating artifact of a 6-week unit. It quickly became apparent, however, that the culture of Norwich, where the Corps does expand to take up every waking hour, sometimes made it legitimately difficult for students to collaborate. However, I believe it is particularly important for a professional and technical writing course to emphasize collaboration, because it reinforces the idea that all writing is a collaborative act and mirrors the type of writing that many of the students who are required to take this course will engage in post-graduation. Furthermore, they will not only produce texts in collaborative environments but they will also work on and be expected to manage projects that span significant time frames. Because groups work on the Discipline Resource Guide over the course of an entire semester, it provides some practice in the type of writing and research that undergraduate students often do not get exposed to.

The practical effect of this approach cannot be understated—and students are quick to recognize it. Not only do students learn from current practitioners but they also make valuable professional contacts that can and do bear fruit. On the other hand, each interaction—from the interviews they conduct to various design decisions they must make throughout the project to the annotated bibliography—is explicitly framed and theorized as rhetoric in our class discussions and in their own reflections at the end of the semester. As a result, the project does a good job of marrying the practical and academic; indeed, I would argue that the project goes beyond including both by blurring the distinction between the two.

Because much recent discourse about the end of higher education and laments about the state of student writing reinforce the divide between industry and the academy, resisting the dichotomy opens up an opportunity to frame professional and technical writing in a yet different way. In "What's Practical about Technical Writing?" Carolyn R. Miller argues, "Understanding practical rhetoric as a manner of conduct rather than of production, as a matter of arguing in a prudent way toward the good of the community rather than of constructing texts, should provide some new perspectives for teachers of technical writing and developers of courses and programs in technical communication" (69). The Discipline Resource Guide asks students to act as ambassadors for the discipline. The audience for the project is clearly defined as new or prospective students, and the goal of the website is to argue that the work is meaningful to an audience who may one day contribute to it substantially. Admittedly, because of the pedagogical focus, this essay focuses on production to a great degree, but connecting to the audience, inviting them to become part of the community, and providing the tools to do so more easily are just as important as the focus on constructing texts.

While collaboration, community, and practicality are important aspects of the Discipline Resource Guide, the multimodal nature of the project is, for most students, both the most challenging and rewarding part of the undertaking. Because this is a 200-level course, I believe it is important to emphasize breadth of writing experiences. For this project alone, students' audience and purpose remain the constant, but they experiment with many different mediums and genres. In fact, while the assignment specifies some of the details, like the requirement to conduct and post two interviews on the website, it does not specify what form those interviews can take. The lack of specificity in that regard (as well as with the video and to a lesser extent the design of the annotated bibliography) requires students to think rhetorically about the medium that is best suited to their audience and purpose, and I have seen students effectively use the interviews in a variety of ways both expected (video, transcript) and unexpected (animation, infographic).

Because learning so many new technologies for a project that accounts for half their grade can be a significant source of anxiety, collaboration is vital to the assignment's effectiveness and it is reinforced throughout the process. It is true that students are empowered to take responsibility for their own learning by becoming the expert and the demand to learn new tools quickly, but it is also true that the collaborative component of the project "can alleviate frustration of learning a new technology and can boost student morale. In groups in which everyone is a novice, experimenting with nonprint modes and new software feels less overwhelming" (Pedersen and Skinner 41). This kind of balance is reflected in much of the rationale for the project and in the development of the pre-writing and scaffolding activities.

In the end, it is easy to see that the Discipline Resource Guide, with its many components, requires a lot of students. In my experience, it offers as much as it demands—if not more. It is at once digital, collaborative, practical, theoretical, physical, multimodal, rhetorical, scholarly, and community-based. And, as with every assignment, it evolves to keep pace with students, Norwich, industry, and technology.

Scaffolding Activities

Mock Informational Interviews

Students usually possess limited interview experience, as either the interviewer or interviewee, and what experience they do have is often limited to job or internship interviews. The interviews I am asking them to conduct, on the other hand, are informational in nature. To gain some practice in informational interviewing, they have class time set aside to draft questions for and engage in two different informational interviews.

For the first interview, each group spends about twenty minutes drafting five questions, which they then use to interview me in class. The goal is to gain some insight into the life of a professor and writing teacher through specific, personalized questions. Understandably, students are sometimes hesitant to ask follow-up questions when they interview me in class. Additionally, for this project, many students conduct their interviews via email, because they are interested in making professional connections where they live. As a result, I ask each group to send me two to three follow-up questions via email. The email should be professional in tone and format, and the questions should either ask for some clarification or specific example to expand upon my earlier in-class response, but they can also ask a new question if they feel that something important was not addressed in the original interview. I then respond to the questions via email, suggesting areas for improvement in both the email itself and their informational interview questions.

While the Discipline Resource Guide requires students with the same major to work together, the goal of an informational interview is to gain insight into the interviewee's profession and background. So, once they have interviewed me, students pair up with someone outside of their group for another interview during the next class period. As I mentioned previously, Norwich University has two student lifestyle options: Corps and civilian. For this activity, it is important that students either pair up with someone who has chosen a different lifestyle at Norwich or a student who has a different major. Norwich's small student population usually means that students in the same major or lifestyle are also often in the same classes and/or share similar extracurricular experiences, which makes an informational interview unnecessary at best and uninformative at worst. They draft five interview questions to ask their partner, then perform their interviews, asking follow-up or clarifying questions during the interview. They then give a short 5 minute presentation to the class reporting what they learned about their partner. After two mock informational interviews, they are better prepared to begin drafting interview questions for the interviewees they have chosen to feature in their Discipline Resource Guide.

Copyright Collage

Because the website and infographic, in particular, bring up copyright and fair use issues, I spend a significant amount of time ensuring that students understand how to use material that they didn't create. After some mini-lectures and class discussions, I bring in materials that groups use to make a "collage": scissors, markers, finger paint, tape, glue, glitter, string, and a huge pile of magazines and catalogs. Groups spend about twenty-five to thirty minutes putting together a "new" composition using images from the materials I have given them. Students can compose any type of text that they choose, but I preface the activity by suggesting ideas such as an advertisement for a different product, a public service announcement, a piece of art, a short zine, a flyer, and so forth. Then each group presents their collage to the class, explaining what they've chosen to create, whether their work violates copyright laws or not, and, when appropriate, how their work is protected under fair use. Students should be able to specifically demonstrate the type, amount, and distribution of materials that fall under fair use. Furthermore, this type of hands-on group activity is helpful for periodically reinforcing effective collaboration within groups, which is especially important because groups will naturally be less productive or interactive at times during this lengthy project.

Pre-Writing Activities

Infographic Mock-Up

The most common problem I see with the infographic is that most of them are too simple. Even though I provide many examples of well-researched infographics that tell a story through text, graphics, and images, students will sometimes default to a few graphs about employment numbers and starting salaries and call it a day. Eventually, I realized that constantly talking about how infographics tell stories was not working; instead, I needed a strategy for complicating their understanding of how information is constructed in an infographic. The strategy I settled on is the mock-up.

Once students have done a significant amount of research on their discipline, I block out about an hour for the mock-up. At this point, students will usually have a vague idea of what they want to include in the infographic. So, to flesh out their ideas, I bring in a stack of blank paper, a wide variety of colored markers, and a glue stick, which I pass out to the groups. I have them start by putting a working title across the top of one page and then label the back of each sheet of paper with the topic or content area that they know they want to include and the elements they think they want to include. Then they draft a rough sketch of each of those elements on the front of the paper. My experience has been that they usually find that they need to add more content and play around with placement, but they are welcome to draw the elements directly onto the mocked-up content section or draw the elements, cut them out, and move them around until they are happy with their final placement and can be glued down.

Once they've gotten some of the individual sections fleshed out, I ask them to look at how those sections relate to one another to determine the overall organization. Often students organize the sheets of paper vertically, mimicking the scrolling style of many infographics. For a variety of reasons, I allow students to use an infographic-builder,[1] though they may also use other tools with which they are familiar. Those who choose to use an infographic-builder will often use a free theme or template, which may not have the vertical orientation. In such cases, I've found that they can shuffle the sections around to approximate the design of something like a flowchart or they can cut the elements out again and arrange them according to the patterns outlined in the template. Either way, having the sections sketched out helps them visualize the infographic more easily and serves to ease some anxiety about diving into designing an infographic—an often unfamiliar and potentially intimidating task.

Storyboard

The rationale, process, and materials for storyboarding the required video are similar to that of the mock-up. While I do teach this course in a computer classroom, using paper and markers for the storyboard is a nice change of pace and makes it easy for the group to work together on the process while also taking some of the anxiety out of the experience—particularly since EN 204 students tend to respond well to hand-on activities. Also similar to the mock-up, I ask them to imagine their video or story in discrete parts such as student interviews, faculty interviews, subdisciplines, history, a significant innovation, the steps in a process, or any other information they want to include. It is important that they do not get waylaid by trying to conceive of the parts in order; instead, they should collectively brainstorm a list of the parts they know they want to include, label each piece of paper accordingly, and draw a rough sketch of it. Next, they need to discuss whether video, photos, graphics, or animations are the best medium for each individual part and label it accordingly. Sometimes students choose to use one medium, like animation, in which case they will still need to storyboard the parts of their animation and consider which graphics to use.

Once each part of their video is labeled and planned, I ask the students to begin rearranging them, putting them in the order they think might work (based on some story-telling principles we discuss). Putting them in approximate order also illuminates what material might still be needed in the video and how they might transition between the units of their story. Finally, the storyboard panels can also be used if the group decides that their movie needs narration, which they write across the bottom of the page to indicate which part of the narration goes with which image, video, or graphic.

Pitfalls and Avoidance Strategies

Procrastination

The scope and length of this project, which have both increased significantly as I have developed it over the years, tend to produce a couple of specific, unsurprising problems. The first is procrastination, which is always a problem, but can be particularly devastating in a semester long, group project. When I first developed the Discipline Resource Guide, it was a 6-week unit with far fewer elements. Though I had due dates for drafts and scheduled workshops at various points throughout the 6-week period, I wanted to emphasize process and, as a result, did not have actual due dates for any of the individual elements. That was obviously a disaster. Because the materials produced for the workshop were not graded, they lacked motivation to not only produce significant materials for the workshop but also to continue working on their portion of the website. With a semester-long project, this problem is even more acute.

Some students were as frustrated with the process as I was. In a number of course evaluations, students expressed enthusiasm for the project as a whole but suggested that I have periodic due dates that are graded separately as a significant part of their homework grade. I now have due dates throughout the semester, to ensure that no one is trying to put together an infographic from scratch or line up an interview at the eleventh hour. That said, when a draft of an element of the project is due, I require that students submit a revision memo as well. In the memo, students outline what they have accomplished on the project to date, what revisions they plan on making to the draft, and a timeline of assigned tasks going forward. The goal is to give students more practice writing memos, keep them on task, and emphasize the composing process. So far, the quality of the projects has increased dramatically, and I have had fewer complaints about uneven participation because the tasks are revisited on a regular basis.

Team Work

The inability of some group members to meet deadlines and contribute substantially to the group is certainly aided by regular due dates, but procrastination is not the only issue that can undermine collaboration. Due to conflicting schedules and personalities, group projects are potentially difficult for everybody involved. I would argue that because the project is also worth 50 percent of the final grade, group dynamics are both more strained and more important.

To avoid what I often refer to as the "imploding group," I have a number of activities that ask groups to perform together throughout the semester. On the day I introduce the project and ask students to form groups, I do some kind of team building exercise in class, usually "The Marshmallow Challenge,"[2] then ask them to reflect on the process of working together and the role each individual played during the exercise. Based on that reflection, they then fill out a group contract detailing contact information, available meeting times, responsibilities, roles, and repercussions for contract violations, which every group member must agree to and sign. Not only does the exercise help the group members connect in an enjoyable manner from the outset, but the contract also outlines expected behavior and removes from me the role of potentially having to step in and police the group. I simply enforce the contract all the group members agreed to.

As is clear from the pre-writing and scaffolding activities, I incorporate a number of in-class activities that require students to work together physically to complete a task related to the project. A lot of the work students complete for this project is done alone in a digital environment. I believe that incorporating hands-on activities is important to acknowledge different learning styles and skill sets, but it is also effective at reuniting groups periodically throughout the semester. It reinforces the idea that the project is a collaboration rather than a digitized collection of individual work, and that the group can enjoy working together even if they have been experiencing frustration related to group dynamics.

Notes

1. At the present time, there are many free infographic builders found online. My students have typically used Piktochart or Easel.ly, though all the infographic tools have improved drastically over the past few years and many new options have been developed as well.

2. During "The Marshmallow Challenge," teams must work together for 18 minutes to build the tallest structure out of "20 sticks of spaghetti, one yard of tape, one yard of string, and one marshmallow" (Wujec). The marshmallow must be on top. I have found that this exercise works particularly well because many of my students are engineers, the students respond well to hands-on exercises, and everybody loves marshmallows.

Works Cited

Miller, Carolyn R. "What's Practical about Technical Communication?" *Professional Writing and Rhetoric: Readings from the Field.* Ed. Tim Peeples. New York: Longman, 2003. 61–70. Print.

Pedersen, Anne-Marie, and Carolyn Skinner. "Collaborating on Multimodal Projects." Ed. Cynthia L. Selfe. *Multimodal Composition: Resources for Teachers.* Cresskill, NJ: Hampton Press, 2007. Print.

Wujec, Tom. "Build a Tower, Build a Team." TED. Feb. 2010. Lecture.

Global Urban Centers
A Rhetorical Analysis of Street Art

Gerald Maki

Supplemental Materials

- Rationale
- Pre-Writing Activities
- Using Street Art to Teach Plagiarism
- Sample Passages from a Student Paper

Global Urban Centers: A Rhetorical Analysis of Street Art

Due Dates

Peer Review Workshop—TBA (Worth up to 40 Points—4 percent of the Overall Grade)

Final Draft—TBA (Worth up to 150 Points—15 percent of the Overall Grade)

Overview

The second writing project asks you to expand your rhetorical repertoire to include analysis, which means to examine in detail the parts of a text, phenomenon, or event to come to a greater understanding of the whole and its wider importance and implications. In this project, you will be analyzing the rhetorical strategies of a single piece of street art (sometimes referred to as graffiti) as found in major city centers around the globe. All of the recommended objects of investigation for this project have been composed by a street artist of some fame or infamy.

To compose a strong rhetorical analysis, one will need to integrate the knowledge gained from our in-class exercises, such as creating effective descriptions by using carefully chosen details, along with supporting a thesis (point) with appropriately selected evidence (particulars).

We will frame our discussion of street art/graffiti against the backdrop of the exponential, on-going growth of megacities. One will want to be sensitive to issues of economic inequality, the role of pop culture, regional political conflicts, and other issues that pertain to the lived experiences of the target audience for these images.

Additionally, street art is often composed by individuals who knowingly break the law to communicate a message to various sectors of society. In deviating from standard social and legal expectations, street artists pose an important ethical question for us: How should one make sense of the fact that these images are illegally produced, especially in light of Broken Windows Theory, which suggests that the presence of graffiti leads to an increase in crime?

As contemporary cultural artifacts, street art provides us with a unique opportunity to consider questions of purpose, audience, and authorship. One will want to discuss not only the effect of the image in question, but carefully detail the various types of rhetorical decisions reflected in the composition of the mural.

Key Questions to Consider in a Rhetorical Analysis

Chapter Eight of our textbook provides a very helpful overview of the types of elements one should examine when analyzing visual texts. For street art, in particular, a strong rhetorical analysis should address the following:

- *Purpose*—What is the purpose of the image? Why might the artist in question have chosen to construct this particular image? Is its goal to entertain, inform, shock, or critique? What type of risk was involved in making the image? What evidence or particulars from the image itself would you highlight to reinforce your claim?
- *Audience*—Who is the intended audience of the image? Where is it located? Is it found on the side of a tall building at the heart of a large city where it can be seen by tens of thousands of people daily? Is the image located in a sewer tunnel where it is visible to only a handful of people, most likely homeless families who are seeking shelter? What role does location play in the image's relationship to the audience?
- *Genre*—One will want to consider the image itself and the conventions

of visual rhetoric as outlined by the textbook, such as color, scheme, imagery. Does the image take the form of a narrative? If so, does it have defined characters? Is it abstract? What type of a mood is evoked by the image?

- *Authorship*—Many street artists create their images anonymously or employ a pseudonym for themselves such as "Faith47" or "Blek le Rat." How does the loss of a legally named author shape the image's rhetorical effect? What does their pseudonym suggest or add to the image in terms of ethos?

Purpose: In a unified, thesis-driven essay, one should provide a detailed rhetorical analysis of a work of contemporary street art. The essay should contain a description of the image and assume that the painting is not available for the reader to view. In composing a description, think carefully about the details you would highlight to help construct a clear and accurate image of the painting in the reader's mind. From there, the paper should contain a thorough, critical examination of the image's purpose, audience, genre, and authorship.

Audience: Your audience for this project is your peers and classmates who may be unfamiliar with graffiti, the artist, and/or the city in question. A slow, careful detailing of important background information as well as the various features of the image will be necessary in order to provide a clear and coherent analysis.

Formatting Specifics: The final essay should be three full pages minimum, 12 point font, double-spaced, stapled, and formatted using MLA. Note: Papers/Drafts not ready at the beginning of class will be counted as late.

General Instructions: Select one (1) piece of graffiti/street art from one (1) of the artists (Blek le Rat, Faith47, *Zezão*, and Banksy) found in the Unit Two folder of our "Class Sessions" page in Blackboard. From there, describe the painting in detail, and analyze the rhetorical moves made and the context in which the painting was constructed. In addition to images from the painters, one will also find links to materials—articles, interviews, videos—discussing the artists and their work in the "Class Sessions" folder. Additionally, we will cover a reading in class on Broken Windows Theory, which addresses the issue of graffiti and crime as well as screen portions of the documentary *Bomb It!* You will want to be sure to incorporate at least two (2) sources into your rhetorical analysis. Incorporating additional relevant research is also welcomed.

Additional Assistance: As always, I am glad to help with any questions you have about the writing process. Feel free to stop by my office or email me questions, drafts, and partial drafts you may have. Full feedback on a given project will require sending me a draft 48 hours before the date of our Peer Review Workshop. After that, I will only be able to provide general feedback and answer smaller questions.

Grade Breakdown

A—(135-150) The paper demonstrates evidence of a strong thesis that unifies the paper's analysis; excellent description highlighting the most important details of the image; body paragraphs provide strong support and direct reinforcement of the thesis; ideas are strongly linked by the thesis as well as the intro, body, and conclusion; topic sentences aid organization; paper engages in dialogue with sources and uses them to enhance the rhetorical analysis; paper utilizes proper MLA formatting to set up the paper as well as to aid the smooth incorporation and citation of outside sources. A grade of "A" is reserved for essays that go above and beyond the minimal requirements for the project by demonstrating strong critical thinking, excellent organization, and/or well-polished writing at the local level.

B—(110-134) Hits the basics of the project; shows evidence of a basic thesis; ties an analysis of the painting to the major questions of purpose, audience, genre, and authorship; provides an adequate organizational structure; generally free of grammar errors but lacking strong polish at the local level. "B" papers demonstrate an understanding of the project's basic requirements but tend to lack the exceptional levels of critical thinking, organization, or local level polish necessary for an "A."

C—(95-109) The project makes an effort at a rhetorical analysis, but may lack one or more of the paper's basic requirements such as a strong thesis, accurately documented sources, well-supported claims, and/or local level writing that is free from grammatical errors.

D—(80-94) The paper barely addresses any of the project's requirements, often due to lack of time spent on the project.

F—(79 and Below) Fails to address most if not all of the project's basic requirements. Ninety-five percent of the time, one knew it was a bad paper when one turned it in.

Rationale

In an English Composition class at Ivy Tech Community College in Bloomington, Indiana, I ask students to write a "Rhetorical Analysis of a Visual Text" by looking at street art, or graffiti, from various city centers across the globe. The unit is part of a themed version of English Composition titled "Global Selves," designed to help students develop a stronger awareness of our increasingly interconnected world and the major issues facing the nearly seven billion people on the planet. The rhetorical analysis appears at the second unit in the course after a section on global labor. It contains a number of different features designed to help students become comfortable writing about visual texts and overcoming a fear of the word "art."

The use of street art for a rhetorical analysis provides a unique opportunity for students to work through the concepts of authorship, ethos, and audience. For example, many graffiti artists deliberately choose not to use their real names, thus challenging conventional notions of the role of the writer/artist. During the unit, students are asked to consider the ethos of someone who is relatively nameless or attaches a pseudonym to their paintings. How do we process our own relationship to a self-proclaimed artist who hides behind a fake name and whose purpose is largely non-commercial?

The use of street art can also help students to consider the role of context and the placement of images. Some painters, such as Banksy, create images in highly visible, highly trafficked areas such as downtown London in hopes of provoking as much of a response as possible. Part of his approach involves an effort to satirize popular culture and ironically expose the media's attempts to create a "buzz" around his images (which he in turn uses to extend his own prankster mythos). A double irony appears when the nameless artist, such as Banksy, becomes a fixture in pop culture as evidenced by his recent successful documentaries such as *Exit Through the Gift Shop* and involvement with television shows such as *The Simpsons*.

Artists such as Zezão, on the other hand, tend to eschew celebrity and focus on more personal expressions of self, such as the abstract, flowing blue lines he placed in the sewers beneath Sao Paolo. Because the students have a chance to select from a variety of artists and styles, they tend to gain a more nuanced understanding of street art and the role of visual rhetoric.

In terms of engagement, perhaps the most important aspect of any assignment, many students felt a sense of fascination in learning more about individuals and images that are closely linked to their own consumption and understanding of culture. Many students readily intuit certain themes about life in the megacities and disparities in global wealth, but they have had little opportunity to develop those ideas in writing. Students working through the project frequently expressed having enjoyed the blend of humor and critique found in many of the images. The notion that anyone, perhaps even themselves, could create images voicing social critique, and that those images might break through into a wider cultural consciousness, can be a very appealing notion to students who, like many of us, live in relative anonymity with regards to larger social debates and discourses.

The very illegal quality of street art itself is not without controversy, and controversy, the placing of students at the edge of an ethical dilemma, can be an excellent resource for educators. Early in the unit we read an article that works through Broken Windows Theory—the notion that the presence of graffiti in a neighborhood increases the surrounding rates of crime—and students are left to grapple with the role these images play as part of a broader social discourse.

Finally, the use of street art may serve as a point of contrast in helping students think about the role of visual rhetoric and public spaces in general, especially that of advertising, by raising questions about what we see, who puts those images there, and what their purpose is.

Pre-Writing Activities

Translating Famous Paintings into Words

One of the biggest obstacles students initially face is their fear and apprehension of the word "art." Even the phrase "street art" suggests a world of high-culture, an area in which many students feel as though they have little knowledge or expertise. To help students overcome this obstacle, I start off with a descriptive writing activity used to introduce the rhetorical analysis.

The in-class activity begins with my giving each student a numbered folder and asking him/her to describe, in one paragraph, as carefully as he/she can, the image contained within. They are not to share their image with anyone else, although they will read their description to the rest of the class. After passing out the folders, I take a moment to allow the class to discuss the key elements of descriptive writing, and we generate a list on the board about the importance of describing the most dominant features of the image, how it is necessary to speak about the tone and mood of the piece, and how the goal is for the rest of the class to have a clear and accurate image in their minds of the picture contained within the folder.

When the students open their folders, a small buzz travels around the room as they realize that they are being asked to translate a famous painting into a few descriptive sentences. The images cover a wide range of art history with a strong emphasis on the 20th century. I project a corresponding PowerPoint presentation on the screen with each slide containing one of the distributed images, although the screen is left blank as the students write. Once the class has completed their descriptions, I will ask the student with folder number one to share her paragraph. After she reads her paragraph aloud, I ask the class how well they can picture the image and if anyone knows the painting that was just recreated through language. After a brief discussion, I show the image on screen, and we compare our mental images with the actual work of art.

The paintings contained within the folders are arranged chronologically. They quickly jump from the Mona Lisa to Monet to the 20th century. Students tend to have some knowledge of art up to the 1900s, but after Van Gogh, the anxiety sets in. We listen to descriptions of paintings by Mondrian, Pollock, Bacon, Dix, Picasso, Dali, and Breton then briefly discuss what is happening with each image and what might be the purpose of these various works. It is at this point that students may feel their strongest sense of dislocation as they bump against the notion that there is a hidden, mysterious world of art criticism, which they are unable to access. However, the discussion is tempered not to reinforce the authority of an art critic, but to help students grapple with the abstractions of the middle of the 20th century. Plus, having to describe a Rothko can lead to a lot a laughs and critical discussion amongst the students.

Towards the end of the presentation, we examine images much more familiar to students in terms of context and style such as the Guerilla Girls' "The Advantages of Being a Woman Artist" before concluding with pieces from Shepard Fairey and, finally, Banksy. Students at the end tend to embrace the humor and irony of these works, and it allows for an enriching discussion of the value of art, its museumification, and the process for deciding what becomes famous.

Screening of *Bomb It!*

In addition to helping the students become comfortable with descriptive writing, I have also found it helpful to screen short passages from the documentary *Bomb It!*, by award winning director John Weiss. The film traces the history of street art as it occurs across the globe. It contains interviews with Blek le Rat, Faith47, and Zezão as well as footage of several graffiti artists in action. The film helps students to see and visualize the actions of these artists, as well as to better understand their diverse motivations. As a whole, *Bomb It!* frames the work of these artists as part of a much larger debate surrounding the use of public space. The sections of *Bomb It!* that cover three of the artists featured in our project are short enough, five to twelve minutes each, to provide an effective overview of their individual philosophies without taking over too much course time. The entire film can be found for free on YouTube and is found in many college and university library collections.

Using Street Art to Teach Plagiarism

Using street art as the basis for a rhetorical analysis has one other advantage—it lends itself well to critical discussions of plagiarism. Often as teachers, we struggle to cover plagiarism in a meaningful way. Sometimes we may find ourselves using a scolding tone and pointing to the official course policies as listed in the syllabus. Many textbooks offer a section on recognizing and avoiding plagiarism, but they are generally situated in the midst of discussions about various formatting styles and examples of paraphrasing vs. quoting. Even the strongest of textbooks do little to engage students to think critically about what is at stake. The history of street art, on the other hand, contains numerous examples of artists who are not only influenced by someone else's visual style, but will go so far as to steal an image then slightly alter it to call it their own. One such case is found in the early works of the now famous Shepard Fairey.

Two weeks into the unit, I assign a discussion board post. The prompt asks students to carefully read an essay where one artist accuses Fairey of stealing from the works of others and failing to give them credit. The students are placed in another ethical dilemma and asked to think critically about what it means to borrow from and/or be influenced by the work of others.

Discussion Board #2: "Shepard Fairey and Plagiarism"

The first lines of Chapter 11 of our textbook state the following: "Plagiarism occurs when writers take credit for work that is not really theirs" (Wilhoit 266). The definition focuses on the written word, but can plagiarism occur when language is not involved? Take the case of Shepard Fairey, one of the most famous street artists today. His popularity propelled him to design the iconic "Obama Hope" image, which become a central visual in a recent presidential election. Below, one will find an article discussing Shepard Fairey's works. In a 250-word minimum initial response, please read the article, then answer the following questions: Can plagiarism occur when talking about paintings? If not, why not? If so—is there a difference between borrowing an idea/being influenced by someone's style and plagiarism? How would a painter or street artist acknowledge or cite his/her source? What might that look like? And, finally, if you think Shepard Fairey plagiarized, what, if anything, should be his punishment?

Link to the original article (with working images): art-for-a-change.com/Obey/.

Excerpts from a Sample Student Paper

The following are excerpts from a student paper based on a rhetorical analysis of street art.

Christine Adkins
Prof. Maki
English 111
1 March 2014

The Street Art of "Banksy": Effective Use of a Public Canvas

Graffiti graces the exterior walls, underpasses, and train cars of every city in the United States and world-wide. This type of vandalism is often associated with the delineation of gang territory or the delinquent behavior of teens in a counter culture. However, in the 1990s, a new style of graffiti emerged in urban centers that was different than gang tagging because the graphics conveyed a social commentary. As critics and the public perceived the works to be significant, spray paint on a wall crossed the line between vandalism and art. The creators were dubbed street-artists and their highly respected work elicited a strong fan base. One such artist is known only by the pseudonym "Banksy." Named one of *Time Magazine*'s 100 Most Influential People in 2010 (*Time*), the work of this artist appears in cities all over the world as well as in museums and private collections, yet no one knows his true identity. According to Will Ellsworth-Jones of *Smithsonian Magazine*, Banksy realizes that anonymity creates its own "invaluable buzz" (3). And Banksy wants people buzzing. Though presented with whimsy or humor, Banksy's art has a lot to say. His political and social themes often include anti-capitalism, anti-fascism, and anti-imperialism. Through striking visual contrast in its aesthetic, the irony of its subject matter, and the chosen placement of this permanent installment, Banksy's untitled piece forces the audience to hear his anti-war message.

This untitled piece is a study in contrasts. Working with stencils for efficiency, Banksy uses mostly black paint in his image. The stenciling allows for precise, crisp lines and a very clear picture. He chose to paint the image on a white-washed wall, lending even more drama to the black paint. The image is that of a young man poised to throw the object he grasps in his right hand. He is wearing a baseball cap turned backwards on his head. To hide his identity, he wears a bandana over his nose and mouth[,] and his gesture suggests that he intends to throw the object with force. His chest is turned toward the audience with his weight shifted back on his right leg and his left arm is extended to the front for leverage[,] his fingers seemingly pointing at his target. His face is turned to the side and with his eyes locked on the destination of the object he holds. His right arm is behind him, cocked and ready to launch the object. Banksy uses heavy, solid black paint on the man's shirt and hat. To give the illusion of a light source over the man's right shoulder, the folds of the back of his bandana and the top of his throwing arm are without paint except to form the creases of the folds. The effect of this technique is to highlight the object in the man's right hand. He holds a large bouquet of flower stems wrapped in a cone of paper, as if purchased from a florist. The delicate lines of the flowers echo the lines of the folds in the man's clothing which contrasts the heavy block of paint indicating the man's sweatshirt. The study in contrasts continues as the flowers are painted using colors. Delicate yellows, oranges, greens, and purples bring the bouquet to life and the viewer's eye is immediately drawn to the flowers. The painting is much larger than life with the bouquet alone standing almost as tall as the height of an average man. Banksy succeeds in creating a work that is visually stunning and demands attention.

Now that the audience is pausing to process the aesthetic of the visual presented in this piece, the irony of the subject matter invites analysis. Banksy plays with stereotypes to make his point. The young man is dressed like a criminal or a protester. The action in the painting suggests that he's in the middle of a violent conflict and his passion for his beliefs is palpable. He universally represents every man highlighted by the media because he's up to no good and he initially evokes a fear response. Given the assumption made based on his appearance, it's a Molotov cocktail that he's expected to hold in his hand. Instead, Banksy gives the man a bouquet of flowers. The delicate pedals and greenery in the bouquet echo that of a lit fuse on a bomb but flowers stereotypically represent peace, happiness, and good will. A Molotov cocktail is designed to have a big effect where it lands[,] and Banksy believes the peacefulness of the flowers can have just as big an impact if thrown and spread with passion. One of Banksy's anti-war quotes is "the greatest crimes in the world are not committed by people breaking the rules but by people following the rules. It's people who follow orders that drop bombs and massacre villages" ([qtd. in] Goodreads). The irony in this quote is transferred to this painting in that it forces the audience to abandon its own complacency. Banksy challenges his audience to evaluate the status quo, or the rules, and passionately, yet peacefully, protest injustices.

In order for his message to reach the widest audience, Banksy paints in large urban areas. Cities offer not only sheer numbers of people to create large audiences, but also immediate access to media coverage when he paints something new [...] Banksy's placement of this piece in the heart of an urban area spotlights his message. It shocks the audience's consciousness regarding the state of their surroundings. Banksy may have planned to use mob mentality when he painted this image. If people in his urban audience see one man taking a stand toward peace, using a gesture that they understand, perhaps they will follow his lead.

With its intense visual presentation, ironic imagery, and brilliant placement, this painting effectively presents Banksy's anti-war message. People are buzzing. Not much is known about the illusive street-artist named Banksy except that he has a lot to say about the state of the world. This installment in Jerusalem is a sample of his unorthodox delivery system. His graffiti is his medium to reach a world-wide audience and his potential canvas is immeasurable. While some critics contend that he is nothing more than a vandal, Banksy is succeeding in starting conversations about difficult subjects; a necessary task in progressive societies. Banksy will continue to use paint on a public canvas to present his ideas[,] and his audience will eagerly await his next message.

WORKS CITED

Wilhoit, Stephen. *A Brief Guide to Writing from Readings*, 6th ed. Boston: Pearson Learning Solutions, 2014.

The Academic Discourse Project

GRACEMARIE MIKE

Supplemental Materials

- Rationale
- Scaffolding Activities
- Pitfalls and Avoidance Strategies
- Grading Rubric
- Student Responses
- Assignment Modifications

Assignment

During our discourse community ethnography project, we investigated discourse practices within communities that came together for social, economic, and spiritual reasons. Through examining these communities' documents, practices, and language, we learned more about these communities' goals and values, especially as they are articulated in our communities' communication practices. Our next project, the Academic Discourse Project, will help us learn more about the use and meaning of language within the discourse communities of our own academic/career fields.

Part One—Annotated Bibliography and Analysis

Annotated Bibliography. First, select a specific topic within your field of study and locate scholarly articles related to this topic through the library website. After reading through these articles and selecting the ones you find most interesting, create an annotated bibliography of 5 *scholarly articles* related to a topic in your field. *Note: Your articles should come from scholarly journals or databases, not websites (unless the journal is online).* Each annotation should contain *a summary of the source* that uses summary language to walk readers through the main points of each source (we'll talk more about this in class) and an *assessment of what makes this article important*. Your summaries should be approximately 5–8 sentences in length, and your assessment should be 2–3 sentences in length.

Analysis. After you write your annotations, write a brief analysis that addresses the following prompts:

- Do articles in your field use the CARS model described by Swales in their introductions? Use examples from your sources to explain the ways that they follow or do not follow the model.
- What ways do authors in your field demonstrate that they are writing into a conversation? That is, how do they demonstrate that their research is in response to the work of others and a calling for future work? Give examples of specific places your authors reference larger conversations.
- What are the major tones and writing styles of the articles in your field? Cite specific examples from your sources. Explain what these factors tell us about the discourse and values of the author/community.
- What are the organizational patterns and techniques used by authors in your field? Again, include specific examples to back up your points.
- Overall, how would you characterize the discourse of your field of study? What are some of the most noticeable features of this discourse community?

Part Two—Website

Now that you have developed a firm understanding of what discourse looks like in your field, it's time to use that knowledge to help others who are interested in entering this discourse community (your peers). For the final component of this project, you will create a website that informs novices in your field about how to go about accessing and gaining authority in the discourse community of your major. We'll talk more about web design in class, but for now focus on gathering information to include for the following sections (each can be its own page on your site):

- Overview of your field of study
- Key ideas and concepts in your field of study
- Specializations and future career options
- Overview of discourse features and literacies

- Advice for current or prospective students studying in this field at Purdue
- Helpful resources/links

For this website, you will draw on your annotated bibliography, your own first-hand knowledge and experiences, websites of professional organizations in your field, interviews with older students/professors, online videos, and any other relevant sources. You will need to include citations for all sources that you draw from.

Purposes: This project aims to (1) give you additional experience with navigating the research process and conducting primary research; (2) help you learn about academic discourse communities and the kinds of research that are valuable in your own field; (3) prepare you to enter (or enter more fully) your chosen field; (4) give you experience with design; (5) give you experience making an argument and backing that argument up with evidence; and (6) allow you to share the knowledge you've created with others.

Resources:

- *Writing Today,* Chapters 17 and 25–28
- Purdue OWL—Primary Research: https://owl.english.purdue.edu/owl/resource/559/01/

Grading: This project is worth 30 percent of your overall grade. You will be assessed on four main categories: content; organization; style, tone, and conventions; grammar, usage, and proofreading. We will discuss these categories in more depth throughout the unit.

Rationale

In their 2013 *Composition Forum* reflection article on their 2007 *College Composition and Communication* piece introducing the Writing-About-Writing approach to first-year composition, Elizabeth Wardle and Doug Downs propose a new vision of first-year composition (FYC) courses as "courses [that] teach students *about* writing and how to learn what they will need to discover to tackle each new and different writing task and situation." This assignment, the Academic Discourse Project, is designed to help students use key concepts in writing studies to explore writing in their own disciplines, thus positioning them to transfer this knowledge about writing into their major courses. In particular, this assignment is designed specifically to help students engage with the concepts of discourse communities and multiliteracies, learn about the characteristics of academic discourse in their own fields (or prospective fields), gain practice analyzing texts, develop primary and secondary research skills, learn the basics of visual design, and gain confidence in researching and writing for public audiences.

Positioned as the culminating project of the semester, this assignment builds on two previous assignments where students explore literacies and discourse communities: a literacy narrative in which students examine significant moments and sponsors in their individual literacy development and a discourse community ethnography in which students analyze the texts and practices of a discourse community to which they belong or have personal interest (some examples include a longboarding club, a sorority, and a daycare). This assignment pushes students to understand notions of discourse conventions, language, genre, and organization in their fields by asking them to explore in depth the writing of an academic discipline into which they are seeking entry. For students who still have not decided on a major, this project gives them the opportunity to explore the discourse practices of an academic discipline in which they are interested, providing them the chance to see if a major is right for them.

The project has two distinct, but related, parts. Part One is a traditional annotated bibliography followed by an analysis, which is guided by provided questions. These questions help students focus not on the content of the articles, but rather on their structure, language, style, and design, therefore helping them to understand the shared characteristics of discourse in their field. Further, these questions give students the opportunity to practice using source material to back up an argument. For question A, students are asked to consider what approach researchers in their field tend to take when they introduce a topic of study by using the CARS model developed by John Swales as a point of comparison. Question B asks students to think about how research in their field is related to past and future work by asking them to point out places where debates, issues, or other research is mentioned. Next, question C asks students to look closely at the kind of language that is used. They assess whether the article is written in passive or active voice and what kind of tone the authors use to draw conclusions about the motivations and values of their field of research. Finally, question D calls students' attention to the structure of academic research articles, asking them to consider various organizational patterns and devices. At the end of this analysis, students must develop a concise, coherent statement about the general characteristics of writing in their academic disciplines (question E). By reflecting on the way published writing in this particular area of their discipline works, students should be able to develop a metacognitive awareness of the moves writers working in their fields tend to make when writing about research.

For Part Two of this project, students use their own first-hand knowledge, conduct additional research, and transform the knowledge they generated in Part One into a website aimed at informing other first-year students and high school students about how to be successful in this field of study at this university. Students create a website that provides an overview of their chosen field, a summary of the discourse style of, and literacies relevant to, the field (such as reading, math, certain computer applications, ways of dressing, etc.), advice for prospective or beginning students, and additional resources for learning more. To generate content for their websites, students combine the results of their annotated bibliography and analysis with their own knowledge, interviews, websites, videos, or other relevant sources for introducing someone to their major. Students often choose to talk with students in grades above them or professors, and they include links to their field's professional organizations, clubs on campus, or other credible websites that provide information about activities that professionals in their field participate in. Websites are designed through Wix.com, though students also have the option of using Google Sites or building a site from scratch if so desired. Through the process of developing their sites, students gain additional research experience as well as experience writing for a well-defined, accessible audience. Peer review works especially well for this part of the project, as students' peers are part of the target demographic for the websites.

This assignment was developed and implemented at a large research university in a first-year composition course. The course enrolls students, both international and domestic, across all majors. Though students come to the university generally well-prepared, they come to this course with a wide range of confidence and ability in writing. One of this assignment's strengths is that it asks students to perform academic analysis (in Part One), while also giving them the opportunity to write for their peers (in Part Two), thus increasing the number of ways in which students can connect to this assignment and develop their skills.

Scaffolding Activities

Scholarly Research

To introduce students to the concept of scholarly research, I brought in hard copies of several journals for students to examine while I explained the academic research, peer review, and publication process. Next, students used the Internet to locate journals in their own fields and explored the contents of these journals. At our next class meeting, we talked about databases and search strategies. After developing lists of keywords and databases to explore, students spent time searching for articles related to their chosen topic in class so that I could assist students with specific questions.

Textual Analysis

Since one of the goals of this assignment is to help students better understand the language and structures of academic writing, it is helpful to spend some time looking closely at sample articles in class, particularly to teach the CARS model described by Swales. To introduce students to this process of textual analysis, I chose a research article students had already read earlier in the semester. (I used Mirabelli's "Learning to Serve: The Language and Literacy of Food Service Workers," but you can select another article for students to read before class.) In class, I asked students to create a reverse outline of the introduction of this piece. After that, I asked them to work in groups to map this article's moves onto those presented in the CARS model. We then discussed students' analyses as a class.

Visual Design

While students may be able to articulate the difference between well-designed and poorly-designed websites, they may not have the vocabulary to describe what distinguishes one from the other. One way I worked to give students a design vocabulary (without being an expert in design myself) is through the C.R.A.P. (contrast, repetition, alignment, proximity) principles. After going through a presentation of these principles, many of which are available online, I asked students to analyze posters from around campus and assess how well they incorporate each of these principles. Then, I had each student choose a website they visit frequently and analyze its effectiveness given the C.R.A.P. principles. As a class, we looked at the best and worst examples of design that students could find on the web.

Pitfalls and Avoidance Strategies

Summary Trouble

Some students seemed to struggle with the summary-writing element of the annotated bibliography, with summaries often being too specific or too general. To help students learn to effectively capture the main points and structure of articles without getting caught up in the details, you can focus on teaching two techniques: reverse outlining and using summary language. To create a reverse outline, have students write down the main idea of each paragraph in the margins of an article. Then, encourage them to use summary language to describe these main points (phrases like "The author argues" or "Next, the authors point out"). It can be helpful to provide students with a list of summary words and phrases or develop such a list as a class.

Web Design

Though students are likely quite familiar with using the web, chances are that they've had less experience doing web design. Though many websites provide easy to use web-design interfaces, one challenge is that students tend to let the options immediately available to them, such as templates, guide all their design decisions. Like more traditional print genres, though, design decisions in web writing should be guided by audience, purpose, context, and other rhetorical considerations. To spark students' creativity and help them create websites based on their own ideas, spend time in class storyboarding. Distribute unlined paper to students, having them fold the sheets into four quadrants. Then, give them some time to sketch possible designs for their site in each of the quadrants in class. Once they have generated some solid design ideas, they can then move on to designing on the computer.

Project Planning

Because this project involves many steps, it's helpful to encourage students to keep good notes on where they are in their research process (for Part One) and their design process (for Part Two). Encourage students to develop a list of tasks for each part before they begin working and to keep a running "to-do" list while they work, so that they can quickly jot down items that need attention without losing focus on the current task. An added bonus of this method is that it will allow students to complete work on their projects even when they only have a short amount of time available.

Technology

The second part of this project is highly dependent on technology. If you don't have computers available in the classroom, if students don't have extended access to computers at home, or if students have low technological literacy, you can modify this assignment by having them create drawings of a website they'd like to design and doing a presentation or report that describes the features and content they would include.

Grading Rubric

Final Draft Evaluation Form: Annotated Bibliography

Content
(60 points: excellent = 60–55; good = 54–45; adequate = 44–40; fair = 39–30; poor = 29)

- Summary of five sources in your field is straightforward and clear; you incorporate effective summary language, paraphrasing, and quotations to help readers get a sense of the main points and organization of each article.
- Analysis demonstrates critical thinking and backs points up with relevant examples from your articles.

Score _____   Comments:

Organization
(10 points: excellent = 10–9; good = 8–7; adequate = 6–5; fair = 4; poor = 3)

- Summaries and analysis flow logically, using transitions to guide readers through your texts.
- Addresses one point of time.

Score _____   Comments:

Style, Tone and Conventions
(20 points: excellent = 20–18; good = 17–16; adequate = 15–14; fair = 13–12; poor = 1–2)

- Uses a range of descriptive, formal language.
- Incorporates appropriate stylistic choices given the audience, purpose, and context (genre of academic annotated bibliography).
- Uses citation style of major field correctly.

Score _____   Comments:

Grammar, Usage and Proofreading
(10 points: excellent = 10–9; good = 8–7; adequate = 6–5; fair = 4; poor = 3)

- Follows academic conventions for proofreading, grammar, punctuation, and usage.

Score _____   Comments:

Total
(100 points: excellent = 90–100; good = 80–89; adequate = 70–79; fair = 60–69; poor = 60)

Score _____ / Grade _____   Comments:

The Academic Discourse Project (Mike)

Final Draft Evaluation Form: Website

Content
(40 points: excellent = 40–36; good = 35–32; adequate = 31–28; fair = 27–25; poor 24)

- Includes each of the following in some form on your website in an easy to understand manner:
    - Overview of your field of study.
    - Key ideas and concepts in your field of study.
    - Specializations and future career options.
    - Overview of discourse features and literacies.
    - Advice for current or prospective students studying in this field at Purdue.
    - Helpful resources/links.
- Incorporates information from credible sources.
- Demonstrates insider knowledge of your field of study.
- Incorporates appropriate images and visuals to aid understanding.

Score _____   Comments:

Organization
(20 points: excellent = 20–18; good = 17–16; adequate = 15–14; fair = 13–12; poor 12)

- Incorporates easy to navigate design.
- Includes logical page design.
- Follows C.R.A.P. principles.

Score _____   Comments:

Style, Tone and Conventions
(20 points: excellent = 20–18; good = 17–16; adequate = 15–14; fair = 13–12; poor = 12)

- Uses a range of descriptive, engaging language.
- Stylistic choices are appropriate given the audience, purpose, and context (genre of informative website aimed at high school and college students).
- Includes appropriate balance of verbal and visual content.
- Uses citation style of major field correctly.

Score _____   Comments:

Grammar, Usage and Proofreading
(20 points: excellent = 20–18; good = 17–16; adequate = 15–14; fair = 13–12; poor = 12)

- Follows academic conventions for proofreading, grammar, punctuation, and usage.

　　　Score _____　　　Comments:

Total
(100 points: excellent = 90–100; good = 80–89; adequate = 70–79; fair = 60–69; poor = 60)

　　　Score _____ / Grade _____　　Comments:

Student Responses

Overall, students seemed to find this project enjoyable and valuable to their future work at the university. In regard to the annotated bibliography portion of this assignment, many students commented in their end-of-semester reflections that they appreciated having the chance to do research related to their majors and to learn more about aspects of their fields with which they were unfamiliar. Even though many students considered the annotated bibliography to be the most difficult task of the semester, they largely agreed that learning how to read and analyze scholarly articles was in the end a productive and useful experience that they believed would serve them well in their futures.

In terms of the website portion of this assignment, students again generally expressed appreciation for the opportunity to learn about their future majors. Students also greatly enjoyed the chance to use their creativity to shape their websites according to their own preferences and the rhetorical situation, rather than having to follow a strict format. Finally, many students explained that they were glad to learn basic design and web building skills since they knew these abilities would be useful for their majors and future careers.

Assignment Modifications

While this assignment's success can certainly be attributed in part to the institutional context in which it was developed and carried out, it can be easily modified to be appropriate for different student populations and settings. For classes where students have lower writing or English proficiency, the number of required sources for the annotated bibliography can be lowered. Another option is to pair students of similar majors so that they can read and analyze articles together. In terms of the technological aspect of this assignment, many students will find today's web building tools to be more intuitive and less intimidating than they might imagine. Even for students without much technological expertise, spending class time simply exploring website builders and learning through trial and error can alleviate much stress. For teachers with less technological expertise, a good strategy is to encourage students to use each other as resources to solve technology problems.

As mentioned above, this project can still be successful even if computer access isn't widely available in the classroom. Presentations, reports, brochures, or booklets can stand in the place of a website. If these still prove too difficult to produce given institutional circumstances, students can simply do research and write or draw outlines of what they would include in such a publication.

Works Cited

Downs, Douglas, and Elizabeth Wardle. "Teaching about Writing, Righting Misconceptions: (Re)envisioning 'First-Year Composition' as 'Introduction to Writing Studies.'" *College Composition and Communication* 58.4 (2007): 552–584. Print.

Luberda, James. "Swales' Three-Move Model for Introductions." *Current Research and Course Materials of James Luberda*. University of Connecticut. Web. 20 August 2014.

Mirabelli, Tony. "Learning to Serve: The Language and Literacy of Food Service Workers." *What They Don't Learn in School*. Ed. Jabari Mahiri. New York: Peter Lange, 2004. 143–162. Print. Rpt. in Wardle, Elizabeth ,and Doug Downs. *Writing About Writing: A College Reader*. Boston: Bedford/St. Martins, 2011. Print.

Swales, John. *Genre Analysis: English in Academic and Research Settings*. Cambridge: Cambridge University Press, 1990. Print.

Wardle, Elizabeth, and Doug Downs. "Reflecting Back and Looking Forward: Revisiting Teaching about Writing, Righting Misconceptions Five Years On." *Composition Forum* 27 (2013). Web. 20 August 2014

Political Cartoons and Multimodal Composition
The Visual Argument Assignment

Erin Dee Moore

Supplemental Materials

- Rationale
- Introductory Video
- Introductory Free-Write
- Peer Review
- Grading Rubric
- Pitfalls and Avoidance Strategies
- Sample Essay and Multimodal Composition
- Instructor Resources
- Student Resources

Writing Assignment

This assignment consists of two parts: a paper and a creative visual image, which will be called a multimodal composition. In the first part of this assignment, you will write a researched essay on either a print advertisement or a political cartoon. In the second part, you will create your own print advertisement or political cartoon. Both parts will be submitted at the same time.

Part 1: The Paper

Overview

Focus: To analyze a visual argument

Aim: To use critical thinking skills to analyze a visual argument; to determine the argument's intended audience, the purpose of the argument, the techniques used to deliver the argument, and the effectiveness of the argument; to conduct research

Length: 400–600 words

Format: Microsoft Word; APA Format

Research: Minimum of one outside source

Required Reading: eBook Chapter 4, "Reading and Writing about Visual Arguments" and "Using Rhetorical Strategies for Persuasion" at Purdue OWL

Submission: Save as an MS Word file and upload to Turnitin.com.

For this assignment, you will be analyzing and critiquing a **print** advertisement or a political cartoon. Using critical thinking skills and credible research, you will determine the ad or cartoon's intended audience, its purpose and effectiveness, and the rhetorical appeals and techniques it uses.

Step One

Find a print advertisement or political cartoon (hereafter "visual argument") to write about. The piece you choose must present an argument, and it should present it in an image. It may include a few—very few—words, but the image must be the dominant focus of the piece. In addition, the image you choose must be relevant and topical; thus, it should have been created in the past two months.

The ad you choose may present an argument about an environmental issue (littering or pollution), a health issue (smoking or obesity), a social issue (gay marriage or gender income inequality), or a political issue (legislation on a particular topic), just to name a few. You should avoid choosing an ad that primarily functions to sell or promote a product or service.

Make sure you completely understand the references in the visual argument before writing about it. For example, most political cartoons are geared toward people who know the background and details of the issue they refer to. If you aren't sure you understand the subject of the cartoon, it would be best to find another one to write about. Of course, you can also research to find out all about it—it's up to you. Just make sure you find something you can write about knowledgeably.

Here are some websites where you might find print ads and political cartoons:

www.politicalcartoons.com/
adsoftheworld.com/
webdesignledger.com/inspiration/most-creative-ads-around-the-world
www.veryfunnyads.com/

STEP TWO

Format your paper in APA Style.

STEP THREE

At the top of your paper, provide either the hard copy version of your print ad or website link to the visual argument you are writing about. Then, respond to the questions below in an essay. This means your work should be one flowing piece; do not include the assigned questions in your paper or number your responses.

Write a well-developed paragraph that responds to each of the questions below. Put the paragraphs in the order the questions are presented. In other words, answer the first question in the first paragraph, the second question in the second paragraph, and so on. Each response must be a full paragraph. Points will be deducted if you write one- or two-sentence paragraphs.

- Describe the audience to whom this visual argument is targeted. This description could include age range, gender, political beliefs, income level, and other demographic information. Explain why you believe that this is the target audience for this argument. What in the visual argument led you to this conclusion?
- What situation prompted the creation of this visual argument? Describe it in enough detail so that the reader has sufficient background to understand the issue and the argument presented.
- What purpose do you believe the argument aims to achieve?
- What rhetorical appeals (logos, pathos, ethos) does the creator use to persuade the audience, and how are they used specifically? Refer to the Purdue OWL resource mentioned above.
- Specifically address the images used in the argument, along with the color, design, and any other visual elements in the argument. Why do you think the creator of the argument chose those specific images, colors, or other elements? How effective are they? Again, be specific.

STEP FOUR

You must include research that supports your answer to question two. This research should be credible and must have an author and a date. Avoid noncredible sites and sources, such as dictionaries, encyclopedias, *Wikipedia*, quick answer sites, and blogs that don't cite their own sources or have a reputable author. Remember to cite this source in your essay by using APA in-text citation.

STEP FIVE

After you have found outside research, you should create a References page. You will need to cite the visual argument and the research that you used.

Part 2: Multimodal Composition

OVERVIEW

Focus: To create your own multimodal composition (cartoon or print ad).

Aim: To use visual elements and rhetorical appeals to compose a multimodal composition; to determine the intended audience of your multimodal composition.

Length: The multimodal composition must be a one-page print ad or a one-panel political cartoon; you must also include a 100–200 word written paragraph.

Format: Microsoft Word; APA Format

Submission: Save in the same MS Word file as your essay (above) and submit to Turnitin.com.

For the first part of this assignment, you analyzed a print advertisement or political cartoon by paying close attention to its intended audience, its purpose, and the rhetorical appeals used.

For the second part, you will take these same topics (e.g. audience, purpose, rhetorical appeals, visual elements, etc.) into consideration, but this time, you will create your own print advertisement or political cartoon.

You will keep the same topic as your original visual argument (the ad or cartoon you analyzed for part one). Therefore, if you found a political cartoon about a certain politician or issue, your own cartoon should also be about that same politician or issue. For example, if the original political cartoon was about President Obama and the Affordable Care Act, then your multimodal composition should also be about the president and health care.

You may not duplicate or reproduce any of the visual elements from the original ad. You should instead think of an alternate way to display the same argument or topic in a visual form. Here are some suggestions for creating your multimodal composition:

- Create a multimodal composition that is intended for a different audience.
- Use different visual elements (e.g., colors, shapes, people/characters, style, design, etc.).
- Show the issue or topic from a different perspective (e.g., show people who are affected by this issue or topic instead of politicians).

- Show a different facet or angle of the same topic or problem (e.g. If the original ad depicts litter on the beach, create an ad that shows animals that are affected by the litter.)
- Use a different rhetorical appeal or appeals.

Once you have chosen your approach, you will need to create your multimodal composition. You may draw your cartoon or advertisement by hand or you may use an online comic generator site. You should not create a video or anything that includes animation; the visual you create must be something that could appear in print, such as in a newspaper or magazine. Whether you choose to draw your cartoon or ad by hand or use a comic generator, make sure that your multimodal composition is primarily visual. There should be few words in it.

Here are some sites that you may find helpful:

- Bitstrips (an online comic generator): bitstrips.com
- ToonDoo (an online comic generator): toondoo.com
- Strip Generator (an online comic generator): stripgenerator.com
- Google Drive: drive.google.com

Step One

You will include your multimodal composition in the same file as your essay and References page from Part 1. Insert a page break after the References page. Make sure that you continue to follow APA style.

Step Two

At the top of the page, write the words "Multimodal Composition." You then have two options:

- Copy and paste a jpeg file of your hand-drawn visual argument.
- Post a link to your visual argument. (You may upload your Visual Argument to Google Drive or use a comic generator site.)

Step Three

Beneath your photo or link, write a 100–200 word paragraph that discusses the intended audience of your multimodal composition, the rhetorical appeals that your multimodal composition uses, and a description of the changes you made to the original visual argument.

Step Four

Edit and proofread your assignment carefully.

Step Five

Upload your assignment to Turnitin.com

REMINDERS
- Use an appropriate tone depending on your intended audience.
- Pay close attention to directions. Be sure you are meeting content objectives and staying within the required word count. Review the grading rubric.
- Proofread your work carefully. Make sure it is error-free.
- Keep the writing center in mind. It is a great resource.
- Review the grading rubric so you know how your work will be evaluated and graded.
- Keep in mind that this assignment is worth 20 percent of your overall grade in the course.

Rationale

The Visual Argument assignment is taught in English Composition II at Full Sail University, which offers accelerated degree programs in Entertainment, Media, and the Arts. Courses at Full Sail are four weeks long and can be taken in person or online. As an online course, English Composition II focuses not only on argument but also on information literacy and academic writing. Students must strive to refine their writing, develop critical thinking skills, avoid logical fallacies, and compose multimodal argument papers. The Visual Argument assignment is often one of the first papers that students must complete. It provides a foundation to later argument essays and projects.

Although this assignment accommodates the interests and aptitudes of students at Full Sail, it would be appropriate for undergraduate students elsewhere. According to Marc Prensky, students today are "digital natives" because their lives have been so influenced and shaped by the media they consume and the technology they use: "Today's average college grads have spent less than 5,000 hours of their lives reading, but over 10,000 hours playing video games (not to mention 20,000 hours watching TV). Computer games, email, the Internet, cell phones and instant message are integral parts of their lives" ("Digital Natives" 1). Prensky asserts that today's students have different thinking patterns than their teachers ("Digital Natives" 1) and as a result traditional teaching methods, such as lectures and reading assignments, are not as effective or engaging for students as interactive activities or educational video games ("Do They Really *Think* Differently?" 4). Twenty-first century students as a whole must be taught differently. This does not mean that teachers should abandon attempts to teach them alphabetic writing but should invent writing assignments that engage them in media and technology. The Visual Argument bridges this gap between what many students are interested in and the skills they need to learn in English Composition.

The Visual Argument assignment does not merely seek to appeal to students but also takes into consideration current scholarship in rhetoric and composition. The New London Group, the New Media Consortium, and rhetoric and composition scholars, such as Kathleen Blake Yancey and Cynthia L. Selfe have concluded that multimodal composition belongs in the English classroom. Technology, which is at the heart of multimodal composition, is vastly becoming more than just a technical tool. As Yancey and Jeff Rice claim, media are not just tools that convey messages and texts; they are becoming integral parts of each text's message (Yancey 83–84; Rice 110). It is imperative, then, that composition instructors begin to teach students how to communicate through alternate mediums, not just the essay. Research conducted by the New Media Consortium in 2005 affirms the importance of multimodality by arguing that twenty-first century communication will require a "set of abilities and skills where aural, visual, and digital literacy overlap. These include the ability to understand the power of images and sounds, to recognize and use that power, to manipulate and transform digital media, to distribute them pervasively, and to easily adapt them to a new form" (2). Therefore, if English instructors fail to instruct students in multimodal composition, they will not be prepared to communicate effectively in the future (Selfe and Selfe 86).

Despite the increased importance of teaching multimodal forms of writing, English teachers must continue to stress traditional, alphabetic writing. Both academic faculty and employers decry the poor quality of recent college graduates' writing. A 2013 survey, conducted by Northwestern University, states that employers prefer to hire graduates who can write well and engage in critical thinking Berrett (par. 1). Good writing is synonymous with career growth and advancement (Miller 20). Instructors must continue to educate students, especially first-year students, on the importance of clear and correct writing so that they can write intelligently and professionally, while paying close attention to issues of tone, word choice, and style.

The Visual Argument assignment combines tradition with innovation: students must write an essay, but they can expand their global communication skills by composing a visual text.

Introductory Video

The introductory video provides a brief overview of the entire assignment. Teachers can show it during class before discussing the assignment in its entirety or can assign it to students to watch at home: youtu.be/c0WEzB_mhrc.

Introductory Free-Write

This free-write can be used to introduce the assignment to the students. The teacher should ask students to find political cartoons in a print newspaper or online and bring them to class. The teacher should collect all of the cartoons and redistribute them among the class. Students should then do a five- to-ten minute free-write on the political cartoon that they received. Finally, the teacher should begin a discussion on the political cartoons and the free-write.

Peer Review

[The following peer review prompt should be used after students have completed a rough draft of their essay and multimodal composition.]

For this peer review activity, you will get into groups of three or four and review your classmates' papers. You should plan to read the essays and multimodal compositions you are assigned two times. The first time, read the essay and multimodal composition as you would anything you were reading. The second time, read with the following questions in mind:

THE PAPER

- What did you like about this paper? Provide a specific example.
- Did the author answer the required questions thoroughly? Where is there room for expansion or clarification? Identify at least one area of the paper that could use more explanation or clarification.
- Were you convinced by the author's analysis of the visual argument? Why or why not?
- Was the research in paragraph two effective? Did the research support the author's argument? Why or why not?
- What grammatical errors did you see in this paper?
- What additional advice or suggestions can you give this writer about revising his or her paper?

THE MULTIMODAL COMPOSITION

- Was your classmate's cartoon or ad on the same topic as the original cartoon or ad?
- Were you able to understand what was happening in your classmate's visual?
- Was your classmate's visual an original take on the issue? Why or why not? If your classmate's visual was not original, what would make it more creative?
- What additional advice can you offer about this visual?

Grading Rubric

Category	Excellent	Good	Fair	Poor
Points Directions Followed (Argument Selection, Format, Submission, etc.): 10 points possible	10 points All directions followed.	8–9 points One minor element missing.	4–7 points Two minor elements missing.	3 points and below Several major and minor elements missing or not fully completed / included.
Points Essay and Critical Thinking: 30 points possible	27–30 points Analysis is thorough and accurate; each question is answered with a thoughtful response written in a well-developed paragraph; strong critical thinking skills are demonstrated and message is clear. Multimodal paragraph is included and is complete.	24–26 points Analysis is clear, thorough, and accurate; each question is answered and responses demonstrate critical thinking but ideas need more support.	18–23 points Analysis is fairly clear, thorough, and accurate; each question is answered; responses demonstrate critical thinking, but ideas / paragraphs need more support.	17 points and below Analysis lacks clarity, thoroughness, or accuracy; critical thinking not clearly demonstrated, and paragraphs are weak.
Points APA Formatting: 10 points possible	10 points Outside source is included in response to question two and is formatted correctly with	7–9 points Outside source is included and formatting is good, but not perfect; references list is	4–6 points Outside source is included and documented, but citations do not follow	3 points and below Outside source not included in response to second question; no references list.

Category	Highest	Middle-High	Middle-Low	Lowest
	an in-text citation; references list is provided that documents this source and the visual argument.	included and formatting is close to perfect.	APA style; references list may or may not be included.	
Multimodal Composition: 30 points possible	**27–30 points** The visual adopts a fresh perspective on the chosen topic and does not duplicate any elements from the original cartoon or ad.	**24–26 points** The visual overall adopts a fresh perspective on the chosen topic. One or two things about the visual might be unclear.	**18–23 points** The visual adopts a moderately fresh perspective on the chosen topic. There may be unclear or unoriginal elements.	**17 points and below** The visual does not adopt a fresh perspective. (0—The visual reproduces the original ad or cartoon)
Grammar and Mechanics: 20 points possible	**20 points** Assignment is free or almost free of errors in spelling, punctuation, grammar, usage, capitalization, and sentence structure; student clearly proofread assignment before submission.	**18–19 points** Assignment contains three to five errors in spelling, punctuation, grammar, usage, capitalization, and sentence structure; student proofread before submission.	**14–17 points** Assignment contains six or more errors in spelling, punctuation, grammar, usage, capitalization, and sentence structure; little evidence of proofreading.	**13 points and below** Assignment contains many errors in grammar and mechanics, so the author's meaning is not clear. Little or no evidence of proofreading.

Pitfalls and Avoidance Strategies

Overall, failing to follow directions is the main pitfall that students face on the visual argument assignment. Students should be encouraged to read the assignment directions and the grading rubric to ensure that they are meeting all requirements. When students do follow all instructions, they generally earn a high grade. Students achieve success on this assignment by following directions, finding credible research, and analyzing the visual argument thoroughly.

One way that students sometimes fail to follow directions is when they choose either a visual image that does not have an argument, or they select an advertisement for a product, which makes this assignment difficult to complete. A commercial or advertisement for a product functions primarily to entice consumers to buy a product or service; thus, these types of ads do have an argument, but it is difficult to answer the required questions and find research on an advertisement or commercial for a product. Teachers should encourage students to choose a visual image that takes a stance on an important, topical issue.

Even when students choose an appropriate visual argument, they can encounter problems if they do not thoroughly understand the issue being presented in the cartoon or print ad. Students should only choose a visual argument that they can talk about knowledgably.

Another pitfall is that students may not address each of the required questions or may not devote equal space to them in the essay. It is important that students write a solid paragraph for each of the required questions. Question four on rhetorical appeals seems to be the topic that most students do not cover well. It might be helpful if the teacher discusses rhetorical appeals during class and provides examples so that students have a thorough understanding.

Failure to include research is also a pitfall that students may face. Students must include an outside source in paragraph two in response to question two. Students should be encouraged to find a credible source that has an author and a date. They should avoid non-credible sources such as dictionaries, encyclopedias, *Wikipedia*, quick answer sites, and blogs that do not cite their own sources or have a reputable author. It might be a good idea to devote some class time to finding credible sources. Teachers should encourage students to first look for potential articles in online newspapers and magazines.

With regard to the multimodal part of this assignment, students can get into trouble if they are too adventurous or ambitious with their projects. For example, students might try to use software or programs that they have never used before in order to create their own political cartoon. Although sites like toondoo.com are relatively user-friendly, students might feel frustrated by learning the new technology. Students should only use software and technology with which they are comfortable.

Finally, it can be tempting for students to make very minor changes to the original visual argument or duplicate parts of it in their multimodal composition. For example, students might be tempted to use similar characters or scenarios, keep the same rhetorical appeals, and speak to the same audience. I encourage students to represent their topic in a completely new way by considering a different audience, different graphics, colors, etc., and a different appeal from the original visual argument.

Sample Essay and Multimodal Composition

The "Calculates Tobacco Costs, Car" visual argument is a stop-smoking advertisement produced for the State of Sao Paulo in Brazil: www.creativeadawards.com/calculates-tobacco-costs-car/. The visual depicts a car in the guise of a stubbed-out cigarette. Consequently, this ad seems geared toward smokers, particularly those who have smoked for years or have a multiple-pack-a-day habit. Basically, this ad asks smokers to contemplate how much money they have spent on cigarettes and think of what else they could have bought. Most likely, only long-term smokers would have spent the price tag of a car on cigarettes. However, smokers in general might be the intended audience, as anyone who smokes spends money on cigarettes that could have been spent on other items.

Smoking cessation advertisements are frequently created to warn smokers of potential health risks, and often are not prompted by a specific situation or event. However, this visual argument was created in response to anti-smoking legislation passed in Brazil. According to Seth Kugel (2009), Sao Paulo, Brazil, released a very strict non-smoking policy in 2009 that includes "just about all enclosed public spaces, including offices, malls and taxis as well as bars and restaurants. Business owners, not the smokers themselves, are subject to fines of up to about $800 for the first two offenses, and temporary shutdowns after that." This law has financial consequences for businesses, an economic consideration that the visual argument presents to smokers as well.

Not only does this ad prompt smokers to consider the financial implications of smoking, but it, like many stop-smoking campaigns, encourages smokers to quit. The ad includes a link to the tabaconomia website where smokers can estimate the total costs of their cigarette habit. The tabacocalculadora (a tobacco calculator) invites smokers to input the amount of cigarettes they smoke and then estimates what else they could have bought with the money they spent on cigarettes. The calculator equates money spent on cigarettes into big-ticket items, such as refrigerators, fashion accessories, and of course, vehicles. Macleod (2009) provides an example: "A person who smoked two packs of Marlboros a day for the past ten years, for example, will find that [he or she] spent the equivalent of a popular car."

Stop smoking campaigns have been around for many years, and many of them do seem aimed at protecting one's health (Grekyte). This ad, however, focuses on the financial and economic effects of smoking. Because this ad focuses on the economic impact of smoking, it employs logos. It asks smokers to consider the amount of money they have spent on cigarettes, not just on a daily basis, but over the course of many years. This type of activity speaks to a person's rational mentality and provides him or her with hard numbers (if they use the tobacco calculator). This ad might also use pathos because when smokers realize the money they have "wasted" on cigarettes, they might feel disappointed, as they reflect on what else they could have bought.

This ad uses a bronze car to signify a cigarette. The car is positioned with the hood facing the ground, and the front bumper is red and smoldering, similar to a cigarette being stubbed into an ashtray. Ash surrounds the hood of the car. The body of the car has been smashed and compressed to mimic the shape of a cigarette. Smoke billows around the body of the car. The visuals are effective in making the viewer conflate the car with a cigarette.

Multimodal Composition

www.toondoo.com/View.toon?param=7747784

The original visual argument depicted a car that was crushed to look like a cigarette in an ashtray. It was geared toward smokers and the money they have spent on cigarettes, money that could have been spent on expensive items, such as a new car. Due to its focus on economics, the original visual argument employed logos. I decided to continue to use logos in my multimodal composition. However, I changed my audience based on research I conducted for my essay in part one. Instead of focusing on smokers, my audience was business owners, those who will be fined in Brazil for permitting customers to smoke. My multimodal project shows a couple, both of whom have a lit cigarette inside a restaurant. A server cautions the viewer that smoking inside will cost a business money.

Instructor Resources

Ball, Cheryl E. "Multimodal Composition (Eng 239)." *Academic Portfolio*. n.d. Web. 26 Aug. 2014.

Barr, Brittany. *Digital Life Place Narratives: Integrating Multimodal Assignments into the Writ 101 Curriculum*. 2011. Web. 26 Aug. 2014.

Borton, Sonya C., and Brian Huot. "Chapter 8: Responding and Assessing." *Digital Media Project*. n.d. Web. 26 Aug. 2014.

Eyman, Douglas, ed. *Kairos: A Journal of Rhetoric, Technology, and Pedagogy*. 2014. Web. 26 Aug. 2014.
Kent State University Department of English. "Assessing Multimodal Student Work." *Kent State University Department of English*. 2014. Web. 7 Aug. 2014.
Lutkewitte, Claire. "The First Digital Native Writing Instructors and the Future Multimodal Composition Classroom." *BWE*. n.d. Web. 26 Aug. 2014.
_____, ed. *Multimodal Composition: A Critical Sourcebook*. Boston: Bedford/St. Martin's, 2014. Print.
McKee, Heidi A., and Dànielle Nicole DeVoss, eds. *Digital Writing Assessment & Evaluation*. Logan: Utah State University Press, 2013. Computers and Composition Digital Press. Web. 26 Aug. 2014.
Moore, Michael R. "Multimodal Assessment Bibliography." *Digital Writing, Rhetoric, and Discourse*. 2014. Web. 26 Aug. 2014.
NCTE. "Position Statement on Multimodal Literacies." *NCTE*. 2014. Web. 26 Aug. 2014.
O'Brien, Annemaree. *Creating Multimodal Texts*. 2013. Web. 26 Aug. 2014.
Prensky, Marc. "Digital Natives, Digital Immigrants." *On the Horizon* 9.5 (2001): 1–6. PDF file.
Schrock, Kathy. "Literacy in the Digital Age." *Kathy Schrock's Guide to Everything*. 2014. Web. 26 Aug. 2014.
Selfe, Cynthia L. *Multimodal Composition: Resources for Teachers*. Cresskill: Hampton, 2007. Print.
Turner, Tim. "Guide to Teaching Visual Rhetoric." *Viz*. n.d. Web. 26 Aug. 2014.
Yancey, Kathleen Blake. "Writing in the 21st Century: A Report from the National Council of Teachers of English." *NCTE*. 2009. Web. 26 Aug. 2014.

STUDENT RESOURCES

Chappatte, Patrick. "The Power of Cartoons." *Ted Talks*. 2010. Web. 26 Aug. 2014.
Donnelly, Liza. "Inside a Cartoonist's World." *TedEd*. Web. 26 Aug. 2014.
Donovan, Jennie. *ProjectAPA.info*. 2014. Web. 30 July 2014.
Moore, Erin. "Visual Argument Assignment Video." *YouTube*. 2014. Web. 29 Aug. 2014.
Paiz, Joshua, et al. "APA Formatting and Style Gide." *Purdue OWL*. 1 March 2013. Web. 30 July 2014.
Rosenau, Matt. "Pathos, Logos, and Ethos in Advertising." *YouTube*. 12 March 2012. Web. 30 July 2014.
Weida, Stacy, and Karl Stolley. "Using Rhetorical Strategies for Persuasion." *Purdue OWL*. 3 Nov. 2013. Web. 30 July 2014.
Williams, George H. "Three Rhetorical Appeals: Ethos, Pathos, Logos." *UMKC Department of English*. n.d. Web. 30 July 2014.
Wisheu, Karen. "How To Analyze Political Cartoons." *YouTube*. 2013. Web. 26 Aug. 2014.

WORKS CITED

Berrett, Dan. "Employers and Public Favor Graduates Who Can Communicate, Survey Finds." *The Chronicle of Higher Education*. 18 Sept. 2013. Web. 29 Aug. 2014.
Greckyte, R. Tabaconomia Campaign: Burning Dreams. *Renata Greckyte*. 2012. Retrieved from www.c2com.up.pt/tm/renata_greckyte/2012/11/tabaconomia-campaign-burning-dreams.html.
Kugel, S. "Sao Paulo, Brazil, Bans Public Smoking." *The World Post*. 2009. Retrieved from: www.huffingtonpost.com/2009/08/07/sao-paulo-brazil-bans-pub_n_253900.html.

Macleod, D. "Tabaconomia Calculates Tobacco Costs." *Inspiration Room*. 2009. Retrieved from theinspirationroom.com/daily/2009/tabaconomia-calculates-tobacco-costs/.

Miller, Nan. "Postmodern Moonshine in English 101." *Academic Questions* 19.3 (2006): 6–36. *Academic Search Complete*. Web. 29 Aug. 2014.

New Media Consortium. *A Global Imperative: The Report of 21st Century Literacy Summit*. 2005. Web. 6 Aug. 2014.

Prensky, Marc. "Digital Natives, Digital Immigrants." *On the Horizon* 9.5 (2001): 1–6. PDF file.

———. "Digital Natives, Digital Immigrants, Part II: Do They Really *Think* Differently? *On the Horizon* 9.6 (2001): 1–9. PDF file.

Rice, Jeff. "Imagery." *Multimodal Composition: A Critical Sourcebook*. Ed. Claire Lutkewitte. Boston and New York: Bedford/St. Martin's, 2014: 891–12. Print.

Selfe, Richard J., and Cynthia L. Selfe. "'Convince Me!' Valuing Multimodal Literacies and Composing Public Service Announcements." *Theory into Practice* 47 (2009): 83–92. *Academic Search Complete*. Web. 29 Aug. 2014.

Waiteman, F. "Calculates Tobacco Costs, Car." *Creative Ad Awards*. 2009. Retrieved from www.creativeadawards.com/calculates-tobacco-costs-car/.

Yancey, Kathleen Blake. "Made Not Only in Words: Composition in a New Key." *Multimodal Composition: A Critical Sourcebook*. Ed. Claire Lutkewitte. Boston: Bedford/St. Martin's, 2014: 628–8. Print.

Researching and Writing a History of Composition-Rhetoric

Lori Ostergaard

Supplemental Materials

- Rationale
- Pre-writing Activities
- Peer Review
- Grading Rubric
- Student Reflective Statements

Writing Assignment

Short Description: For your second major project this semester, you will take what you have learned about the field of composition and its values as an academic discipline, and apply that knowledge to the study of a single moment, movement, individual, or theory in the field's history. To construct your history, you will be working with a variety of primary sources or artifacts, similar to those that we have been working with all semester.

The artifacts you choose to collect and analyze for your history of the field may be textbooks, journals, conference programs and/or proceedings, dissertations or theses, or primary source materials from a single institutional site of instruction or from a single individual. Your history should span a significant, but short (51–0 year), period in composition history. In other words, you will not tell the big history of the field; instead, you will research a single aspect of the field and analyze that aspect during a single moment in the field's history.

Project Goals:

- Gain further experience analyzing primary source material and working with disciplinary artifacts.
- Construct a short history of the field through a careful study and analysis of the field's historical artifacts.
- Synthesize what you have learned about the field and its values through a discussion of a single movement, individual, approach, or moment.
- Provide future writing studies students with historical studies that will introduce them to one important aspect of the field they are joining.

Project Weight: 20 percent

Project Audience: Your audience for this project is future writing studies students, and the purpose of your research is to show them some important aspect of the field they are joining, to use a very small piece of our history to explain this field and its values.

Extended Description: Your archival project may investigate a number of questions from any era of composition: for example, how a variety of textbooks from a particular era taught one thing (peer review, personal narrative, rhetoric, letter writing); how an early educational journal addressed a single topic; what major topics/issues were covered by a single journal over the course of a decade and what this says about the field at that time. You might also examine:

- how a particular method was discussed over multiple years at a single conference;
- how a subdiscipline like new media or professional writing has evolved to become important to the discipline;
- how a single movement (expressivism, process, rhetoric) was discussed in a single period;
- how a single topic or issue (grammar; punctuation; assessment; basic writers; advanced writing classes; race, gender, and ability/disability studies) was discussed in a single period;
- the transformation of writing instruction at a single high school or college over a decade or less;
- the self-sponsored (extracurricular) writing of students at a high school or college (newspapers, literary magazines, writing clubs);
- the self-sponsored writing of community clubs or literary societies;
- how the field has dealt with the professionalization of graduate students;
- how the field has talked about the use of contingent (part-time) faculty to teach first-year writing;
- how the field has discussed PhD, MA, or BA degrees;

- the work of an individual writing teacher or professor over her/his lifetime;
- the work of an individual student;
- the evolution of WAC/WID programs or Writing Centers;
- the composition dissertations composed during a single period in our history and what they tell us;
- the topics explored at a regional or national conference during a single decade; and
- the influence of a single disciplinary organization (English Club in Chicago, NCTE, CCCC, WPA, etc.) over a short period of time.

You might examine the following (partial list) of artifacts to construct your history:

- course catalogs of a high school or college
- college or high school newspapers
- college or high school literary magazines
- the complete works of a single theorist or researcher in the field
- journal issues from a single 5- to 10-year period
- conference programs (or summaries) from a single 5- to 10-year period
- conference chair's addresses from a single 5- to 10-year period
- textbooks
- dissertations and theses
- individual archive collections
- obituaries

Paper Requirements: Your archival research will result in a 5–7 page academic paper, using APA style (a better style for historical work than MLA because of its use of dates in the main text and its use of the past tense). Your paper will be divided into at least four main sections: introduction, review of literature, research methods, and discussion. Your introduction should set the historical scene for your readers, providing a rationale for investigating your topic. Your review of literature will both locate your primary research within current conversations in the field and demonstrate your understanding of the history of the field as well. Your paper will also include a section outlining your research methods. This section should describe where you located your archival sources and what sources were available to you, but it should also provide a reflection on the limitations of the archival record, specifically addressing possible biases within the record and noting what, if anything, may be missing from that record. Finally, your paper will include a discussion section that synthesizes the primary and secondary research you have collected to provide an informed analysis of your research topic. Because this type of research writing may be new to many of the writers in this class, we will conduct individual peer reviews for each section of your paper before you submit the entire paper for a final peer review.

Some of you may wish to expand your research topic into a thesis, writing sample for graduate school applications, article for an undergraduate journal, or presentation for an undergraduate conference, and I will be happy to help you do that.

Rationale: Why Ask Writing and Rhetoric Majors to Work with Historical Artifacts?

Oakland University's (OU's) Writing and Rhetoric major provides advanced students with the option of focusing their study in one of three major tracks: Professional Writing, Writing for Digital Media, and Writing Studies. Students pursuing the professional writing track take classes in editing, business writing, science writing, legal writing, and grant writing, and they frequently pursue careers as writers in business and industry immediately following graduation. Students in our digital media track take classes that introduce them to writing for digital media, podcasting, web design, and social networking, and they have had some success finding jobs as writers and social network coordinators.

By contrast to these two tracks that train students for careers as professional writers and digital media composers, the Writing Studies track prepares our majors for graduate work in composition-rhetoric through course work in research methods, rhetorical history and theory, and pedagogy. WRT 329, Writing Studies, is the required gateway course for this track, providing OU's Writing and Rhetoric majors with a survey of composition-rhetoric as an academic discipline, including an examination of the history, theories, research, curricula, and pedagogies associated with composition-rhetoric in the university. The course seeks to introduce our students in the writing studies track to both the intellectual and the mundane features of the discipline, helping our majors recognize the disciplinary values that underlie our field's history, research, service, and pedagogy. I view this gateway course as a way of moving our majors beyond simple disciplinary identification—beyond gaining just enough disciplinary knowledge to know their Bartholomae from their Elbow—and towards a vision of the "'future tense' of their lives as rhetoric and composition professionals" (Miller et al. 397). Students work with primary artifacts as well as secondary sources throughout the semester, and their work with these artifacts culminates in this final history paper. This assignment requires that they consult a number of primary archival documents, synthesizing those documents with published histories of the field, and offering their own analysis that locates their history within current disciplinary conversations and contexts.

Rather than encounter only other people's interpretations of the field, the artifact approach allows my students to produce their own critical evaluations. Rather than read historical accounts of the field as definitive and authoritative, I believe my students begin to recognize that those histories were stories constructed, often, from incomplete archives and shaped as much by gaps and silences as they were by the available materials.

While my students have had some success with this project, the process was not very smooth the first time I taught it. I originally assigned this as the first project of the semester, before students knew much about the contemporary field, and when their introduction to disciplinary history was somewhat shallow and they had little experience working with and analyzing disciplinary artifacts. As a result, my students had difficulty placing their historical analyses into the larger context of the field, and they struggled to synthesize their research with the research of historical scholars in the field. The second time, I assigned it at the end of the semester. By this point, my students had studied both the current state of the field—through artifacts ranging from job postings to listservs, journal issues to conference CFPs—and the field's early institutional history. Students' archival research projects from both sections have included an analysis of a collection of bound essays preserved in the archive by a political science professor whose students wrote about the need for increased student engagement with university governance, a collection of first-year writing student essays from the early 1980s, a history of a much-loved English professor's role in promoting writing support services on campus, and a history of the development of our (very recent) writing major.

Pre-Writing Activities

Most of my students have little experience reading or analyzing disciplinary artifacts, and few have ever entered their university's archives when we begin the semester. We work with current disciplinary artifacts in the major projects leading up to this history project: conference programs, job ads, program descriptions, websites, journals, etc. They also read and discuss works composed by a number of historians in the field (Connors, Goggin, and Ritter). Finally, students engage in a variety of warm-up activities designed to provide them with a better understanding of the kinds of materials they will encounter in the archives, as well as the audiences of, purposes for, and methods employed in archival research.

Pre-Writing 1:
Playing with Historical Artifacts

The first of these warm-up activities requires that students work with a small collection of historical artifacts that I bring to class a week before our first trip to the university's archives. These are artifacts I have collected from different institutions and publications, and all are from the late nineteenth and early twentieth centuries. Students work in groups to analyze different collections of these artifacts, making only casual notes and sharing what they discover with their group members.

We spend the next class period making connections between their individual notes and the notes their classmates made. For example, students who examined early composition textbooks might connect their discoveries to the work of a group who examined published textbook reviews. Other groups begin to make connections between early faculty biographies and obituaries and the descriptions of MA theses written by those faculty. Groups discuss and attempt to historically contextualize letters from a university president to a female student interested in attending his university, college and high school newspaper articles, college and high school club and publication descriptions from yearbooks, course catalogs, journal articles, and conference proceedings. This exercise provides students with a sense of what materials they might encounter in our university archives and what kinds of materials (textbooks, obituaries, theses) they may need to locate elsewhere.

Once they have visited the archives and begun collecting data for their projects, students conduct rhetorical analyses to determine how archival histories are organized and how the arguments in these histories are made and supported. The first rhetorical analysis asks students to choose three proposals from the history section of the CCCC—the course is offered in winter, so these proposals are available online. The second analysis students conduct is of Lisa Mastrangelo's "Learning from the Past: Rhetoric, Composition, and Debate at Mount Holyoke College." Students read the entire article, individually summarize what Mastrangelo is doing over the course of just a few pages of that article, and apply what they learn from those summaries to their own work. The assignment descriptions for both of these activities are included below.

Pre-Writing 2: Rhetorical Analysis
of History Conference Proposals

Conference proposals may be useful in helping us to understand the discourse of a particular field because proposals have to do a lot of disciplinary and rhetorical work in a very short amount of space.

For this forum, I'd like you to spend a little time reviewing the history conference proposals we looked at on Monday[1] to discover the different types of persuasive and disciplinary (academic) work these proposals do.

To begin, take a look at two (or three) of the CCCC proposals at this site. It might be helpful if, rather than choosing the first few proposals you find or choosing them randomly, you identify two or three proposals that seem somewhat similar to the topic you're researching.

So if your research examines student texts/papers/newspapers, you might want to look at panels that do something similar. If your research speaks to women's roles in comp-rhet, see if any of the proposals deal with this topic as well. If you are examining new trends in the field (like new media), you might not find a history panel addressing that specific trend, but you might find a suitable example of a proposal addressing a different trend from history.

Next, identify three or more strategies the writers use to persuade proposal raters that their history panel and their topic will be interesting, relevant, and significant to the field.

- What roles do ethos, pathos, logos, and kairos play in these proposals (do these appeals show up in these texts)? How is secondary research used here (is it)? How is primary research used (is it)?
- What general academic rhetorical strategies can you identify? Are there any strategies that seem to be unique to people who study composition history?

For each strategy you identify, please also provide us with direct evidence of this strategy at work in a proposal (so give us a quote or an example that makes a direct reference to a specific proposal).

Finally, I'm going to ask you to discuss what you found with a couple of classmates and specifically to think about how you might incorporate the strategies they discuss into your own history project for this class.

Pre-Writing 3: Analysis of Lisa Mastrangelo's "Learning from the Past"

As promised, for this online discussion, you will need to read and outline Lisa Mastrangelo's article before outlining your own archival history project.

Begin by reading Mastrangelo's article and summarizing what she is doing (not "saying") in the pages you have been assigned to summarize below. Note that you will need to have read the entire article to make sense of what she is doing in the section of the article that you are outlining.

Next, read through your classmates' outlines of their sections of Mastrangelo's text. Once you have done this, outline your own history project, providing not just what you plan to do in each section, but some of the details you will use, sources you will include, and claims you will make.

Finally, read through two of your classmates' history project outlines and provide them with some feedback on their organizational strategies.

Peer Review

Because most of my students are new to archival research, I require that they attend paper conferences with me. These conferences focus on their first full, but still rough, drafts, and these meetings provide us with an opportunity to discuss both the research my students have gathered and the rhetorical strategies they will need to think about as they revise. Students also engage in a series of peer reviews involving individual parts of their projects—their outlines, methods sections, reviews of literature—and of the whole projects. The description that I provide to students for the first peer review of their full projects is included below.

Peer Review of Full Drafts

This peer review is going to be a little more structured than our other reviews in this class because I'd like you to be able to really intervene in your classmates' research and writing processes and begin to identify small problems for these writers before they become large problems.

Begin by finding the two questions your peer asked you to respond to below. Click "reply" to those questions, read them over, and then read over the questions below before you begin to read your peer's paper.

When you're done reading, answer all of the questions below and both of your peers' questions. Remember that the more information they have from you at this stage in the process, the stronger their final drafts will be. So please provide kind, but also thought-provoking, detailed, and constructive answers.

When you have finished answering all of the questions, provide any additional feedback you have for this writer.

Remember that answers like "I think this looks fine," or (in answer to the "What should they do next" question) "I think you should just continue researching and writing" are not in the least bit helpful to writers who are looking to strengthen and expand their drafts.

Here are some questions for peer reviewers.

- What's the thesis? What point is the writer making with this work? If you aren't sure, say this and suggest what the main point might be.
- What's the most interesting aspect of this research? Why do you find it interesting?

- How does the author establish the relevance or importance of this research to the field?
- Does the writer fully employ/use his/her primary sources in this work? If not, where could s/he add the primary source material s/he has collected to support a thesis?
  - If this were your paper, what research would you try to find next?
  - If this were your paper, what would you do next?

Grading Rubric

4.0—This project demonstrates both the writer's advanced understanding of the specific history s/he researched and his/her ability to locate and use historical artifacts to tell that history. The project also suggests the writer's ability to make his/her local or focused history speak to the larger historical context of the time. The work synthesizes primary and secondary data to create a new, different, or more nuanced history of the field. While the writer may have struggled some to develop the review of literature, methods, or discussions sections of the text, his/her project illustrates a concerted effort to meet the rhetorical challenges evident in composing histories of the field.

3.0—This above-average project demonstrates both the writer's understanding of the specific history s/he researched and his/her ability to locate and use historical artifacts to tell that history. The project also suggests the writer made some attempts to connect his/her local or focused history with the larger historical context. The writer had some success synthesizing primary and secondary data to create a new, different, or more nuanced history of the field. While the writer struggled to develop the review of literature, methods, or discussions sections of the text, his/her project illustrates his/her efforts to meet the rhetorical challenges evident in composing histories of the field.

2.0—This average project suggests that the writer may have understood the specific history s/he researched and may have had some success telling that history through a reflection on historical artifacts. The writer may have struggled to incorporate primary source material and/or may have experienced some difficulty connecting his/her history to a larger historical context. The writer may have had some success synthesizing primary and secondary data and may have struggled with one or more of the required sections of the text: review of literature, methods, or discussion.

1.0—This below average project suggests that the writer may not have understood the specific history s/he researched and may have had little success locating historical artifacts and/or using those materials to construct a local history of the field. The writer may have chosen not to incorporate secondary source material or connect his/her history to a larger historical context. One or more of the required sections may be missing or poorly constructed.

0—The writer may not have had time to complete the research and writing required for a passing grade for this project. The researcher may not have gathered any historical artifacts beyond what was collected during the class visit to the archives. His/her history may indicate an attempt to formulate a thesis based on limited primary source material, or it may suggest that the writer was not aware of the larger context for his/her local history. Required sections may be missing or poorly constructed.

Student Reflective Statements

In their portfolio introductions, students in this class suggested that their work with disciplinary artifacts was an entirely new research activity. While most students commented on the research they did in the class, one summed up her experiences by noting that the history project had introduced her to "some research forums and pathways that I would have never considered in the past" (Mockford).[2] She also suggested that she "liked working with the direct materials. I loved looking through all those old books! It was quite a lot of fun looking at old pictures and documents that were very important to people in the past. It was effective and got the point across on how far back the debates of composition had been going on for" (Mockford). Another student suggested that "by looking at these artifacts from the field, it became clear what the field valued at different points in time. Seeing these different values and how they were expressed was far more beneficial than reading a secondary text which spelled out what the field believes to be important" (Romlein). In their responses to course evaluations, none of the students in either class suggested that the archival work they did was unnecessary or uninteresting. Instead, those students who reflected on the history assignment mentioned this assignment in response to a question about what made the class a "good learning experience." For example, one student listed archival work first: "archival activities and looking at artifacts made this class a great learning experience for other methods of finding information." Others liked "the fact that the history of comp-rhet was explored," and they enjoyed "the physical research and studies of previous scholar[s'] work."

Notes

1. center.uoregon.edu/NCTE/20124C/program/search_results.php?text_search_bool=AND&keywordid%5B0%5D=602117&keywordid%5B1%5D=602191&keywordid%5B2%5D=&keywordid%5B3%5D=&orderby=DATE&Search=Search...

2. Student participants have provided informed consent, agreeing to have their

work cited here (IRB 622663-1). Student evaluation comments were collected anonymously.

WORKS CITED

Connors, Robert J. "Journals in Composition Studies." *College English* 46.4 (1984): 348-365. Print.

―――. "Overwork/Underpay: Labor and status of composition teachers since 1880." *Rhetoric Review* 9.1 (1990): 108-126. Print.

Goggin, Maureen Daly. "Composing a Discipline: The Role of Scholarly Journals in the Disciplinary Emergence of Rhetoric and Composition Since 1950." *Rhetoric Review* 15 (1997): 322-348. Print.

Mastrangelo, Lisa. "Learning from the Past: Rhetoric, Composition, and Debate at Mount Holyoke College." *Rhetoric Review* 18.1 (1999): 46-64. Print.

Miller, Scott L., Brenda Jo Brueggemann, Bennis Blue, and Deneen M. Shepherd. "Present Perfect and Future Imperfect: Results of a National Survey of Graduate Students in Rhetoric and Composition Programs." *College Composition and Communication* 48.3 (1997): 392-409. Print.

Mockford, Emma. "Personal Statement." 17 April 2013. TS. Oakland University E-portfolio, Rochester, MI.

Ritter, Kelly. "Archival Research in Composition Studies: Re-Imagining the Historian's Role." *Rhetoric Review* 31.4 (2012): 461-478. Print.

Romlein, Jeanne. "Personal Statement." 17 April 2013. TS. Oakland University E-portfolio, Rochester, MI.

Critical Analysis of a *Wikipedia* Entry

GWENDOLYNNE REID

Supplemental Materials

- Rationale
- Pre-Writing Activities
- Grading Rubric
- Pitfalls and Avoidance Strategies
- Follow-Up Multimodal Assignment

Writing Assignment

ASSIGNMENT SNAPSHOT

Assignment: Analyze and evaluate a *Wikipedia* entry to shed light on the role the encyclopedia can play in academic writing.

Audience: Undergraduate writers and those who care about their writing.

Sources: Any sources you need to develop an insightful analysis, including, at minimum, the *Wikipedia* entry (with its "talk" and "view history" pages), the sources it links to, and 3+ scholarly sources on the same subject as the entry.

Documentation: MLA.

Length: 1,250+ words, without your works cited.

LEARNING OBJECTIVES

- Practice critical thinking about writing and research choices.
- Practice balancing original thinking and argument with source work.
- Practice analysis, synthesis, and evaluation.

RHETORICAL PURPOSE

For a variety of reasons, students are often told to avoid *Wikipedia* for academic research. Yet *Wikipedia* tends to be a source most of us consult regularly in our personal lives, relying on it as a quick source of information on most subjects we can think of. Your rhetorical purpose in this paper will be to analyze and evaluate a *Wikipedia* entry of your choice to shed light on the role *Wikipedia* can play in academic research and writing. Because this is a more limited context for *Wikipedia*'s use, you should imagine your audience as undergraduate writers and those who care about their writing (e.g., composition instructors, composition scholars, writing center staff, librarians, etc.).

FOCUS

While you will include some content on the subject of your chosen *Wikipedia* entry, keep in mind that it is not your primary focus. Also avoid making your scholarly sources your focus (e.g. through extensive summary); use your sources to further your own analysis and purpose. Ultimately, your focus should be on *Wikipedia*'s potential role in academic research and writing.

RESEARCH AND EVIDENCE

Your first research task will be to select a representative *Wikipedia* entry that you find interesting and that you think you can analyze insightfully. If you choose a particularly lengthy entry, you might focus your analysis on a manageable section of it. As part of your inquiry, you will need to develop criteria for evaluating your chosen entry and brainstorm which resources you'll need to help you analyze and evaluate its potential role in academic writing. While this will differ for each entry, at a minimum you should plan on including among your sources (1) the *Wikipedia* entry itself (with its "talk" and "view history" pages), (2) the sources the *Wikipedia* entry cites and links to, and (3) at least 3 scholarly sources on the same subject as your entry. To lend depth to your analysis, you might also consider including sources on *Wikipedia* itself. Since part of what you are examining is the language of the entry, some direct quotes of your research will be necessary; however, to avoid a paper that is too quote-heavy, try to balance quotes with paraphrases and summaries when the language is not your object of focus. Aim to balance all these forms of source material with your own analysis and evaluation. Think rhetorically about your source use and follow MLA guidelines for documentation.

GLOBAL FEATURES

You have two main tasks to accomplish in this project, analysis and evaluation, offering you a variety of organizational options. For example, you may decide to analyze your entry before you evaluate it, or analyze and evaluate together as you go. Along the same lines, you might decide to organize paragraphs according to elements you have chosen to analyze or the evaluative criteria you developed. You might even organize according to the concerns raised about the use of *Wikipedia* in academic research and writing. Whatever organizing pattern you choose, make sure that it is logical, that it supports your rhetorical purpose, and that you guide readers through it with adequate signposting (e.g., transitions, signal phrases, etc.). You may even opt to use subheadings. Regardless of structure, you will need a thesis that offers your main finding about your chosen *Wikipedia* entry's potential for use in academic work; you may also include a more general recommendation for *Wikipedia*'s academic use or keep this sort of reflection solely for your conclusion, which should address the broader implications of your findings and of *Wikipedia*'s role in undergraduate research and writing.

LOCAL FEATURES

In making stylistic choices, consider what will be effective for your rhetorical situation. Terms related to writing studies or library science, for example, may not need definition, while specialized concepts from other fields (e.g., if your *Wikipedia* entry is about a specialized topic) may require brief definitions or concrete examples. In general, strive for a clear, specific style and a reasonable tone, appropriate for an academic audience including both undergraduates and faculty. Follow MLA guidelines for formatting your paper.

SUGGESTED PROCESS

You will likely move between these phases recursively (possible activities in parentheses):

- Entry selection. Reflection. Exploratory searching. Skimming. Pre-searching on related sources. Exploration of the entry's subpages.
- Research. Keyword brainstorming and refinement. Database and Google Scholar searching. Following links on your entry and citations on possible sources. Skimming. Reflection.
- Inquiry. Reading. Note-taking. Looking for patterns. Developing evaluative criteria. Rereading. Gathering evidence. Asking questions. Examining features. Reflection.
- Planning. Reviewing notes and reflections. Freewriting. Listing. Clustering. Reflection. Developing possible plans. Developing a rough main finding. Gathering evidence.
- Writing. Drafting. Rereading. Reworking your plan. Finding more evidence. Refining your thesis.

- Revising. Rereading. Self-evaluation. Seeking feedback. Letting the draft rest. Reverse outlining. Talking it out. Rewriting.
- Editing. Reading aloud/backwards. Seeking proofreaders and help. Working on style and grammar. Checking documentation. Checking formatting.

Rationale

While describing today's students as digital natives has become a common trope, a substantial body of information literacy research has problematized assumptions about what students born in the digital age know how to do with digital resources and what they understand about contemporary information ecologies. Alison Head, for example, reporting on results from Project Information Literacy focused on first-year college students, stresses the diversity of students' research experiences and the challenges many of them face in transitioning to college-level research resources and expectations. Gregor Kennedy and Terry Judd similarly complicate the concept of the digital native, with research revealing that few students wholly match that label (133). In their estimation, ubiquitous access to more information, "places more not less onus on faculty" to actively support students' development as digital researchers (132).

At the same time, a number of scholars from both library science and composition have argued for understanding research and writing as part of a single process (e.g., Artman, Frisicaro-Pawlowski, and Monge; Bowles-Terry, Davis, and Holliday; Elmborg; Norgaard, "Contributions"; Norgaard, "In the Classroom"). These scholars also tend to stress a rhetorical understanding of sources as important for both parts of this process, helping students pay attention to everything from the conversations authors and sources are part of to how students' own work relates and contributes to those conversations. Research instruction is rhetorical instruction.

Together, these lines of inquiry suggest a need or space for more explicit attention to digital resources and research in the composition classroom. This assignment is one step in that direction, asking students to critically examine a digital resource they are likely to use quite regularly. At the same time, *Wikipedia* is also a source students are regularly warned off of by educators, sometimes to the point of becoming a taboo in academic contexts. Welcoming *Wikipedia* into the classroom and giving students a space to critically examine it through guided inquiry invites students to explore its affordances and construction in ways many of them might not do on their own, potentially developing a more critical understanding of it. Doing so also tells students that the composition classroom is a safe space for interrogating these sorts of writing taboos and the anxieties that come with them. While some students may have examined *Wikipedia*'s affordances, such as its talk and history pages, perhaps even contributing to the site, most students likely won't have; regardless, those affordances give students a particularly concrete look at how knowledge and writing are socially constructed. Finally, because the assignment asks students to analyze *Wikipedia* as a potential resource for academic contexts and inquiry, the assignment continues their rhetorical development, encouraging them to think about sources and source use contextually rather than absolutely.

Because the assignment allows them to choose their own entries for analysis, most students have found the assignment engaging as a means for exploring their interests and building on their prior knowledge. Student topics have ranged from internet addiction and cyberbullying to continuous tracks and even the Wright brothers. Although students typically develop a range of stances on *Wikipedia* through the assignment, most arrive at a more critical approach, putting emphasis on the contexts and purposes within which *Wikipedia* might be used effectively, and those where it might be counterproductive.

While developed in the context of a FYW course at a large research university with a WID-based curriculum, the assignment is also appropriate for a range of other institutions and curricula, including Writing-about-Writing, and potentially new media or multimodal writing (see the description of a multimodal project based on the inquiry). The assignment also has room to be developed into a more complex inquiry for a collaborative version of the project. Although the assignment is flexible enough to fit in a variety of assignment sequences, it will be more likely to lead to deep critical thinking if incorporated after students have been introduced to rhetorical concepts. Because it requires students to find, analyze, and synthesize multiple forms of evidence, it is also more likely to be successful after students have had some practice with research-based writing.

Pre-Writing Activities

The pre-writing activities suggested below are designed to help students delay judgment on *Wikipedia* and engage in deeper inquiry on their entry and the site:

Exploring *Wikipedia*'s Affordances

A particularly important part of encouraging students to think critically about *Wikipedia* is simply giving students space to explore its affordances.

Many students will not have noticed anything but the main tab for *Wikipedia* entries. Pointing out some of the other tabs within each entry, such as the "talk" and "view history" tabs, can be eye-opening for students, giving them a glimpse of the social and technical dynamics behind how the information they've consulted in the past is generated.

To keep this exploration student-centered, dividing students into groups responsible for examining and then presenting on a particular affordance of the site can be productive. For a larger class, this activity could include groups responsible for reporting on some of the important community pages on *Wikipedia* (examples below), also important elements for thinking critically about the site. Alternatively, this sort of exploration could be integrated in students' entry selection phase, with individual students writing descriptions and summaries of what they're finding in the various tabs of their entries. If done with potential entries under consideration, this could help students make their entry selections, as well as giving them a more comparative view of the possible variations across *Wikipedia*.

Readings from *Wikipedia*

Along with affordances and elements of individual *Wikipedia* entries, students benefit from exploring *Wikipedia*'s own descriptions of itself and of its policies, as well as looking at some of its important community pages. While many of these exist, the following are some of the most notable and relevant to the assignment:

"Administrator Noticeboard: Incidents" (en.wikipedia.org/wiki/Wikipedia:Administrators%27_noticeboard/Incidents)—This dynamic list of ongoing incidents on the site demonstrates that problems like vandalism occur, but also that the community is fairly vigilant and speedy in addressing those problems.

"Core Content Policies" (en.wikipedia.org/wiki/Wikipedia:Core_content_policies)—This page defines *Wikipedia*'s core policies on the content included in its articles, with links to more detailed pages on the policies of verifiability, neutral point-of-view, and "no original research." This pairs well with Garfinkel's article on the site's epistemology (below).

"Good Article Criteria" (en.wikipedia.org/wiki/Wikipedia:GA)—Reading about *Wikipedia*'s criteria for selecting "good articles" (directly below the "featured article" rating) can help students start thinking about the site's values and their own evaluative criteria.

"What *Wikipedia* Is Not" (en.wikipedia.org/wiki/Wikipedia:What_Wikipedia_is_not)—Primarily meant for potential contributors to the site, this entry clarifies what the site is intended to be, as well as what it is not meant to be.

Readings on *Wikipedia*

An inductive, hands-on approach to examining *Wikipedia* and thinking critically about it as a potential source tends to work well for students; however, some issues with the site will still remain opaque without outside readings on particular cases and dynamics. While there is no shortage of articles on *Wikipedia*, many of them are not particularly accessible to first-year students. The following readings are fairly accessible and could be used toward the beginning of the unit to help students think through some of the issues related to the site, including issues related to its academic use (Cohen), its demographics and purpose (Dee), and its epistemology and accuracy (Cross; Garfinkel; Giles; Roth).

Cohen, Noam. "A History Department Bans Citing *Wikipedia* as a Research Source." *New York Times* 21 Feb. 2007. NYTimes.com. Web. 8 Aug. 2014.

Cross, Tom. "Puppy Smoothies: Improving the Reliability of Open, Collaborative Wikis." *First Monday* 11.9 (2006): n. pag. firstmonday.org. Web. 14 Aug. 2014.

Dee, Jonathan. "All the News That's Fit to Print Out." *New York Times* 1 July 2007. NYTimes.com. Web. 8 Aug. 2014.

Garfinkel, Simon L. "*Wikipedia* and the Meaning of Truth." *Technology Review* 111.6 (2008): 84–86. Print.

Giles, Jim. "Internet Encyclopaedias Go Head to Head." *Nature* 438.7070 (2005): 900–901. Web. 1 Dec. 2013.

Roth, Philip. "An Open Letter to *Wikipedia*." *New Yorker Blogs* 7 Sept. 2012. Web. 1 Dec. 2013.

Entry Selection

Since students are likely to be more critical readers on topics they are personally invested in or have studied extensively in the past, assigning reflective work to elicit some of those topics can be a productive pre-writing activity. This can be combined with some exploratory searching for entries on *Wikipedia*, as well as group or class brainstorms of criteria for selecting a productive entry. Because students might not think of important criteria until they are exploring possible entries, keeping a dynamic crowdsourced document of criteria could be a useful strategy here (e.g. in a shared Google document). Encouraging students to follow links and explore subpages, such as the "talk" and "view history" pages should be an important part of this process. Students may also benefit from some "pre-searching" on related academic sources to make sure meeting this part of the assignment's research requirement will be feasible.

Mock Debate

Noam Cohen's *New York Times* article (above) describes a campus-wide discussion on *Wikipedia* as a source after the history department at Middlebury College decided to ban its use in student work. Faculty and students on all sides of the issue came together for a discussion that included arguments and evidence presented from a variety of perspectives. Holding a Middlebury-style mock debate on the policy can be a good way to engage students who are motivated by competition and role-playing. It is also a useful invention tool for thinking through a range of factors to be considered in deciding how *Wikipedia* can or should be used, as well as encouraging students to support claims with specific reasons and evidence. To promote this sort of specificity, assign roles with clearly articulated tasks and goals, outline the order of events during the debate, and give students adequate time to prepare. Highlighting students' "available means" of presenting evidence can also encourage them to be specific in how they support claims (e.g., document cameras, projectors, etc.). At a minimum, divide students into three groups, one supporting a ban, one opposed to a ban, and one serving as a panel of "judges" or college faculty and administrators responsible for crafting the ultimate policy. Judges may seem to have the least preparation to do, but having them develop the criteria and factors they consider to make their policy decision and requiring that they present a statement on their decision can help focus their task.

Library Research

An important part of thinking through how *Wikipedia* might be used in academic work includes examining alternatives and comparing their affordances with those of *Wikipedia*. In addition to database research that will lead students to original research on their topics, help students find the sorts of informational sources scholars might use, including specialized encyclopedias. Most academic libraries have a number of these available, both in the library and online. For example, a student analyzing the *Wikipedia* entry on President Kennedy might include one or more entries on Kennedy from the *Encyclopedia of the U.S. Presidency: A Historical Reference* among the academic sources used in their paper. A student studying ADHD might include the *Diagnostic and Statistical Manual of Mental Disorders* (DSM-5) among their sources. This sort of nuanced look at the range of sources scholars might consult, including informational sources, helps develop a more contextual, rhetorical understanding of sources and what each type is "good for." If your institution has the resources, a librarian-led session on finding appropriate reference works for academic research can be a valuable activity during this unit. This is also an opportune moment for introducing students to peer review and other academic practices designed to regulate knowledge construction, an important point of reference for students as they examine how the *Wikipedia* community regulates the construction of "common knowledge."

Reflection

For composition instructors, the importance of including reflective writing throughout the writing process generally goes without saying. For this assignment, reflection early in the inquiry process and interspersed throughout can be especially valuable for deepening students' analyses and capturing (and promoting) the evolution of their thinking. For example, students might benefit from reflections on many (or all) of the following:

- their prior use and understandings of *Wikipedia*;
- what they discovered while exploring the site's affordances;
- what they learned when reading outside sources on the site;
- what they predict they'll find when researching their chosen topics;
- what they found during research and any surprises;
- the similarities and discrepancies they found between their academic sources and their entry;
- what factors or criteria to consider when deciding whether to use a source for a scholarly project (and/or *how* to appropriately use that source); and
- what prior experiences and expectations their readers might bring to reading their analysis.

In addition to promoting deeper inquiry, many of these types of reflections will also yield material students can use during their planning and drafting. For example, their own surprises during their inquiry can give them ideas for effective essay openers.

Elements for Analysis

Because most students have more practice with informational or persuasive writing than analytical writing, many will benefit from support in noticing more features of their entry to analyze. This support can take many forms, including "lab" time to work in class with built-in peer response during the session, an ongoing crowdsourced list of elements in a shared Google document, or even an instructor-provided list of "areas" to pay attention to during inquiry (e.g., substantive, global, local, intertextual, visual, etc.). Some students may benefit from printing out their entry to mark it up with notes, highlighting, and post-its. Others may appreciate a studio-like, collaborative invention session with a station set up for each student/entry (i.e., with a laptop or print-out of the entry and a pad of paper for peer notes) and time to move from station to station adding thoughts on interesting features noticed in peers' entries.

Developing Evaluative Criteria

Similarly, students may need support in thinking through the criteria writers should consider when deciding whether and how to use resources in academic work. Many handbooks and library guides provide lists of evaluative criteria for students to run through when selecting sources (e.g., the CRAAP test), but these sometimes do not include more rhetorical, contextual concerns. One approach to eliciting rhetorical concerns along with other concerns is to have students reflect on the factors they consider when deciding whether to "cite" a source in exchanges with friends and family (including on social media) and to compare those factors with the criteria they might consider in academic contexts. Like with the analytical elements, crowdsourcing a class list of evaluative criteria could be a productive approach, perhaps even challenging students to critique a popular source evaluation tool or propose one of their own. Once students have developed a set of evaluative criteria, they should be encouraged to apply it to their *Wikipedia* entry, perhaps comparing this with application to one or more of their academic sources.

Grading Rubric

The rubric included below does not assign points to elements of students' papers, instead breaking the paper down into several levels or views, starting with the most important—its rhetorical purpose. The bullets describe what a successful paper will look like in an area, while allowing for diverse approaches in each area. Finally, the evaluative scale is meant to emphasize process and the idea that a rhetorically effective paper is achievable given enough time and effort spent developing it. An added benefit to this approach is that the rubric can also become a helpful tool for responding to early drafts, visually indicating through circling, underlining, or highlighting which areas are already effective and which could use more attention during revision.

Purpose—Critical Analysis   Unacceptable   Discovery   Rough   Shaped   Polished

- Analyzes a specific *Wikipedia* entry and evaluates its potential for use in academic research and writing, basing this evaluation on a set of criteria sensitive to an academic context.
- Goes beyond summarizing the entry or making a general argument about *Wikipedia* to providing insight on how the entry's features and affordances work in context of academic research and writing.
- Demonstrates sensitivity to the concerns and values of undergraduate writers and those who care about their development as writers.
- Adds insight to readers' understandings of the entry, of *Wikipedia*, and of today's research and writing landscape.

Research and   Unacceptable   Discovery   Rough   Shaped   Polished
Evidence

- Focuses on an entry that lends itself to an interesting and useful analysis of *Wikipedia*'s role in academic work.
- Fulfills academic readers' expectations for evidence, basing analysis on, at minimum, the *Wikipedia* entry (with its "talk" and "view history" pages), the sources it links to, and 3+ scholarly sources on the same subject as the entry.
- Any additional sources included contribute positively to the goals of the critical analysis and to the author's *ethos*.
- Balances evidence from the entry and additional sources with at least as much analysis and evaluation, connecting evidence clearly to the paper's claims and conclusions.
- Source material is signaled in an easily-retraced manner that orients readers and helps put evidence in context.
- Choices about quoting versus paraphrasing versus summarizing are made based on rhetorical purpose and effectiveness.
- Consistently follows MLA conventions for documentation.

Global Features   Unacceptable   Discovery   Rough   Shaped   Polished

- Elements of the paper (e.g. title, introduction, thesis, body sections/paragraphs, conclusion, etc.) demonstrate attention to reader needs and expectations, guiding them clearly and logically to achieve the paper's rhetorical purpose.
- Opening elements (title & introduction) engage readers with the paper's purpose, object of analysis (the *Wikipedia* entry), and main finding (thesis) on the entry's potential for use in academic work.
- Organization helps readers progress logically through the analysis and evaluation, supporting the rhetorical purpose.
- Paragraphs (& sections) are focused, balancing evidence and critical analysis and building up logically to the conclusion.
- Conclusion summarizes and reflects more broadly on paper's findings and *Wikipedia*'s role in academic work, possibly offering general recommendations for *Wikipedia*'s use in academic research or raising new questions.
- Makes effective use of signposting to guide readers through paper's logic (i.e. transitions, signal phrases, headings, etc.).

Local Features   Unacceptable   Discovery   Rough   Shaped   Polished

- Adopts clear, engaging, but serious style and tone appropriate for intended audience and context.
- Defines any specialized terms related to the entry that may be unfamiliar to an audience of undergraduate writers and those who care about and support their writing.
- Uses formal and stylistic choices to further the message and rhetorical goals of the paper.
- Follows MLA guidelines for formatting.

Pitfalls and Avoidance Strategies

Entry selection is a particularly important moment for students, with some potentially drawn to entries that are too underdeveloped for a complex analysis and others drawn to entries that are much too lengthy and detailed to examine in the time allotted for the assignment. The *Wikipedia* entry on Leonardo Da Vinci, for example, is quite lengthy and (at the time of this writing) includes 111 references. Since the assignment asks students to examine the sources their entry references, this would be an unmanageable task. A strategy for avoiding these sorts of problems is to build in time for the class to develop selection criteria for entries and to engage in peer response on entries peers are considering. Instructor feedback on selected entries is also important. For particularly lengthy choices, instructors might encourage students to choose a manageable portion of a longer entry. In the case of Leonardo Da Vinci, this might be the "Engineering and Inventions" section, which only cites 8 sources. Another option would be to turn the assignment into a collaborative assignment, which could allow students to tackle lengthier entries. Building on a topic students have researched and written about in one or more previous assignments (e.g. an annotated bibliography) can also make the process more manageable.

Later on in the process, some of the pitfalls instructors might encounter will relate to students' inexperience with analysis. Many students have prior experience with persuasive or informational writing, but not with analytical writing. For some, this inexperience will lead them to either build a general persuasive piece on *Wikipedia* or to summarize their entry and sources with no analysis. Many of the pre-writing activities described are meant to extend the inquiry and invention phases of the project to give students the ideas and material they'll need to avoid falling back on these more familiar forms of writing. Encouraging students to organize their papers according to analytical elements or evaluative criteria can also help them avoid these pitfalls and stay focused on their rhetorical purpose.

Follow-Up Multimodal Assignment

Assigning students a multimodal version of the assignment either after or during project development can be a productive way to extend the rhetorical learning taking place during the unit. Thinking about the rhetorical choices they made (or are making) in the paper in comparison with the choices they need to make in a short video on their inquiry, for example, can shed light on how both work rhetorically and semiotically. Shifting the target audience can also help students think more critically about rhetorical choices in both. While a number of genres and media could be tapped for a follow-up adaptation of the assignment described above, this example asks students to develop a short video:

Short Video Assignment

Use the findings and conclusions you developed in your Critical Analysis of a *Wikipedia* Article paper and adapt them to a new medium—a short, 3–5 minute video—and to the wider audience you might reach on YouTube or Vimeo. Your goal in this video is to engage viewers with the issues surrounding *Wikipedia* use for serious inquiry and use your evidence and analysis to help viewers become more critical *Wikipedia* users. Your video should be engaging, informative, and supported, using a wide range of rhetorical resources to make your point—images, music, spoken words, written words, etc. While evidence looks different in a video, it is still important as support for any claims you make; to help viewers connect evidence to your claims, attribute sources clearly through strategies like oral signaling, visual signaling, credits, etc. You do not need to actually publish your video for the public, though you may do so for extra credit. Make this decision before creating your video as this will impact the choices you make in terms of fair use and copyright. At the end of the unit, we will have a class video screening during which you will briefly discuss the choices you made in transposing your work to a new medium and audience, sharing aspects of the experience such as challenges, victories, learning, etc.

To minimize discrepancies in students' comfort with the technical aspects of developing a video, instructors might make the video assignment collaborative, encouraging groups to identify and use each other's strengths. An additional benefit to doing so is that students will have access to more evidence and analysis for the project. Regardless, the experience of adapting their inquiry to video and reflecting on their choices gives students a nice way to share and celebrate the results of that inquiry while continuing their learning about research, composition, and rhetoric.

Works Cited

Artman, Margaret, Erica Frisicaro-Pawlowski, and Robert Monge. "Not Just One Shot: Extending the Dialogues about Information Literacy in Composition Classes." *Composition Studies* 38.2 (2010): 93–110. Print.

Bowles-Terry, Melissa, Erin Davis, and Wendy Holliday. "'Writing Information Literacy' Revisited: Application of Theory to Practice in the Classroom." *Reference & User Services Quarterly* 49.3 (2010): 225–230. Print.

Elmborg, James K. "Locating the Center: Libraries, Writing Centers and Information Literacy." *Writing Lab Newsletter* 30.6 (2006): 7–11. Print.

Head, Alison J. "Learning the Ropes: How Freshmen Conduct Course Research Once They Enter College." Project Information Literacy Research Report (2013): 14–18. Print.

Kennedy, Gregor E., and Terry S. Judd. "Beyond Google and the 'Satisficing' Searching of Digital Natives." *Deconstructing Digital Natives: Young People, Technology, and the New Literacies*. Ed. Michael Thomas. New York: Routledge, 2011. 119–136. Print.

Norgaard, Rolf. "Writing Information Literacy: Contributions to a Concept." *Reference & User Services Quarterly* 43.2 (2003): 124–130. Print.

———. "Writing Information Literacy in the Classroom: Pedagogical Enactments and Implications." *Reference & User Services Quarterly* 43.3 (2004): 220–226. Print.

"In the Year"
Using Website Design for ePortfolios

Katherine Robbins

Supplemental Materials

- Rationale
- Website Contents
- Scaffolding Activity
- Evaluation and Rubric
- Student Writing Samples
- ePortfolio Tips

Website Assignment

Individually or in groups, you will develop and launch a website using the program *Weebly*. The website is meant to help you engage with the Composition Theories you have learned throughout the semester: Intertextuality, genre theory, verbal and visual rhetoric, and digital literacy. Through creating a website, you will be implementing these theories in practice. Since you will be individually graded on your own essays through the Writing Portfolio, the Website Grade comes with criteria that relates to both the content and the design of the website.

The goal of the website is to turn your individual essays into a unified website on the year. You will look at the collection of essays from the semester (Essay 1—In the Year, Essay 2—Rhetoric in the Year, and Essay 3—Visual Rhetoric in the Year) and assemble them in a way that puts the essays together to create a presentation of the year under discussion. This may mean linking readings by content, subject, analysis approach, etc. Whichever way you choose to lay out the essays, the website needs to show cohesion and clear purpose.

Since this is meant to be a functioning, usable website, part of the grading criteria relates to the appeal to its audience. Because of that, I'll be looking at the site and grading it on how well it would appeal to the web browsing audience. In other words, is the look and aesthetic appealing and engaging? Is the website easy to navigate and use? Is there some interactive piece that gets the audience to engage with the content? To grade the website, I'll use the attached Website Grading Rubric.

Rationale

When I was teaching at James Madison University in Harrisonburg, Virginia, I attended a *Teaching and Learning with Technology* conference. One of the presenters was Andrew Witmer, a professor who teaches "Race and Religion in the Antebellum South" at JMU. At the start of the presentation, he discussed using WordPress to create student websites. Then, he handed the presentation over to former students and let them discuss their experiences. As each group presented their website, I was impressed by the pride in all of their faces, the strong sense of ownership, and the meaning that their respective topic held for each student because of this project. During the presentation, I wondered, "Why am I not doing this with my first-year composition students?"

Watching how innovative the history department was being with technology reminded me of Kathleen Blake Yancey's "Made Not Only in Words" CCCC presentation from December 2004. Her paper reflects on the role of composition in an age of technology, visual rhetoric, and multimodal means of communication. In "Quartet Four," Yancey addresses composition that is devoid of the opportunities of technology. Instead she thinks about all the ways meaning could be created for composition students: "These spaces—the intertextual, overlapping curricular spaces—between the school and the public, including print and screen, are still ours to study, to examine, and to claim" (321). By having his students create websites, Witmer was teaching his students the type of composition for which Yancey advocates. Although I was teaching my students about writing study theories, the history students were not actively engaging with these theories. While I listened to the history students present their projects, I started scribbling down ideas on how to start a website project for my composition students.

Deciding to do a website project was easy; figuring out how was another matter. Landing on a hook to unify the project was probably the trickiest part. In a "Race and Religion in Antebellum South" class, the parameters of the class determine the website topics. With a freshman composition class, there are no contextual parameters. If my students were going to be successful with their websites, I knew I had to pick an angle that offered them freedom to pursue their own interest but came with enough parameters to help them develop purpose and establish an audience.

The epiphany moment was deciding to have students pick a year in history. This angle became the origins of my *"In The Year..." ePortfolio Project*, which I have now used for two-and-a-half years with first-year composition students enrolled in 10- and 12-week long writing courses at a university and a community college. I used this project as both a solo project and as a group project in which 3–4 students pool their essays for one website. To help them create a unified website, the papers have to focus on one year in history. While some students pick the year they were born, others start with an event that fascinated them. Throughout the semester, I assign essays designed to help the student further explore the year's themes (Essay #1), Verbal Rhetoric (Essay #2), and Visual Rhetoric (Essay #3). The students then take these three essays and use Weebly, a free website builder, to feature their essays in a unified, thematic way.

The *"In The Year..." ePortfolio Project* fits well into current composition theory. On a practical level the project is important for life skills like computer and Web 2.0 (i.e., Weebly, Dipity, Popplet, etc.), digital citizenship, and professional development. Additionally, it helps students see writing as not just flat text, but living, interactive material. By creating websites, papers transform into multimodal works that integrate spatial, linguistic, visual, aural, and, possibly, gestural meaning. Transitioning the papers from written works to web essays helps students to understand how genre theory influences how we write and the purpose of writing. The opportunities of the add-ons, layout, aesthetic, and functions of Weebly alter the way that the audience experiences and engages with the essays. Students have to understand the audience for which they are writing and consider various discourse communities with which they are in dialogue. Lastly, it uses core writing studies theories of visual and verbal rhetoric since the writing, website, and visuals all work together to create one core meaning.

Another benefit of using ePortfolios is the technique of hypertextualizing. In traditional ePortfolios, hypertextualizing occurs through the linking of words to texts, websites, or images. In "Down the Yellow Chip Road: Hypertext Portfolios in Oz," Katherine Fischer found that the benefit of hypertextualizing is that it "requires that the writer provide metaphorical ways of moving from piece to piece because there are no paper pages to turn and because scrolling alone is not the norm" (340). Instead of engaging with turning pages, ePortfolios utilizing hypertexts ask the writer to make more active choices on the sequence, timing, and direction in which the reader experiences the works. With websites, students utilize the medium to control the order of the pages, use buttons with links or embedded hyperlinks to direct the viewer within the site. There are also links that open supplemental information that takes the viewer away from the site or to download materials. As Marshall McLuhan writes, "the medium is the message" (qtd. in Fischer 353), and with websites, the student gets more power over the dimensions of those messages.

The website project is also consistent with the dual goals of First-Year Writing courses: to teach composition theory and to prepare students for college writing. My hope is that the assignment succeeds in the combination of college writing goals (i.e. research, thesis statements, analysis, primary vs. secondary sources) while also teaching students about composition theory (i.e. discourse community, genre theory, rhetoric, and intertextuality). Given the public nature of creating a website, the way websites engage with other sites through hypertexting, and the way websites engage with global audiences, using websites for the ePortfolio helps students enter into larger dialogues.

These larger dialogues are what I enjoy most about this assignment. Instead of being a static paper on 9/11, there are slideshows, interesting YouTube montages that splice together and sync news coverage from six broadcasts, links to poems, inclusions of art, and interactive timelines. By engaging with endless options of artifacts, students end up inadvertently positioning themselves in the broader rhetoric surrounding their paper topic and extending knowledge beyond the sources of the paper and into a more global conversation. Cynthia Selfe, in her article on technology and literacy, advocates for "helping [students] learn how to become critical thinkers about technology and the social issues surrounding its use" (1180). Student created websites blend learning the technology while also teaching students to engage in global rhetoric by situating the website in larger dialogues, selecting artifacts, and contributing to rhetorical conversations. Meaning is moved out of being "situational and relational" and out of the "specific institution where the discourse takes place" (Clifford 862). The life-world of the paper extends beyond the meaning attached to the paper by the class and into the meaning attached by positioning themselves in larger conversations. Instead of being constrained by the limitations of page and word processor, a student has all of the affordances of their imaginations.

Website Contents

The website combines the three essays composed throughout the semester; here are brief descriptions of the assignment for each essay.

"In The Year...": This first essay asks students to find the theme of the year based on three things that happen in the year. This is a somewhat arbitrary task because in any given year there are infinite themes. This makes the goal then to not worry about "the right" theme, but the theme they can prove through research, analysis, and connections. It also encourages students to be specific in their theme to make it easier to connect evidence. Ultimately, the essay teaches students how to use primary and secondary sources. It also teaches building specific thesis statements, focusing research, arguing with strong logic, and choosing quality sources.

"Rhetoric in the Year": For this essay, the main objective is to use knowledge of rhetoric to analyze an event/article/primary source/video from the year: i.e., political commercial, ad campaign, speech, news story, etc. Whatever source the student chooses, the end goal is to find rhetorical meaning that will help them better understand the year and works as a follow-up to the theme discussion in the first essay.

"Visual Rhetoric in the Year": In the last essay, the students pick an image that was created in that year: i.e., movie poster, commercial, film poster, political poster or ad, etc. Then, they analyze the picture by looking at aesthetic meaning, use of pathos, visual connotations, or a combination of these elements to figure out what is the meaning the visual rhetoric is attaching to the image and possibly to the themes of the year.

Scaffolding Activity

By the time the students get to the ePortfolio, the essays have received plenty of feedback. Each essay is turned in as a draft that receives both feedback from peers and a 5-minute screencast review from me. With community college students, they also submit outlines, which I review in class. The outlines and review activity work well for them because some students may have been out of school for a while and need more help organizing the paper. By reviewing the outlines as a class, I can facilitate a discussion in which students provide each other with feedback, get ideas on where to go next, and help each other brainstorm ideas. Finally, before the Portfolio is due, I offer students the opportunity to have one-on-one conferences with me to discuss peer and instructor feedback and review their revision goals. When they begin transitioning the essays into websites, the content, research, analysis, and themes of the websites are already developed, which allows the student to focus more on the multimodal development and interpretation that comes with designing the site.

For scaffolding the website build, I incorporate in-class work, and a good portion of the base and structure of the website is developed in class.

I reserve computer lab space for two class periods (for 50-minute classes) and one for classes that meet once or twice a week. This gives students the opportunity to start the project when I am around to ask questions. For most, creating a website is a new thing. Because of the newness, it is more valuable to use class time to address questions, to intervene early, and to allay fears or concerns. Plus, the in-class work days are also good days to teach students how to use Weebly, showcase previous websites, and show them additional Web 2.0 tools they can incorporate. Although interactive tools like Dipity, Meograph, Voki, Popplet, ThingLink, etc., are not required elements, they do help with the "Interactivity" and "Interest" requirement of the rubric. Plus, incorporating Web 2.0 tools often helps students get more excited about the website and encourages them to think about their essays in alternative ways.

Evaluation and Rubric

Students submit their portfolio and websites for separate grading. I could provide one grade, but some students elect to take the essay content and divide it as needed over different webpages or to create the basis of new content. So it makes more sense to treat the portfolio and ePortfolio as separate entities, although there is similar textual content. Also, while the Portfolio is graded on written quality, the ePortfolio is graded on execution.

Because of this emphasis on execution, Matthew Davies and Kathleen Blake Yancey offer the "IDA" model created by Moss, Girard, and Haniford as an approach to assessing ePortfolios. "IDA" places Interpretation, Decisions, and Actions (13) as a means of combining this idea of content, design, and execution to help measure success. With multimodal web-based projects, this combination makes sense as a model. Using IDA requires asking the questions: (1) how did the student interpret the portfolio in multimodal ways; (2) what decisions were made concerning which written content to supplement with hypertexts, illustrations, etc.; and (3) what actions did the student take in engaging the viewer or in the development of the piece. Although I came across Davies and Yancey's article after designing a rubric for the *"In the Year..." ePortfolio Project*, the rubrics dual focus on content and design relate to the "IDA" theory. In designing the rubric, I wanted one that evaluated the site as a functioning site. However, the rubric also needed to reflect the "interpretation" and "decisions" of transitioning their textual portfolios into interactive websites, a process that requires making meaning out of their portfolios.

Because grading multimodal works like websites has a balance of interpretation and decisions, I make sure to use a rubric that reflects two parts of creating a website—*Website Content* and *Layout and Aesthetic*—as well as acknowledges interpretive efforts within those two parts. These two sections remind the students that they have to be cognizant of not just what they write but how they showcase the product. It also reminds me while grading that a student had to approach this activity, like most multimodal projects, as both an intended plan and an executed plan. As someone who often allows websites, films, and multimodal reflective pieces, I learned early that grading these types of pieces brings a challenge. There is the respect and admiration that comes from seeing such creative efforts and from appreciating the layers of disclosure and personalization that multimodal projects demand. Yet there is also the logistical side of evaluating such efforts in a way that does not punish for lack of technology knowledge or for lack of creative abilities.

For these websites, I wanted to use a rubric to create the evaluations component so I was not blanketly responding overly positively to the efforts. However, the rubric had to be one that allowed space for encouraging and responding to creative efforts, personalization, process, and decisions while also holding the builder to basic expectations. For grading, I adapted several rubrics I found online that were created to grade a website. These rubrics provided criteria for evaluating the quality of the website: font, color choices, layout, working hypertext, etc. The main changes I made were part of balancing grading for execution and decisions with rewarding interpretation and efforts. These latter rubric lines focused on theme, intertextuality, use of multimedia, and interactivity.

Website Content

	Excellent	*Satisfactory*	*Needs Improvement*
Theme	The site has a well-stated, clear purpose and theme that is carried throughout the site.	The site has a clearly stated purpose and theme, but may have one or two elements that do not seem to be related.	The purpose and theme of the site is somewhat vague.
Intertextuality	Website shows a strong understanding of how all essays relate to each other. Website author(s) successfully thought about how best to build the content to show interconnectivity.	Website thought about how the essays relate with each other, but wasn't able to successfully display/lay out individual essays in a way that build onto each other.	Essays are simply dropped into website in a way that doesn't show reflection on how essays connect.

Layout and Aesthetics

	Excellent	Satisfactory	Needs Improvement
Use of Multimedia	All multimedia relate to content. Enhances the understanding of the content.	Most of the multimedia contributes to the understanding of the concepts, ideas, etc.	The multimedia does not contribute or seems irrelevant. Detracts rather than aids.
Interactivity	Website has interactive element to make it fun and exciting. It provides another way to present content in a meaningful way.	The website makes some attempt at an interactive component, but doesn't really enhance or relate to the source content as strongly as an "Excellent" website.	Website makes no attempt at providing any interactivity with user.

Student Writing Samples

In the numerous sections that I have done this project, no two websites have come out alike. When the websites are done as a group, the website theme is trickier because it has to encapsulate all of the papers. In the individual projects, students can pinpoint a more focused theme, which will guide the design and development. While some students take an event (i.e., Cuban Missile Crisis, Hurricane Katrina, or 9/11) and focus all of the three essays on understanding and finding meaning in that one event, other students start with the theme (i.e., sex scandals, technology innovations, and fear). Some students have decided to use the site to expand their projects to include additional information about the year to (i.e., popular movies and songs, timeline of the year, etc.) to give larger context to understanding the more focused essays. To help get a stronger sense of the final products, here are brief descriptions of three websites:

1. 2012: Missteps and Negative Role Models
    a. Three Events: Psy and "Gangnam Style," *Fifty Shades of Grey*, and Lance Armstrong
    b. Rhetorical Analysis: AT&T commercial about texting and driving
    c. Visual Rhetoric: the movie poster for *Django Unchained*
    d. Website Features: use of buttons to house papers and to click to other pages, an "Oops Moments of 2012" page that has pictures of celebrities with stories about their mishaps and links to the

full stories, YouTube video of the AT&T commercial, and an images of the year Popplet
2. 1962: "Cuba and the Missilettes"
   a. Three Events: Fidel Castro excommunicated by the Catholic Church, Cuba suspended from the Organization of American States, and the embargo
   b. Rhetorical Analysis: *New York Times* article that uses "either-or" fallacy about weapons in Cuba
   c. *Daily Mail* political cartoon of Kennedy and Khrushchev arm wrestling
   d. Website Features: pictures of the Cuban Missile Crisis in all of the website headers, "About Me" page, Dipity Timeline on the Cuban Missile Crisis
3. 1976: "Year of Women Making History"
   a. Three Events: Unita Blackwell becomes first black mayor in Mississippi, women allowed in the US Naval Academy, Nadia Comaneci wins a perfect 10 in the uneven bars
   b. Rhetorical Analysis: Barbara Jordan's speech to the Democratic National Convention
   c. Visual Rhetoric: True Cigarette Ad
   d. Website Features: Popplet Timeline of major events, music and movies from the year, quick facts (i.e. cost of milk, president, etc.), "In the Year" collage, and 70s-style font and colors

Each of these websites shows a different approach. The 2012 site tended to put more focus on visual interpretation of the essays. The viewer accessed her essays by clicking a button that would take the viewer to GoogleDocs to read the essay. So the site itself was more dedicated to pictures, videos, and the aesthetic of the site to understand the theme. The 1962 site mainly focused on the essays. Each of the subpages contained a picture from the year and then the essay with additional images. The strongest component was the cleanness of the aesthetic. In looking at it, a viewer could tell right away the theme was Cuban Missile Crisis. The main weakness of this site was it needed to include more hyperlinks to connect between essays, but its strength as a site that clearly interpreted the year was the redeeming component. The 1976 year had a website that did not carry the theme of "Women Making History" as the website theme; instead, the main focus was designing a site that presented the year itself. Through factoids about the year and the 1970s color palette and font, the site asked the viewer to engage at first with the year as a whole and then with specific components, like "Women Making History." With all three websites, a person outside of the class could find fault, and they show as first attempts at creating sites. But, and this goes back to the "IDA" model, I can see the way each thought about interpreting their papers, the decisions they made in how images, layout, and design could influence the way a viewer experienced the year they chose, and the actions used to get the technology to execute those goals.

ePortfolio Tips

As I have gone on to teach other classes, I have had time to reflect on the *"In the Year ..." ePortfolio Project.* In writing for this collection of assignments, here are some discoveries I have made about the project and tips to consider while adapting the assignment to other classroom settings:

Choosing a Website Builder

Cost	Weebly Education is mostly free, with some features as pay "Pro" features.
Privacy	Can password protect certain pages
Layout	Large selection of themes and templates
	Layout locks with zooming; proportions stay the same
Intuitive	Yes
Design Options	Yes: wide variety that look more up-to-date
Can Embed HTML	Yes and always works
Blog Option	Yes
Mobile Design Option	Yes
Best ePortfolio Use	Web design and multimodal projects

As imagined, the biggest execution issue for the assignment is the technology itself. In her article, "Migration Patterns: A Status Report on the Transition from Paper to ePortfolios and the Effect on Multimodal Composition Initiatives," Christine Tulley categorizes ePortfolios program into four types: LMS systems, commercial software, homegrown ePortfolios, and open source (Tulley). These software function as electronic binders to house text, are template driven programs designed by writing programs, or require bottom-up construction. Open Source Software, like Wordpress, Weebly, Wix, Google Sites, Moveable Type, etc., offer greater flexibility, are often free, provide equal access, more design freedom, and greater multimodal potential (Tulley 106–108). Open Source programs like Weebly and Wix place focus on creation, development, and multimodal integration in a more guided, scaffolded program that focuses more on interpretation than technological knowledge. Thus, the website project uses technology in a way that makes technology "a positive influence that will promote a social construction of knowledge in which teachers and student are all learners-in-progress, collaborating together to form new communities of learning" (Hawisher and

Selfe 305). With Weebly, I noticed increased student satisfaction in the final website and lower technology anxiety levels. It also contributes to the final product because good programs, like Weebly, have design elements built in that will help give students ideas on what their websites can do.

Time Frame

For this assignment, my students really only have over a week after turning in the Portfolio itself to complete their site. When I first started doing the assignment, everything was due at once: the Portfolio, the in-class presentation of the website, and the website. Eventually, I moved the due dates to make the Portfolio due before students began the process of building the ePortfolio. With this new timeline, the ePortfolio gets to have sole focus, but I do wonder if the project needs more incubation time. Although I tried one semester teaching the technology at the midway point, what I found was that most students forgot how to use the program in the interim. In adapting this assignment for other classrooms, timeline is an important consideration because of students' need to digest the technology and reflect on how to transform the text.

Guidelines for Transforming the Written Content

One of the guidelines of the ePortfolio is that it has to contain the essays from the Portfolio in some form or fashion. The essays did not have to appear all in one place, but they had to be included. Because of this, the essays tend to appear as embedded documents, as a link to a GoogleDoc, one entity that could be downloaded for future reading, or copied and pasted in its entirety. However, what tends to be more interesting is when the essays are integrated in more creative ways. For instance, one student broke the body paragraphs into separate pieces of information that were separated by a horizontal line, included a picture, some sort of hyperlink to a video or article, and a quotation to transition between segments. The page then ended up reading more like a series of information segments that was linked together by the common theme. As an exercise in making text multiliterate, this ended up being a strong use of the original portfolio content and suggests there needs to be more emphasis on remediating the texts, featuring portions of essays, and creating interactive spaces to accompany the text portfolio.

Reflection Component

As is, the assignment is missing a metacognitive piece to round out the project. At the time of the assignment, I used presentations as the reflection component, but think there are stronger and more interesting ways of encouraging critical thought on digitizing the Portfolio. Before adapting this assignment for your class, I'd recommend reading "Reflection and Electronic Portfolios" by Kathleen Blake Yancey for research on reflection pieces and options for incorporating metacognition.

Presentation Day

To share and reflect on the ePortfolio, I had students present their websites to the class. However, the limitation is that websites are meant to be engaged with, and the presentations limit audience interaction and engagement with each of the sites. Instead, interaction with the website can be done through surveys built in to the websites or through allowing students to do peer-review. These surveys and peer-feedback could be included as a portion of the final grade or as a "soft launch" in which a student gets feedback from peers, revises, and then turns in the final website for grading.

Works Cited

Clifford, John. "The Subject in Discourse." *The Norton Book of Composition Studies.* Ed. Susan Miller. New York: W. W. Norton, 2009. 861–873. Print.

Davis, Matthew, and Kathleen Blake Yancey. "Notes Toward the Role of Materiality in Composing, Reviewing, and Assessing Multimodal Texts." *Computers and Composition* 31: 13–28. *ScienceDirect.* Web. 24 July 2014.

Fischer, Katherine. "Down the Yellow Chip Road: Hypertext Portfolios in Oz." *Situating Portfolios: Four Perspectives.* Ed. Kathleen Blake Yancey and Irwin Weiser. Logan: Utah State University, 1997. 338–356. Print.

Hawisher, Gail and Cynthia Selfe. "Wedding the Technologies of Writing Portfolios and Computers: The Challenges of Electronic Classrooms." *Situating Portfolios: Four Perspectives.* Ed. Kathleen Blake Yancey and Irwin Weiser. Logan,: Utah State University, 1997. 3053–21. Print.

Selfe, Cynthia. "Technology and Literacy: A Story About the Perils of Not Paying Attention." *The Norton Book of Composition Studies.* Ed. Susan Miller. New York: W. W. Norton, 2009. 1163–1185. Print.

Tulley, Christine. "Migration Patterns: A Status Report on the Transition from Paper to Eportfolios and the Effect on Multimodal Composition Initiatives." *Computers and Composition* 30: 101–114. *SciVerse ScienceDirect.* Web. 27 July 2014.

Witmer, Andrew, Grace Caudle, and Paul Fait. "Digital History in the Classroom: Strategies for Student Learning." *Teaching and Learning with Technology Conference.* Festival Conference and Student Center Ballroom, James Madison University, Harrisonburg, VA. 6 Oct. 2011. Pre-Conference Presentation.

Yancey, Kathleen Blake. "Made Not Only in Words: Composition in a New Key." *CCC* 56.2 (2004): 297–328. Print.

_____. "Reflection and Electronic Portfolios: Inventing the Self and Reinventing the University." *Electronic Portfolios 2.0 Emergent Research on Implementation and Impact.* Ed. Darren Cambridge, Barbara Cambridge, and Kathleen Blake Yancey. Sterling, VA: Stylus Publishing LLC, 2009. 5–16. Print.

Workplace Document Analysis and Evaluation

Melissa Vosen Callens

Supplemental Materials

- Rationale
- Pre-Writing Activities
- Scaffolding Activities
- Pitfalls and Avoidance Strategies
- Grading Rubric
- Student Writing Sample

Workplace Document Analysis and Evaluation

Length: 5–6 pages, single-spaced
Value: 20 percent of final grade
Purpose of assignment: In this assignment, you have the opportunity to read and analyze the kinds of documents you might see in your career in the health professions. This assignment asks you to carefully read and analyze a healthcare document found in a facility of your choosing. After you read and analyze the document, you will produce an evaluation and recommendation report for the facility's manager.

This assignment will have some of the features of a rhetorical analysis assignment you might have done in English 120, but it adds in analysis of a healthcare document. It requires you to ground your analysis in the concept of "health literacy." You can make this assignment relevant to your academic and professional goals by choosing an interesting document to analyze in your field. In the next unit, you will also get experience writing and designing a professional healthcare document. While you might not end up designing your own documents in your career, you will be a valuable employee if you can provide informed opinions on these elements of the healthcare experience.

The final report should be written in a professional style and tone (if you are critical of the document, be constructive with your criticism). The final document should combine the document design features of a workplace report with the citation style appropriate for your major (i.e., APA, MLA, AMA, Chicago, etc.).

You will have to:

1. Chose a healthcare document to analyze. This document could be found at your current place of employment, a place you'd like to be employed, a facility you visit as a patient, or a convenient but relevant location. Chose multiple documents if most of the documents are simple, one-page fliers or posters.
2. If possible, talk to an employee about the clientele and the documents used. Get the employee's perception of how and why things are as they are. Talk to clientele about the documents used, if possible.
3. Write a thorough draft.
   - Come up with a title for your report that is both informative and engaging.
   - Write an introductory paragraph that engages readers, provides background information on the facility, and forecasts the structure and purpose of your paper as well as your evaluation.
   - Describe the document you are analyzing with concise and relevant details.
   - Analyze the place and document based on criteria established from your understanding of health literacy. Make good use of your observation and document research.
   - Evaluate the document. Once you have analyzed the document based on health literacy criteria, you should be able to evaluate them.
   - Include scanned images of the document you are analyzing.
4. Revise. This draft should conform to the documentation guidelines in your field (i.e. APA, MLA, CBE), but it should also use professional document design: single spacing, headings, etc. It should be of appropriate length and depth.

Analysis Suggestions:

1. Establish who comes to the healthcare facility you are studying, with a specific emphasis on understanding the range of health literacies these patients will represent.
2. Then consider questions like:
   - What health information is available in this location?

- Where is it located, what medium is it available in, is the information appropriate for the clientele?
3. What is appropriate for clientele can be broken down further:
    - Is the purpose of the document clear?
    - Is the document well designed? Eye-catching? Information clearly chunked? Inviting or threatening, or just too dull?
    - Is it well written? Is it comprehensible to an appropriate range of readers, or is it appropriately focused on the right audience?
    - Is the author (likely a group or organization) well-known? Respectable? Does that matter? What does the identity of the author do for the document?
    - Is it "useable"? Does it help users find additional information?
    - How does the document fit (or not) with the rest of the organization's mission?

Audience and Voice: Your prose style should be professional—appropriate for others in your field.

Social context: The social context for this assignment will be this class, but also your profession. Remember to be respectful to any staff members (or patients) both in person and in your writing. Even when you critique documents, you should avoid insulting people or institutions.

This assignment draws on an assignment originally created by Dr. Kevin Brooks.

Rationale

At North Dakota State University (NDSU), a land-grant research institution, I teach several upper-division writing courses: Writing in the Health Professions, Business and Professional Writing, and Visual Culture and Language. Unlike first-year composition courses, upper-division writing courses at NDSU require students to engage in discipline-specific research and writing. In each of these courses, I ask students to identify, analyze, and evaluate a document they would likely find in their desired place of employment.

For example, in my Writing in the Health Professions courses, students often obtain documents from clinics, hospitals, pharmacies, nursing homes, etc. Most of these students are already working as pharmacy technicians or licensed practical nurses and choose to obtain documents from their place of employment. In my Business and Professional Writing courses, students obtain a variety of documents from the industry in which they hope to be employed: banking materials, marketing documents from retail stores, company contact forms, etc.

Most students in my Writing in the Health Professions courses, the focus of this essay, choose to examine a brochure, flier, discharge instructions, or drug information sheets for their document analysis. To analyze the layout and readability of the document, students are required to use registered nurse and health literacy advocate Helen Osborne's plain language principles and graphic designer Robin Williams's basic design principles. These principles require students to examine many different aspects of the document: tone, format and layout, graphics, sources, sentence structure, and word choice, among other things. In addition, students research the accuracy of the content in the document.

Eventually, after analyzing and evaluating the document, I ask students to create their own, using the knowledge they gained through course readings and completing their document analysis. In the course, we talk extensively about health literacy: what it is, why it is important, and how it is a collaborative relationship between a patient and a healthcare provider. Since health literacy is the ability to understand health information to make informed health-related decisions, documents are a common part of this exchange of information in patient education. When these students seek employment, they will likely not be creating their own educational materials; most will work for large hospitals or organizations that have a health communication/marketing team. My hope, however, is that they will be able to provide informed opinions on these elements of the healthcare experience. They will be able to make recommendations to those creating the documents as well as have a better understanding of how patients might interpret these materials.

Pre-Writing Activities

To start thinking about health literacy, students are required to research health literacy in their field and document what health experts are saying about it. They present their findings to the class on an online discussion board forum. In addition, bringing research to practice, students are asked to identify and describe a personal health literacy story—a time when a healthcare situation or instructions were misunderstood. This story could be about them or a family member, or it could be something they have observed at work (so long as no privacy/HIPPA issues are violated). Students also share these stories on an online discussion board forum. These small assignments are crucial because they help students understand why it is so important to have effective, easy-to-understand educational documents for patients or customers. It also helps them critically think about what causes misunderstandings in the first place.

Scaffolding Activities

In class (or online—in an online course), students practice analyzing a variety of workplace documents in groups prior to writing their paper. One of my favorite scaffolding activities follows. After students get some practice working with the plain language checklist and basic design principles, I split them into groups, and they draw different "document creation" scenarios from a hat. For example, one group might draw "a document on diabetes for a nursing home in Los Angeles." The group would then have an opportunity to ask me questions—as I pretend to be the supervisor of the facility requesting the document. After their short consultation with me, students have the rest of the class period to create a rough sketch to present to the class. When finished, groups should be able to justify their content and design choices. The class then provides feedback, and the activity allows students to think about how different elements work together (or against one another). This helps them hone their critical analysis skills before they analyze their document for their paper.

Furthermore, this assignment builds upon the rhetorical analysis assignment taught in our first-year courses at NDSU. In addition to the scaffolding assignment above, students read several examples of student papers from previous semesters to get a better understanding of how to complete and write a document analysis.

Pitfalls and Avoidance Strategies

The biggest problem I have had with this particular assignment is students having difficulties obtaining a document. As I mentioned before, this isn't usually a problem for students in the Writing in the Health Professions course, but in the business writing course, students typically don't have the same connections to professional workplaces and thus workplace documents. It is important to spend time brainstorming with the students where they might obtain these documents—and how they might obtain them.

I typically talk to the students about how to approach businesses (or healthcare facilities). We talk about being respectful and how to best explain/pitch the assignment. In the beginning, I had a few complaints from healthcare facilities, but this is no longer a problem. It wasn't so much that my students were disrespectful when obtaining documents; it had more to do with the number of requests being submitted to facilities. Because of this, we also talk in class about who is going where to obtain a document, so one facility isn't inundated with requests. In addition, I have a list of people at different healthcare facilities that students can contact. Finally, we also talk about "other" places, places that students don't necessarily think about: dentist offices, urgent care clinics, nutrition offices, etc. I also remind them that they can look to their own healthcare providers for documents.

Grading Rubric

After completing the assignment, students are able to recognize how both content and layout can aid (or detract) patients' understanding of crucial health information. In the next unit, I ask students to create their own document and apply both the plain language principles and design principles. I do not expect perfection, as they are not graphic designers; however, I do expect to see a demonstration of their understanding of these basic tools that support health literacy.

Qualities and features of the report	Feedback
Informative and catchy title	5 4 3 2 1
Strong introductory paragraph: background on facility and documents (history, location, demographics); good forecast of report's content and structure	5 4 3 2 1
Detailed description, analysis, and evaluation of document. Avoid simply reproducing the plain language checklist; identify strengths, weaknesses, and include only relevant information	5 4 3 2 1
Conclusion: summarize findings, make recommendations. The organizational structure of the report is clear and easy to follow: follows through on forecast, makes logical sense	5 4 3 2 1
The design elements are professional and effective: header and/or footer with page numbering, font choice appropriate, single spacing with block paragraphs, appropriate margins and good use of white space, informative section headings, bullet lists if appropriate, photos and images placed effectively and labeled correctly, reference page formatted correctly	5 4 3 2 1
You should draw explicitly on Helen Osborne's definitions of health literacy, plain language, and/or other secondary sources (Robin Williams' design principles) that can help you analyze and evaluate your space and documents	5 4 3 2 1
Properly introduce and cite sources in-text and end of text. Appropriate professional style is used; final report is well edited and relatively free of errors	5 4 3 2 1

Grade: _____ / 250

A = excellent document in all aspects—some slight room for improvement.
B = good; some aspects of the document or project might be excellent, others will be good.
C = acceptable completion of the assignment. No major problems, but room for improvement in most areas of the assignment.
D = a major aspect of the assignment has not been completed. Elements of the assignment might be quite good, but with unsatisfactory completion of certain elements, the assignment will remain a D.
F = incomplete assignment because page length was not met, proper research was not completed, proper documentation conventions not followed, genre conventions not adhered to, etc.

Student Writing Sample

Below is an excerpt from a student paper. Please note that the name of the facility as been changed for privacy purposes.

Anytown, USA Drug Store: Caring for Patients Through Accessibility and Literature

Introduction: Background, Feng Shui, and Plain Language

Anytown, USA Drug Store is a pharmacy and flower shop located on Front Street in Anytown, USA. It serves as the major pharmacy in the surrounding area. This is generally the final stop for patients after a [doctor's] visit or a monthly stop for refill prescriptions. Through Anytown, USA Drug Store, patients are able to pick up their needed medications, learn how to take them properly, and be on their way home.

Anytown, USA Drug Store was founded in 1951. The pharmacy is run through the Anytown franchise program, which has thousands of facilities across the United States. The pharmacy has a flower shop, as well as various goods including beauty products, jewelry, candy, Hallmark cards, and office supplies. In the summer of 2012, Anytown, USA Drug Store underwent a major renovation, expanding the small space into nearly double its size. This gave the drug store the opportunity to expand the cashier area, give the flower shop more space, and move the pharmacy to the center of the store, which allowed patients easier access to get their medication. The space was not only expanded to give it more space and room for more items, but the store also changed the décor. Now, it is more welcoming and easier to navigate through.

Healthcare facilities are generally uninviting, intimidating places for patients or visitors. According to Osborne, healthcare facilities are places where personal and often emotional conversations about healthcare matters occur. These conversations can be difficult when taking place in environments that feel cold and impersonal. Osborne also discusses the importance of Feng Shui and Plain Language to achieve appropriate healthcare environments and literature to ensure comfort and understanding for all visitors. Now, I will use these two concepts in relevance to Anytown, USA Drug Store to analyze a document that is offered to patients. I will use visual and textual examples of how Anytown, USA Drug Store's environment and documents create a positive visit for patients.

Health Literacy: Does Anytown, USA Drug Store Meet the Standards?

Anytown, USA Drug Store's patients come from the surrounding area, have a wide age range, exhibit different literacy levels, and have different backgrounds and beliefs. This being said, health literacy is an important concept to the drug store. Health literacy is the degree to which individuals have the capacity to obtain, process, and understand basic health information and services needed to make appropriate health decisions. In order for all patients to understand health literacy, plain language should be used as medical terms are not widely understood. This plain language should not only be spoken, but used in documents as well. During this section, I will describe and analyze a diabetes document given to patients at Anytown, USA Drug Store. This document is shown below on page 10, Figure 5. Using Osborne's plain language descriptions, I will evaluate the text, use of design, and organization of the document. First, I will evaluate the text of the document to see if it uses plain language concepts, and then I will describe the design and layout of the document.

Readability: Is There Too Much Information?

This document is written at a reading level for most people. Readability is the ease at which a text can be read and understood. This document discusses diabetes, so the terms used should be common terms to diabetics, but not necessarily terms that every patient would understand. For example, the article, shown below on figure five page 3, explains [...], "The American Diabetes Association recommends an A1C test every 2–3 months, blood pressure every time you visit the doctor, and cholesterol levels measured at least one per year." While this is simple word usage, not everyone is going to understand what an A1C test is, but because it is a diabetes document, it is more likely that the reader will understand it because it is a common term associated with diabetes.

This document is written in a manner that should be understandable to all customers. There are some large words, such as "The Affordable Care Act (ACA)," [which] some people might not be familiar with. However, the document breaks the ACA into chunks and focuses on what the patient actually needs to know. Under it, there is a true or false quiz about the Affordable Care Act, and on the next page, it describes why each question is true or false. This strategy of word choice keeps a reader interested [...] and answers questions that a patient might be too afraid to ask. Osborne explains that using jargon, abbreviations, acronyms, idioms, and simple words that aren't so simple [sic]. The document uses words that are easy to understand for the audience[,] and it gets the reader to interact with the text by taking the quiz on the first page to simplify the tougher to understand concepts that are discussed within the document.

As I said earlier, this document describes each point very well, so a reader does not get confused. The front page of the document depicts what is inside by stating, "What You Need to Know" with four topics underneath. Here, we find out that four things will be discussed. The document discusses each topic in [the] order that it was written in the first page, giving less room for confusion. Four topics [are] a lot of information to cover in four pages, and at times, the document gets a little wordy. Most of the space is covered with text that is simple to read, but it is time consuming given the ample amount of information given, and the text may not be easy to read for audience with bad eyesight, as it is a lot of information to take in.

Design and Layout: Meeting the C.R.A.P. Standards

In *The Non-Designer's Design Book* by Robin Williams, it explains that there are four basic principles of design that occur in every well-designed piece of work. These principles are: Contrast, Repetition, Alignment, and Proximity[,] C.R.A.P. for short. These principles are to ensure that a document is easy and enjoyable to read. Anytown, USA Drug Store has a variety of patients, so the audience varies. This document targets diabetics, who are of all ages, so the document is designed in a simple manner with pictures that appeal to all ages as seen on page 10, Figure 5.

The pictures in the document are a small element compared to the amount of text. They occur on the tops and bottom of pages, and with various graphs throughout the document. The pictures depict what the articles are going to discuss. For example, in the section, "Five Fake Foods to Avoid," images of the food appear to the left of the text about each item. The images are not a main element of the article, but they add color and relate to the text.

The document follows the C.R.A.P. principle of contrast in several ways. Contrast is used in the document by making important elements larger and describing each element in smaller print below. In the document, each main point is a bright color including: green, orange, or bright blue, and black is used underneath to describe each point [sic]. The colors attract the eye and tell the audience what is about to be discussed. Each section is separated using a color border that is the color of the text in that section.

The second principle, repetition, was also used throughout the document. The larger font for main points is used, even in different sections and topics. The document is consistent. The audience's eyes are meant to go to the bold and colorful print, and they do. The audience is guided through the page through consistent use of repetition.

The third principle of design, [alignment], is consistent throughout most of the article. The document is unified through organization of the pages. The document is all left aligned, except for the ad on the last page. This feature gives the document a sense of organization. The document includes sticky notes on page 2 and 3 to connect the reader to what the page as a whole discusses. The article discusses a topic, and the sticky note gives tips on what the reader can do to get control over his/her life.

The final design principle, proximity, is used in the document as well. Proximity gives the document a well-rounded look. Each section is grouped together by a certain color, and that color forms a border around the section. Related items are grouped together in the article through numbers. The article "Five Fake Foods to Avoid" groups items together by numbering five foods to avoid eating for a healthier life style. Each sub point is given by bold, colorful text, and each main point is quite larger than the sub point and description.

Evaluation: Keep the Text to a Minimum
This document meets the wants and needs of many diabetics. It provides quality information on several things including healthcare, how to choose healthcare plans, and foods to avoid. There are many positive aspects of this document, and below, I am going to review them:

- Gets the audience to interact by including a quiz
- Visual examples
- Appropriate font text, font size, and alignment
- Correct use of proximity, contrast, repetition, and alignment
- Well separated topics

The elements above give the patients at Anytown, USA Drug Store an informative, readable text that is easy to follow. This document educates patients on important things including recommended healthcare and foods to avoid to maintain good health.

However, there are some things the document could improve on to provide an even better document. The improvements that could be made are listed below:

- Using less text so the readers can understand all of the important information.
- Explaining what page each topic is going to be talked about on the cover of the document so it is easier to navigate through.
- Give the document more white space.

With these improvements, the document could be better understood by the readers and allow for them to learn more, even though there is less text. Overall, the document achieves the goal of educating patients about diabetes and explaining how to acquire a healthier lifestyle.

WORK CITED

Osborne, Helen. "Plain Language: Writing in Ways Others Can Understand" *Health Literacy Consulting*. www.healthliteracy.com

William, Robin. *The Non-Designer's Design Book*. 2nd ed. Berkeley: Peachpit Press, 2004.

The Partner Project
Advanced Argument

Karma Waltonen

Supplemental Materials

- Rationale
- Pitfalls and Avoidance Strategies
- Professional Samples
- Sample Student Annotations

The Partner Project

Divide into groups of two. Choose a topic that you want to write a *persuasive* essay about, meaning your essay thesis must be debatable/arguable (your partner will choose an entirely different topic). Argue something specific! Local and small works better than global and big.

Part 1: Write your persuasive essay. Give this essay to your partner on the day assigned. No more than five pages. (If you do not give your essay to your partner on the day assigned, you will lose at least a quarter of the overall essay grade—that is, you cannot get more than a 75 percent, which is a C. It is unfair to hold up your partner's work.) Make this essay good—you do *not* get to revise it after you see your partner's evaluation. Use reliable sources, especially peer-reviewed sources, as appropriate, for this essay.

Remember that writers know they're already in a conversation about topics—there are people who have argued this before you. What are their arguments and counter-arguments? If you use outside research, cite it correctly. As you're writing this for a general educated audience, you will want to define terms, address warrants, and situate yourself in the argument. In other words, consider *the rhetorical situation* for your paper. Your audience should be people like me and your classmates—educated, but not necessarily specialists in your topic. If you think we might not be interested in your subject, work to make us care. (For example, if you intend your audience to be sports fans, but your audience isn't, you're going to have problems.) If you think we won't understand the background of the subject or some of the terminology, define it. You are trying to be persuasive—so persuade. Use ethos, logos, and pathos effectively. Use your "public voice."

Understand which of the *five types* of persuasive essays you're writing. Are you arguing that we should classify x as a certain type of college class so that it counts towards y requirement? (Then you're doing an evaluation/proposal.) Are you arguing that the limit on characters in tweets contributes to further misuse/misunderstandings of the English language (punctuation rules, etc.)? (Then you're doing a causal argument.) Are you arguing that *X-Men* toys should be considered human rather than non-human (as opposed to the recent court case, which said they were non-human)? (Then you're doing definition/proposal). Are you arguing that Shakespeare's wife actually wrote his plays? (Then you're doing an argument of fact [meaning not that your assertion is the fact, but that there is a factual answer in reality to the question.]) Are you arguing that middle school English classes should teach certain YA classics rather than classics originally intended for adults (like Dickens' stuff)? (Then you're doing a proposal.)

Note that many of the other four argument types inevitably need to lead to a proposal. (Why do an evaluation where you argue that x works better than y if the ultimate point isn't that we should do x?)

All proposals must address three things: the why, the how, and to what effect.

For example, if you want to argue that we should stop using the SAT/ACT for college admission purposes, there are many reasons *why* you might think so (test anxiety, cultural bias inherent in standardized exams, etc.). However, a successful proposal will consider the *how*. You can't just do away with the only standardized aspect of college applications—you have to replace that aspect with something else that all students could be measured by. You must also consider how that would be implemented, how it would change the application process, how it would change the process and staffing to review and select applicants, etc. And you must consider what all the effects of your change would be.

It is not possible to write a strong partner project without dealing with *counter argument*.

Ultimately, your success will depend on if you are clear about your purpose, if you're persuasive, and if you address the needs of your audience.[1]

Part 2: Pretend you do not know the author personally. You are going to write an evaluative response essay. You will need to give a brief, coherent, and fair summary of the author's work before you begin to analyze the piece. Remember that you can discuss any aspect of the piece—the evidence, the main claims, the sub-claims, the logos, ethos, pathos, logical fallacies, tone, warrants, organization, bias, clarity, grammar, etc. Review the guidelines for conceding and refuting in our handouts. Remember that your own evaluative essay is persuasive and must have all three appeals operating to some degree. Note that you may also discuss what this essay has NOT said about the issue. If you use outside sources, cite them. Give examples of specific passages from the first essay. Give this essay to your partner on the day listed (the same late penalties apply; return part 1 with it). No more than five pages. Do *not* just argue the opposite position of your partner on a topic—that's not the point. Your thesis will be about *whether the piece was effective or not and why*.

Part 3: Read over the rebuttal essay (your partner's Part 2). Remember not to take anything personally. This person is agreeing and/or disagreeing with an essay—s/he is not personally attacking you. (S/he is not required to sugarcoat criticism—that doesn't indicate s/he is disrespecting you or being mean.) Take some time to think about what s/he has said. Write an essay responding directly to this piece. You may find yourself disagreeing with everything. You may find yourself acknowledging some of the critique. Perhaps you find yourself in a position to say, "X said I didn't do Y, but that's not what I was trying to do in the first place." (If so, ask yourself if you made your intentions clear.) As you respond, quote/paraphrase from Parts 1 & 2 where appropriate. No more than five pages. Give this essay, along with Parts 1 & 2 of this topic thread, to me. Weak Part 3s simply attempt to make the original argument again. Strong Part 3s address the criticism in Part 2.

Order for turning it in: Your Part 1, your partner's Part 2, your Part 3, Out of Class Essay Memo (your partner will give me your Part 2).

A plea from the grader: please try to find original topics; I do not want to read the same old arguments about abortion rights, legalizing marijuana, gun control, gay marriage, sports controversies, and political diatribes.

Also, make sure that you're not making an overly obvious or overly vague argument. Students arguing that American children are too obese (and "something" must be done about it) won't be successful. Arguing that we should "do more" to stop something won't work—if you're making a proposal, you should actually *propose something specific*. That said, try to propose something practical if a proposal is your goal. Many students get themselves into trouble by saying that "x should be mandatory" when they can't really defend it or when it would be impractical, illegal, or unconstitutional (in the case of the last two, the argument should actually be that the law or constitution should be changed).

If you use outside sources, cite them according to MLA or APA style.

Please look back over MLA/APA handouts and the plagiarism sheets, especially the section on the most common problems. Getting citation format wrong can lose you points. If it's unclear where ideas are coming from, you could get an F.

This project is a last chance to show me you've assimilated the knowledge from the course, including style and grammar.

Rationale

This assignment is the last project in an upper-division writing class: Advanced Composition and Rhetoric.[2] The sequence of the class: narrative essay, basic argument/analysis, partner project. (There are also a timed-writing midterm and a take-home final, which is a short satire.)

Thus, with this assignment, students are able to put together the skills from the course: style, grammar, details, rhetorical analysis, persuasive argument (including counter-argument, addressing warrants, etc.), proper research and citation techniques, etc.

When I gave a presentation on this assignment at a writing teachers' conference, I called my presentation "The Partner Project: Beyond Peer Review." By the time my students encounter this project, they've done traditional peer review of their basic argument/analysis essays. Thus, they've gotten some help from peers and have discovered the limitations of traditional peer review. (They have also gotten two papers and a midterm back with my comments, whether or not they really read, much less integrated, my suggestions.)

This essay challenges them in an entirely new way. Students often write something very similar to their second essay for Part 1—an evaluation or proposal that hasn't been well thought out and that doesn't address the needs of the audience. Most students do not think about what their audience already knows or believes prior to this assignment. (For example, one student wrote Part 1 arguing that Filipino veterans of World War II should still receive veterans' benefits. Her partner was completely confused, not understanding why we would grant benefits to foreigners. The first student, a Filipina, had assumed her fellow students knew that the Philippines are a former colony.)

Receiving Part 2 is usually a shock. While they've had comments on their writing before, they've never had an essay written about their writing—a formal review that goes into detail about multiple aspects of their persuasiveness.

While I have students turn in memos with all of their assignments (telling me about their perceived strengths, weaknesses, challenges, and choices), Part 3 allows and forces students to think critically about their own writing on a new level. The responses in this part tend to be short—most students write about how their partner was correct ("My obsession with persuading my audience that domestic shoeless-ness is preferable placed blinders on my perspective. I was both unable to think about and appreciate the depth counterarguments add"; "In my head it makes sense, but I understand I need supportive examples to help influence the reader effectively"). My favorite line from a Part 3 is "as I cannot rewrite the first part of the project, I can only bury my head in shame into these hands that have stacked the deck."

Some correctly point out that while much of what the partner said was correct, the partner got something wrong too (like "my partner said I overgeneralized, but I said 'a few'").

A few students realize how important the details can be in an argument. One student was rather stunned when her partner's response revealed that her plan to keep UC Davis on the quarter system, but to make the quarters as long as semesters was flawed in that it would require adding several weeks to the year—she simply hadn't done the math. Another student discovered how one typo can ruin a piece: "I have to admit that I made a terrible mistake […] what I meant to say is the Chinese will *not* fire the first shot. This is a very important lesson for me as I realize how big of the difference one word, like 'not,' can make in the entire article" (italics mine).

Although the students find this project difficult, the memos they write and the teacher evaluations speak highly of the challenge. One student noted, "It seems as though it is often easier to spot logical fallacies in other works than it is in one's own writing." Another said, "I'm glad we [critiqued each other] because it was a much needed reality check."

Many noted the uniqueness: "Reading someone else directly critiquing my work is a strange experience, since we judge other people in our minds everyday but do not get feedback from others that often. Part three of the essay felt like my debate competition at high school, that I [respond] to attacks from the other side and defend my points, while [remaining] calm and rational."

Others commented on how difficult it was to take an honest, thorough critique of their work: "This essay was really hard because it is hard to take criticism from another student. I found myself getting mad, or saying that my partner had no idea [what] she was talking about. However, the more times I read her essay, the more I realized that she was partially right. Therefore, it was a great learning experience." Another stated:

> It is always difficult reading someone else's response to your own work. I felt partially hurt and a little angry. I immediately started picking out the flaws in her response. Obviously there was no way I was at fault. My first reaction was that she completely missed the argument of my paper, but upon noticing this I realized this was more a fault of mine than hers. By not making my argument clear and backing it up with substantial evidence I had

opened the door for criticism. I didn't provide enough counter arguments to justify my claim. While it was tough to read someone picking apart my paper I did realize that I could have written a stronger paper that would have made a clearer argument.

I particularly like how one student summed up her experience: "I have definitely heard 'cliché' before when referencing my writing, but it felt different hearing that word from my fellow classmates. A hammer shattered my soul. All the pieces too sharp to pick up, but my teacher encouraged growth. The tough criticism was meant to push our minds to places that we may have never been before. Gradually, I picked up the pieces and created a mosaic."

The overall response to the essay can be summed up by one particular student: "Seriously, I had a lot of fun doing this project. I've never done anything like it at Davis [in my five years], and I found it both enjoyable and educational. Getting students to actually engage in real discourse is great. It really makes you look at your paper objectively, and reviewing a peer's paper lets you see what your own writing can be like."

In addition to the benefits listed above, this project also aids in avoiding plagiarism. Unfortunately, it is all too easy for students to find or buy argumentative essays online (how we long for the days when all we had to worry about was the proverbial file cabinet of papers in a dorm room or fraternity house). Students are also able to sometimes "double-dip" papers—using one paper for two classes—especially when we assign papers that fall within their discipline. I take great care to explain that double dipping is considered plagiarism, as per their code of conduct. While there's a chance that students might cheat in one way or another on Part 1, it is virtually impossible to do so with Parts 2 and 3.

While the project certainly increases critical reading and argument skills, it also encourages students to perfect their annotation skills. Often, when I receive the full project, I can see arguments forming in the margins and in the way students underline certain words and phrases. In fact, when the Partner Project is returned, some students will see me answering these comments in the margins with "Exactly!" or "That's a misreading!" A few pages with sample annotations are reproduced in the last section of this essay.

Another benefit is that you can track the students' progress through the project and reward growth in your grading. If Part 3 is much stronger than Part 1, I weigh it more heavily. If, however, the student simply tries to make their argument again (this sometimes has the same feeling of watching an English speaker try to talk to a foreigner—they repeat themselves, but louder), repeating the same mistakes even, then you have solid evidence that the student is not applying the lessons of the class or the assignment.

Many instructors have expressed interest in this assignment but want to give their students the option to revise Part 1 when the entire project is completed. This could certainly work. I don't do so, though, for two reasons.

First, I am teaching on the quarter system, so time is already crunched.[3] Second, I have found that many of my students turn in awful papers when they know there's an option to revise. I suggest that if you want to do a Part 4, where they revise Part 1 at the end, you consider not telling them about this until after Part 1 is turned in.

You might also consider allowing the students to revise in multimodal ways—turning their essay into a presentation, a conference paper, a blog post, a podcast, a fact sheet, etc.

While I don't do a workshop or formal pre-writing activity for this assignment,[4] you might consider having them workshop thesis statements, outlines, etc. They might, for example, present their idea in a five-minute presentation to the class, with a brief question/answer session in which the students can trouble-shoot the ideas before the student finishes Part 1.

Pitfalls and Avoidance Strategies

Even with the best assignments, there are potential drawbacks and pitfalls:

Uneven dividing: My classes are capped at 25. However, by the time we reach the partner project, I have usually lost at least one student. If, however, you have an uneven number, there are three options.

- Give your spare student an argument from something like *Newsweek*'s "My Turn" (short essays written by non-professional writers). You critique their Part 1.
- If you have two sections running, both with uneven numbers, you can pair up your spares.
- Offer extra credit to a student for writing two Part 2s. That student would give a copy to both of his/her partners, write two responses, and then have the option to either write Part 3 based on one partner's response or to combine the partners' responses for Part 3.

Occasionally, I have also had a student decide to drop (for a medical reason, etc.) or to discontinue participating in the class during the Partner Project itself. It is vital to stress to the students that they must inform you of such decisions so you can protect their partners. You must also check to make sure the parts are being turned in on time to their partners.

Irresponsible students: As noted in the assignment above, the penalties for turning in Part 1 and/or 2 are great. I explain to the students that this is because it is grossly unfair to one's partner to cut down on the thinking/writing time.

Dishonest students: One student attempted to cheat by turning in a Part 1 on time, but then emailing his partner later in the week, asking the student to respond to a very different version of the paper. The partner alerted me to the problem. Problems like this can be avoided in two ways.

- Have students physically or electronically give you the parts of the project as they go, even though you won't be reading them until the project is over. (I do this, but also make them give me the paper copies they've worked with, as I like to see their marginalia.)
- Stress to the students that you must receive unaltered portions of the assignment. If, for example, a student decides to revise Part 1 based on criticism of Part 2, Part 2 will seem to make no sense.

Awkward pairings: I allow my students to partner themselves, although I do discourage allowing best friends, roommates, and lovers to partner for this. Sometimes a very strong student pairs with a very weak student, which can be problematic, in that the weak student will not give constructive feedback to his/her partner (and, in some extreme ESL cases, will not even be able to understand his/her partner's essay). The weak student benefits by having a solid critique. In the cases where a strong student does not get a desirable level of feedback, I have had the strong student acknowledge that in Part 3 and then state what the partner should have said (the strong student, by doing part 2, has gotten better at catching flaws in an argument). For example, one strong student noted that his partner admitted that she didn't understand the word "ironic" and also didn't call him on several potential problems: "[She did not discuss] my point about using Uranium as a monetary standard. I totally glossed over this as a potentially awesome idea and then left it wide open [...] she should have asked more of me here." This might be avoided by having the instructor pair students based on ability, but I am reluctant to do this, as two weak students together usually accomplish little in learning/improving.

Professional Samples

As we go into the project, we read a variety of essays that fits each of the projects. As I'm sure you have plenty of articles already on the syllabus that would fit Part 1, I won't list mine here.

Part 2

- Margaret Werthiem, "Born to Rape?" www.salon.com/2000/02/29/rape_15/: a response to *A Natural History of Rape: The Biological Basis of Sexual Coercion* by Randy Thornhill and Craig Palmer.
- Al Franken, "Ann Coulter: Nutcase" from *Lies (and the Lying Liars Who Tell Them)*: a response to Ann Coulter's *Slander*.
- John Horgan, "No, War Is Not Inevitable," discovermagazine.com/2012/jun/02-no-war-is-not-inevitable: a response to E.O. Wilson's "Is War Inevitable?" discovermagazine.com/2012/jun/07-is-war-inevitable-by-e-o-wilson.

- Eric Klinenberg, "Facebook Isn't Making Us Lonely," www.slate.com/articles/life/culturebox/2012/04/is_facebook_making_us_lonely_no_the_atlantic_cover_story_is_wrong_.html: a response to Stephen Marche's "Is Facebook Making Us Lonely?" www.theatlantic.com/magazine/archive/2012/05/is-facebook-making-us-lonely/308930/.

Part 3

- The Oatmeal's (a web comic writer) "Tesla Response," theoatmeal.com/blog/tesla_response: a response to Alex Knapp's critique on Forbes.com (www.forbes.com/sites/alexknapp/2012/05/18/nikola-tesla-wasnt-god-and-thomas-edison-wasnt-the-devil/) of The Oatmeal's comic, "Why Nikola Tesla Was the Greatest Geek Who Ever Lived," theoatmeal.com/comics/tesla.
- The Preface to the paperback edition of Richard Dawkins' *The God Delusion*, in which he responds to criticism of the hardcover edition.[5]

I also give the students samples of past Partner Projects from the class.

NOTES

1. Your audience needs something clearly written with good grammar.
2. I have also used a modified version of this assignment in other upper-division courses, such as Writing in International Relations. The modifications are just narrowing the subjects they can write about (making sure they fit the focus of the course) and changing some of the readings we do in conjunction with the assignment.
3. I give my students a week between each part in the regular quarter.
4. Other than the occasional time for a freewrite on potential topics.
5. I stress that we're discussing this only in terms of the project—that we're not debating Dawkins' central thesis about atheism. I also pair this reading with Julia Sweeney's "Letting Go of God," in which she discusses her difficult, soul-searching journey to atheism. The students are able to appreciate the difference between the pieces in terms of tone and of purpose (Sweeney is writing a narrative, not a persuasive piece; thus, since the topic is sensitive, the students realize that readers will be less put off by her approach).

Sample Student Annotations

(*Images appear on the following 9 pages*)

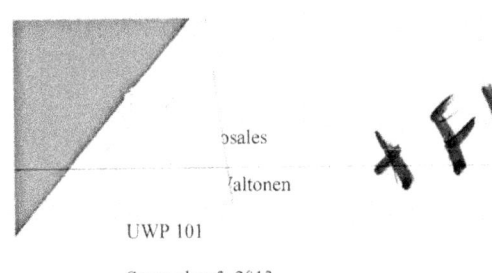

osales

altonen

UWP 101

September 5, 2013

2812

eSports: A Real Sport?

Thousands scream and bang their plastic Thundersticks together in a loud, upheaving roar. The lights dim in the arena as the opening band takes stage. Thousands of die-hard fans pack the Staples Center as they anxiously wait for the Finals to start. The audience had been preparing for this event for months and come with decorated posters shouting out to their favored team. No, this isn't the NBA Finals, this is the *League of Legends* World Championships Finals.

League of Legends, developed by Riot Games, is the biggest video game in the world (MacManus). Its viewership rivals that of the NBA (Nunnely) (NBA News) and its player base in the U.S. dwarfs that of baseball (Dave). For eSports, a term coined for "electronic sports" played competitively, naturally, League of Legends is the king. And as of July 2013, *League of Legends* is officially recognized by the U.S. government as a professional sport (Dave).

By drawing parallels and differences between eSports and universally accepted sports, I will evaluate the legitimacy of *League of Legends* being a professional sport, and on a broader spectrum, eSports being considered sports. There are several controversial terms when in the context of eSports. From here on out: "professional sports" will refer to universally accepted sports such as basketball, baseball, and football; "athlete" will refer to the players of professional sports; "sport" will be redefined multiple times.

Not a Simple Definition

The definition of "sport" varies depending on who is asked. Merriam-Webster defines it much differently than Oxford. Some believe it requires physical exertion along with inherent danger. Some believe sports require honed skill, not necessarily physical. Others believe sports can be any activity that is performed with the intent to entertain oneself or others. Thus, the set "sports" includes and excludes a wide variance of activities, also depending on who is asked. Professional sports including hockey, tennis, and track and field are of course sports. Many include NASCAR and golf in "sports". To a lesser extent, billiards and poker can be considered sports. And to some, chess is even considered a sport (Norman). Are video games sports?

Similarities in Events

"eSports" is a broad term used to define competitive video gaming. *League of Legends* is an eSport. Collectively, *League of Legends* and *StarCraft II* (arguably the second-largest eSport), are eSports. "eSports" can also be used to describe the competitive gaming scene as a whole. In this sense, eSports is competitive video gaming presented in the same fashion as professional sports (42analytics). For example, Riot will be hosting the *League of Legends* World Championships in October at the Staples Center. Tickets for the competition sold out in under an hour, possibly an unofficial record for the most tickets to a live event sold in the shortest amount of time (Tassi).

Forms of mediation such as rules regulating clothes and shoes professional athletes can wear are also present in eSports. Computers used in the competition must obey the competition guidelines, and professional gamers use personalized and calibrated mice and keyboards, similar to how cyclists have preferences in their bikes and tennis players have preferences in their rackets. Referees are also common in both (Taylor 623). Events are professionally commentated live and broadcasted live as well. These broadcasts exhibit similar viewer numbers to professional sports. The 2013 *League of Legends* All-Star event had 18 million viewers (Nunnely); Super Bowl XLVII had 108 million viewers (ESPN.com News Services); the 2013 NBA finals averaged at 17 million viewers per game (NBA News); the 2012 World Series averaged at 12 million viewers per game (Paulsen).

The fans of eSports are also very similar to the fans of professional sports. They gather at these large venues and are as captivated and as dedicated as fans of professional sports. Fans show up in special attire to mimic and flatter their favorite players or teams. After the event, fans of eSports seek to meet their favorite players and request signed paraphernalia and photographs (Russell).

Differences in Events

Unlike fans of professional sports, fans of eSports can *aspire* to be like the professional gamers seen at live competitions. This is because it is a participatory activity. Not all Miami Heat fans play 5-on-5 basketball during their free time and barely any Baltimore Ravens fans play full on contact football following Monday Night Football. Fans of eSports have easy access to and play the exact same game they enjoy watching (42analytics).

There are some differences due to the nature of video games. Because eSports encompasses all competitive gaming and new competitive video games are released frequently, video games that could be considered "professional games" change annually. With dozens of video games considered "professional games" at one time, tournament schedules sometimes are not friendly with each other. In July 2013, the finals for *StarCraft II* and *Dota 2* occurred at the same time, competing for the same viewers (Gonzalez). No organization in their right mind would host a football-like championship at the same time as the Super Bowl, intended for the same audience. This is something not seen in professional sports.

Rosales 4

Additionally, as a consequence of eSports being a participatory activity, developers have [*caters to the fans (b/c consumers?)*] to care for the general public playing their games more so than caring for the professional gamers. Due to this, rules and regulations within a game are changed often, regardless of how far [*other than the player*] into the competitive gaming season it is (Magee). Prior to 1955, when a ball-carrier's knee in the NFL touched the ground, the ball was *not* considered dead and the player could keep on running. This kind of rule change happening mid-season would be devastating to both players and fans of the game (Hoffman).

However, the aforementioned differences do not prevent eSports from being recognized as a sport. Fans' increased participation in their favorite professional sport certainly would not deny any professional sport from being considered so. Although multiple professional sport finals airing at the same time and groundbreaking mid-season rule changes would be extremely detrimental to the sport, they would still be considered professional sports. [*→ contradicts p. 3 line 2*] [*→ But what about purists? couldn't a new sport evolve*]

Are Professional Gamers "Athletes"?

Much of the debate on whether *League of Legends* is a professional sport and whether eSports are considered sports is based on the professional players themselves. The definition of "athlete" also varies depending on the source. Oxford defines an athlete as: "a person who is proficient in sports and other forms of physical exercise" – a cyclical argument for this case. Merriam-Webster defines and athlete as: "a person who is trained or skilled in exercises, sports, or games requiring physical strength, agility, or stamina". Professional gamers may loosely fit this definition.

Jung "Mvp" Jong Hyun is currently the 8th most successful professional gamer and has made nearly $400,000 over his five-year-long career (Liquipedia). His team, LG IM, short for LG (the well-known consumer electronics and home appliances company) Incredible Miracle, is comprised more than a dozen other teammates and their coach. They all live together in a "professional gaming house" with a house cook. His diet and (yes, physical) exercise is strictly monitored (Jackson). The professional gamers start their day by being handed a training agenda of what they will be practicing for the day. They are dressed in uniform: matching attire branded with all of their sponsors. They are encouraged to – and do – think about the game every waking moment – not just fantasizing, but constantly strategizing. They spend the day practicing the game, criticizing their teammates while they play the game, analyzing their own game footage with their coach, watching footage of their opponents, and adapting their strategies to those opponents they will face in the near future. A usual day of training will last twelve straight hours, and sometimes reach over twenty hours. Their motivation: every moment that you're not practicing, your opponent could be practicing. During the week, professional gamers sleep, eat, take care of bodily functions and hygiene, and train – nothing else. Aside from their physical appearances, these professional gamers could be mistaken for professional athletes.

These late-teens and early-twenties have sacrificed a higher education, a social life, and their friends and family to pursue a career of professional gaming. Ahn "Seed" Sahng Won, a member of team LG IM, states, "I do feel it's unfair sometimes not having [everything I've sacrificed, but] whining is not what pros do… I am supporting myself which is pretty cool at my age… I am exchanging [everything I've sacrificed] for priceless experiences" (TeamStarTale). There's no doubt that training for twelve hours per day isn't easy and that having twenty-hour training days is a feat of endurance, especially when these professional gamers have to keep up this training regimen throughout the whole year.

In contrast, NFL players have different training regimens for season, offseason, preseason, and training camp. Their daily schedule can range from: driving two hours for a ninety-minute scrimmage, signing some autographs, driving to grab some lunch, heading back to the field for another scrimmage, doing an interview, hanging around, and then a two-hour workout at night; to all-day training, as described by Ryan Riddle, former defensive end in the NFL:

> "Your body has likely been bashed and trampled so much that you can no longer distinguish bruised flesh from normal. With muscles so stiff and fatigued, the brief walk from hotel to locker is a challenge. Your body is screaming for rest; your mind is constantly at the breaking point." (Riddle).

"For me, I want to put my body through the most pain it's ever been through." - DeAngelo Hall (Back To Football).

That feeling is something professional gamers will never feel in their gaming career. Professional gamers are able to train twenty hours a day because when training isn't prohibited by the limitations of the physical body – training doesn't stop. Although professional gamers are more dedicated to their career than athletes, professional gamers do not experience the extreme mental and physical pain that is required of professional athleticism. Professional gamers are not athletes.

The Government's Controversial View

The U.S. government, however, claims that professional gamers are indeed athletes. Prior to July 2013, in eSports tournaments held in the U.S., foreign players and teams could travel here, compete, and then leave with the prize money. Now, specific to *League of Legends*, players can reside and practice with their teams here in the U.S., along with earning a salary. They get a P-1A visa "'to enrich the nation's cultural landscape' by welcoming 'diverse talent'". Thousands of athletes in professional sports get a P-1A visa each year, while entertainers such as actors or singers get a P-1B visa. *League of Legends* is recognized as a major sports league because they have clear rules, at least six teams, and pulls in revenues of at least $10 million. Daniel Cosgrove, a U.S. Citizenship and Immigration Services spokesman, referred to the P-1A as a "'highly specific visa'" for "'internationally recognized athletes'" (Dave). "The P-1 classification applies to you if you are coming to the U.S. temporarily to perform at a specific athletic competition as an athlete, individually or as part of a group or team, at an internationally recognized level of performance." (U.S. Citizenship and Immigration Services).

There's no question that the U.S. government recognizes eSports as a sport and professional gamers as athletes. Dustin Beck, Riot Games vice president of e-sports, states "'It validates eSports as a sport… It's like David Beckham coming to the LA Galaxy.'" (Campbell). There's no doubt that eSports is big. Annual salaries of top players average around $100,000 (Campbell). Major companies such as Nissan, American Express, and LG sponsor professional gamers.

Not an Argument of Definition

There's no common definitive answer as to whether professional gamers fit the definition of an athlete or whether eSports fits the definition of a sport. It seems like the question: "is eSports a sport?" could be answered by asking: "how do *you* define a *sport*?" People who believe that golf, ping pong, bowling, billiards, and other not-so-strenuous physical activities are sports, also believe that eSports is a sport. People who believe that the aforementioned activities aren't sports and that sports require extreme physical exertion and inherent danger, don't believe that eSports is a sport.

Perhaps the best way to answer the question, "is eSports a sport?" is to see that eSports aren't treated like sports. Americans don't think it's a sport and Americans don't treat it like a sport. Advocates for believing that eSports is a sport aren't confident in their beliefs. If a college football fan was challenged with, "football isn't a real sport," he would scoff and dismiss the accusations. If a fan of eSports was challenged with, "eSports isn't a real sport," he would get defensive. Fans of eSports are insecure about their belief that eSports is a real sport (Sterling).

By extension, I am arguing that "questionable" sports such as billiards and poker aren't sports, as they aren't overwhelmingly accepted as sports, but specifics of that is best reserved for a different essay. The future of eSports seems to be heading away from professional sports as well. Beck in a recent interview, stated that unlike traditional professional sports, that the current eSports audience consumes media more through Netflix, Hulu, and other internet-based sources rather than through TV, so Riot is not aiming at bringing eSports to U.S. televisions (Tack).

Without giving a concrete definition to "athlete" and "sport", it will be impossible to see if professional gamers and eSports fit those definitions. And unless people on the forefront of eSports, such as Riot, push specifically towards gaining eSports' acceptance as a sport, the American public will never consider it a sport.

EVALUATION of aspects
  similarities in:
  - PRESENTATION (e an arena is a large gathering, tickets are sold, there is an event fans pay $ to see)

  - MEDIATION
    - rules & regulation on gear } customization within these guidelines
      ex: (cyclists, bikes)   ⇒ (gamers, personalized/calibrated
          (tennis players, rackets)   mice & keyboards)

    - referees
    - live commentaries/broadcasts
      → w/ similar viewer #s

  - FANS

  differences:
  GAMING/ESPORT   "PROFESSIONAL" SPORT
  challenges{ · participatory, fans play the   · fans cannot play 5 on 5 w/
  this   same games   Miami Heat

  applies { · scheduling conflicts/   · no one would schedule a football
  to   finals/tournaments occurring @   championship same time as
  ranges   same time   Super Bowl
              schedule coincides   → But this is probably @ diff
                                                 levels · b/c NFL is highest prof.
                                                 league... does Esports have this? (PG.?)
                                               · Ⓐ b/c would be detrimental
            · rules & regulations Δ often b/c
              videogame is for consumers

  ARE THE GAMERS ATHLETES?
  If under the definition of athlete = someone who experiences extreme
  mental & physical pain during training for the sport ... then NO
  (why dwell on this. IS THE (COUNTER ARGUMENT) → needs to be more strongly
  emphasized that this def is used b/c it doesn't match w/ conclusion

Captain Discourse and Other Heroes
Learning about Writing Research through Comic Books

Courtney L. Werner *and*
Nicole I. Caswell

Supplemental Materials

- Rationale
- Scaffolding Activities
  - Writing and Rhetoric Research Methods
  - Drafting Research Proposals
  - Three Panel Comic Strips
  - Storyboarding Activity
  - Peer Critique
- Evaluation
- Student Responses

Writing Assignment

Objective

This assignment is to help you think about the relationship between text and images. Also, this assignment requires you to have a deep understanding of the research you have done so that you are able to share it with your audience in a unique manner—a skill much harder to master than you think. Finally, this assignment pulls together all of the College Writing II course objectives.

Audience

Your audience for these comic books is future College Writing II students who are unfamiliar with ways to research writing and rhetoric. You can safely assume that your readers have already conducted traditional library research but are seeking out more information on your research method. Assume, too, that readers are unfamiliar with the texts you discuss, so you will need to provide extra information to help them understand. See below for a discussion of the prompt.

REQUIREMENTS/PROMPT

- With your partner, create a comic book that identifies a particular research method for writing and rhetoric research. Your comic book should address how to use this particular research method. In addition, your comic book will address why writing is difficult to research as well as the affordances and constraints of the particular method you chose for your book.
- Since comic books utilize different page sizes and formats, there is no page length requirement, but you should envision this as an in-depth treatment of the topic.
- Images should complement your written text. If you use images you found online, be sure to cite them (and consult the fair use/copyright of the image—just like we read about in *Bound by Law?*).
- Be creative with your comic book. Think of creating a story that helps you address the topic.
- Design and final presentation—consider having a company bind your comic book (like the local Kinkos) or find an online site to pdf or physically produce your book.

Note: You will not be assessed on your artistic ability, but you will be assessed on your use of images with text and quality of presentation.

Rationale

While reading comic books has great value for students (we frequently assign *Understanding Comics* and *Bound by Law? Tales from the Public Domain* in our first-year composition courses), we find greater value in assigning students to compose their own comic books. At the four-year public research university where we piloted this assignment, students are required to take a first-semester and a second-semester writing course: the first-semester course is an introduction to analytic essay genres while the second-semester course prepares students for research-driven writing. We created the comic book assignment as the final of four major writing projects for the second-semester writing course, which culminates with an in-depth understanding of a particular research method students use across the university curriculum. The project effectively challenges students, developing both their awareness of writing research and their abilities to utilize various modes of communication and multiliteracies while showcasing their understanding of research design and practice.

For this project, students were asked to collaboratively produce comic books that teach future college writing students how to conduct writing and rhetoric research. The entire course was themed around research questions (and how to discover "answers") that revolve around composition and rhetoric. For this particular project, students were asked to get into groups and ask an appropriate research question about a type of research method or methodology. Student groups, therefore, selected a method/methodology of research (discourse analysis, feminist methodologies, surveys, focus groups, think aloud protocols, etc.) that could be used to answer a variety of writing and rhetoric research questions. In this way, students learned about the research method in great detail—especially since they needed to explain the method to another student via a comic book.

This assignment further challenged students to consider multimodal writing in various ways. First, students had to consider how they would use a variety of modes to write their comic: how would they utilize and combine pictures and words? would they use color? would font changes or speech bubble styles offer visual cues to readers? Students were asked to use their own artistic abilities, digital software, or Web 2.0 comic book generators to complete the assignment.

Additionally, this assignment challenged students to think critically about a diverse range of writing concerns and accomplished many of our writing program's course objectives, including teaching students to build upon rhetorical principles, design effective research questions, identify appropriate methods for answering those questions, critically evaluate and use sources for research, develop technological literacies and familiarity with digital composing environments, and understand the relationship between text, image, and design in multimodal compositions. Although the assignment meets these goals, it can easily be adapted to achieve goals and objectives in other types of writing courses and writing programs. Creating student-generated comic books allows students to explore the writing process outside of producing traditional academic essays while strengthening essential academic skills.

Scaffolding Techniques

As a research-focused course, each of the four major projects incorporated research. Projects one and two introduced students to integrating secondary research in their writing, whereas project three (a research proposal, including a literature review, on a research method) directly led into the comic book assignment. Some of the scaffolding activities we used throughout projects three and four included defining writing and rhetoric research methods, drafting research proposals on specific methods, writing three-panel comic strips, using storyboard techniques, and engaging in peer critique. Our scaffolding activities enabled students to feel more confident in their abilities, tackle the project more willingly, and consider the rhetorical concerns of comic books.

Writing and Rhetoric Research Methods

One of the earliest in-class activities associated with this project centered on having students understand what writing and rhetoric research methods exist and how to define those methods. We distributed handouts with a list of eighteen different methods of research. During class, students were asked to use internet research and their *DK Handbooks* (Wysocki and Lynch 98–107) to generate 3–4 sentences for *each* method. The handout has been reproduced below.

As you define the following research methods, consider answering these questions:

What is the method? What does the method help you get at with research? How do you use that method?/What do you do?

- Surveys/Questionnaires
- Interviews
- Focus Groups
- Think Aloud Protocols
- Content Analysis
- Textual Analysis
- Discourse/CDA/Linguistic Analysis
- Observation/Field Notes
- Thick Description
- Screen/Activity Recordings/Captures
- Rhetorical Analysis
- Grounded Theory/Coding
- Design Experiments
- Visual Analysis
- Ethnography
- Case Study
- Feminist Methodology
- Archival Research

Drafting Research Proposals

After students were in groups and had picked a method to study and describe (each group had a different method), they worked together to compose research proposals. The research proposal had a few goals. First, it gave the groups a chance to work with each other and figure out how and when to work together before they began working on the actual comic book. Second, it forced the groups to create a schedule for completing the project. We knew that group projects can go very well or very poorly, and planning a schedule was one way to help ensure a positive group work experience for our students. Thirdly, this project allowed students to do most of the research they needed to complete their comic books. In addition to being a scaffolding assignment, it also helped spread students' work over a longer period of time instead of an end-of-semester rush. Below is the drafting assignment as handed out to students.

Purpose

The goal of the research proposal is to help you plan out your research for your final comic book project. At the end of the proposal, you should have a clear idea about what your topic is, what research is out there, what you need to do, and how to do it. Think of this as your plan of attack for your project.

Your proposal should be 6–8 pages long, with 3–4 pages dedicated to the literature review. Points will be deducted if your proposal does not fit within the page requirements. Your proposal should cover the following headings (detailed below): Title, Rationale & Purpose, Description, Literature Review, Timeline, and Presentation.

Headings

- Title: Pick a title for your final project. This can be a working title that you change later.
- Rationale and Purpose: This section helps provide a brief introduction to your research as well as answering the following questions.
    - What is the purpose of your research?
    - What are you trying to figure out?
    - Why is your research important?
- Description of Topic:
    - What is your topic?
    - What all do you need to consider within your topic?
    - Are there any specific terms that you need to define?
    - What will your audience learn from reading your comic book?
- Literature Review: A literature review is an analysis and critique of the research related to your project. It should provide the reader with an understanding of how your specific project is related to the research already done on the topic. Your sources should be relevant to your topic. Your lit-

erature review should synthesize the results of your reading into a summary that lays out clearly what you know about your topic and what you need to know (which is why you are doing this project).
- Timeline:
    - How are you going to go about completing this project?
    - What are your personal due dates?
- Presentation:
    - How do you envision your final copy of your comic book?
    - Will it be in a digital format or hard copy?

Your proposal should include at least 3–4 library sources (journal articles, books, book chapters), 1–2 web sources if needed, and follow APA format. Remember to be creative. Be descriptive. Sell your comic book idea in your proposal.

THREE PANEL COMIC STRIPS

Our main goal in this activity was trying to get students used to showing how something can *happen* in a comic strip. Unfortunately, we didn't write a specific assignment sheet for this activity, but the activity did follow a particular format that we detailed in our lesson plans.

At the beginning of class, we asked students first to write down five things that happened to them over the past week. These could be literally any situation. Then, we handed out five blank comic strips to each student. The strips were composed of three separate frames, and they were large, 4" × 11" strips (each frame was roughly 4" × 3.5"). We asked students to illustrate each of the five things they listed at the start of class, and we gave them about twenty minutes to do so (allowing for four minutes per strip). At the end of the time limit, students exchanged their strips with their groups and talked openly about what was easiest for them or most difficult. For the last ten minutes of this forty-minute activity, students engaged in a classroom dialogue to explain what they had learned from the activity.

This activity afforded students a low-stakes environment to test out their abilities with a comic format. They had practice drafting images, considering how text and image might work together, and telling a basic narrative. This activity was a precursor for the storyboarding activity.

STORYBOARDING ACTIVITY

This activity came late in the semester after students had collected most of their research materials and were starting to think about how to write their actual "how-to" comic book. The activity was split into three distinct parts and took up two class periods.

Part 1: Set up

In your comic book groups, analyze some of the story-line features of *BOUND BY LAW?* using the chart below.

Character Name/Features	Personality Traits	Purpose

Next, analyze the story. You can refer to this link to a narrative map that we discussed in class to help you: s.spachman.tripod.com/Narrative/storymap.htm. Trace the storyline of *BOUND BY LAW?*, and indicate places in the text where "learning" takes place. How are issues of fair use "taught" throughout the storyline? Fill in your answers for each narrative piece below.

Exposition:
Rising Action:
Climax:
Falling Action:
Resolution:

Part 2: Application

With your group, brainstorm your characters and storyline. Who are the characters? What are they like? What is your storyline? What is the purpose? What is the progression of the story? Use the same or similar charts that we used to analyze *BOUND BY LAW?* for this activity.

Part 3: Storyboarding

Review the helpful links below if you are interested in making your comic book digitally. If you are designing your comic book by hand, pick a few of the blank layouts (which can also be found via these links) to use. Think about what text and dialogue you'll want to include and the placement of text with the images. Take 15 minutes to list out some possible scenes and the structure of your storyline based on the work you did in Part 2. Use Part 2 as the basis for your quick drafting to create this fun storyboard (which is really just a rough draft of what you plan to make later).

Helpful links:

- www.creativecomicart.com/step-by-step.html
- marvelkids.com/games/play/75/create_your_own_comic
- www.scholastic.com/amulet/makeyourown/
- w ww.designcomics.org/

These links will help you think about designing the pages, characters, text, and dialogue of your comic book.

PEER CRITIQUE

For the peer review, we first had students work together to develop a rubric (see the Evaluation section below for a description of how students developed a rubric for the assignment). Then, we asked students to bring their rough drafts of their comic books to class; these rough drafts could be anything: storyboards, detailed outlines, brief artistic illustrations with narrative arc descriptions, or more finished products (especially the digital projects). Each group joined up with another group and swapped comic book drafts. After students had swapped drafts, we passed out the rubric to each group, and students graded each other using the rubric. Finally, each group was required to compose an editorial letter to their partner group detailing the questions, concerns, thoughts, ideas, and suggestions they had for the other group's comic book. Both the comic book draft and editorial letter were returned to the authoring group by the end of the class.

Evaluation

Throughout the course, we focused on building a community through various collaborative projects (such as this comic book assignment). Part of our community building included making sure students had a voice in evaluation; by allowing students to help generate evaluative features, we, as a class, were able to understand how we were all interpreting the assignment. Thus, we detail our process for developing appropriate evaluation standards for the project.

One technique for designing an effective rubric is to ask students to actually construct a rubric. When students create the rubric, they have the opportunity to critically analyze the prompt; in groups, they can hash out misunderstandings, and they have the opportunity to specifically ask for clarification on prompt requirements. This technique is also beneficial for the instructor: once students have presented a rubric to the instructor, she sees more clearly what areas of the assignment students find unclear or even unnecessary. Although students have real input for this rubric, the instructor maintains the final say in the rubric used to assess the projects.

Rubric Activity

Get into your podcast groups.[1] As a group, define how you think the projects should be assessed: what's most important to have in the comic book?

What types of things should "count" for more? You should assign points to each category. Points will be negotiated between the class and me. For example, you should not assign 100 points to one category and then 10 to all the others. Be prepared to argue for the decisions that you make. The project is worth 200 points. You should draft this by hand on actual paper because you will be moving around, and we all know how unreliable the computers can be.

Your rubric must include the following categories:

- 30–60+ pages (should you include page sizes? amount of pictures per page? other?)
- cover original comic book;
- be directed at College Writing II students;
- teach a method of research: in your groups, define some criteria for this and what it will look like/how it will be assessed;
- explain how/why writing is difficult to research;
- explain affordances/constraints of THIS method for researching writing and rhetoric;
- use images that complement written text;
- use design techniques and methods from class readings;
- demonstrate storyline and character development;
- demonstrate creativity;
- include a final presentation;
- include citations—both in-text and references page (images need to be cited, too, if you take them from another source instead of creating them yourself!).
- LIST YOUR OTHER CATEGORIES HERE (at least 5–7)
  - consider things like grammar, overall design, research, etc.

Class time break down:

- First round with your podcast group: you have 20 minutes.
- Second round with combined groups: you have 15 minutes.
- Final round, the three final group rubrics on board: we will have 15 minutes. If necessary, we will finish at the beginning of class on Thursday.

Note: This *is* the rubric that I will use to grade your projects, although it may be lightly edited. You will have the approved rubric well before your project is due.

Sample Rubric Generated with Student Input

Final Presentation	The overall appearance of the comic book: • follows through with assignment • looks clean, neat, and organized • uses design techniques • grabs an audiences' attention Binding or PDF (such as zooming on images) has a professional feel and flow.	/30
Teaching Method	The comic book teaches the audience about a specific writing research method and how to use that method. In teaching the method, you should: • include as close to as many points from the research proposal • enact a creative way of relaying information (not just copy and paste research proposal into a spoken part) • include references • explain the method	/30
Images	The images within the comic book: • pertain to text • complement the text • relate to each other • are easily followed • are presented in effective balance with other images/text	/25
Length	The final comic book should be: • 30 pages for 8½ × 11 or 60 pages for 4¼ × 5½ ◦ Layout and spacing are very important, so there should be a minimum of two illustrations (with text) on each page. Up to four pages of the comic book can be single illustration pages if relevant to the story.	/20
Affordances and Constraints	Within the comic book, authors: • include two affordances of the research method • include two constraints of the research method • explain how the research method is used and what can hold researchers back	/15
Citations	Throughout the comic book, authors • have at least three separate cited sources (5 pts each) • follow APA format	/15
Storyline (and characters)	The storyline of the comic book is: • consistent, clear, and easy to follow • cohesive and complete (easily identifiable beginning, middle, and end) • understandable and meets the assignment guidelines The characters of the comic book have: • a steady personality for each character	/15
Original	The comic book is not: • plagiarized • copied from another idea	/10
Audience	The audience of the comic book: • pertains to College Writing II students	/10

Writing Technique	The comic book appeals to the audience because it is: • not too simplistic • appropriate for educated young adults The comic book incorporates: • an understanding of what we learned from the readings in class • a layout that includes consistent fonts • elements that contrast to visually show the difference between images and scenes • a clean look	/10
Creativity	Overall, the comic book: • is creative • pertains to audience • uses images and text in creative and interesting ways	/10
Language | Grammar	The text of the comic book is: • appropriate for characters (slang if necessary) • fits characters • follows standard punctuation and grammar as applicable	/5
Writing Difficulty	The comic book includes: • a paragraph or conversation talking about the confusions and complications of researching writing and rhetoric	/5
Total Grade		/200

Student Responses

Finally, we bring students' voices[2] to bear on the conversation through their "finished products" and reflective writing, allowing student words to demonstrate the project's importance and level of success.

As part of our last day of class, during our final exam period, we had a gallery day where every group showed off their comic books. The students went around the classroom reading, reviewing, and chatting about the other comics they were seeing. Due to the size of the class (25 students, 12 total groups), students were given two minutes to briefly review each comic. Then, they were given a prompt to respond to and post to our course's online platform. The prompt they responded to read, "In 250 words or less, what stood out to you the most in terms of design and layout? In other words, what are you still thinking about (in terms of visual layout) at this particular moment? What are you most impressed with in regards to your classmates' work? You may want to discuss examples of things you have found interesting or exemplary, or examples of approaches you didn't quite understand."

Many students gave positive feedback about what the class did overall: "[E]veryone had some really good ideas. [One student's] group was really well done and the artwork was well drawn. [O]verall[, I] think this project was a big success." Other students specifically talked about techniques they thought were interesting: "What stood out to me the most was the comic with the actual pictures. [I] never would of [sic] thought of doing a comic like that. [I] also thought the clue comic was really well drawn. [I] was most impressed with those two comics as well. [I] thought they were both really good, and it seems like they worked really hard"; "I saw designs from the [McCloud] assignment that [I] could easily dicipher [sic]. But a lot were new to me and looked fantastic in almost every way. The only bad spots I saw on any were empty spots not colored in. My top 3 comic books [I] saw were number 3 the actual picture comic book [sic]. That in my opinion was the most creative idea of the class. [...] Overall[,] everyone did great on these, and they turned out so much better than I thought."

Although we received positive feedback on the project, there were also a few students who did not learn as much from the experience as we hoped they would, and they don't seem to have enjoyed the experience as much as other students did. Some students particularly felt the time constraints of the project were two tight: "I'm still wishing that I maybe had a few more days to work out all of the kinks in our project." Other students did not enjoy reviewing their classmates' products and wished for more specific digital requirements: "I didn't like those with stick figures, that caused them to kind of loose [sic] the comic book feeling, and threw me off a little." This student's response also specifically detailed a desire to require students to use digital composing tools and drawing software. Another student critiqued others' uses of multimodality, saying: "Some of the other comic books could have been a little more better to look at [sic]. They could have incorporated color and some different fonts or bolded letters." Comments like these helped us understand that for some students, our program and course objectives centering on multimodal composition had not been fully met.

Still, many students remained surprised and excited by what they were all able to produce for this assignment. A common theme in reflections on the project is summarized by these two students' responses: "Looking at my classmates' comic books, it actually impressed me"; "Overall, I found it really cool how everyone was assigned the same project and came out with completely different comic books." One resounding comment that came across in students' reflections was that the project was, in hindsight, worthwhile: "I know everyone struggled through this project and in the end the comic books turned out really well (headache or no headache included). [...] I think everyone did well for this project." A few students took extra time to explain why they thought the project was so beneficial for them, such as the student who thoughtfully wrote:

> It was a lot of work but there was a lot of creative aspects of it that made it harder to lose interest in. I know that I enjoyed constructing the actual comic book and coloring it and lettering it was work that I did not mind doing. Not only that but by having to hand draw

and letter the comic book I know that I will ever forget what we spent so much time on. The information about feminist research is something I know I will not forget. This is something I do not think would have happened if I were to have just written a paper. I feel as though I went into this project having no understanding of the feminist research method but know [sic] I feel like I could explain it to someone and use it properly to conduct research. Through this project[,] I learned a research method that previously I did not know existed. If we had been assigned a group paper instead[,] I think that I would not have worked as nearly as hard as I did on our comic nor have learned as much.

Finally, student responses to the assignment were so positive that several students complained about not having enough time to read everyone's comics cover-to-cover. One student critiqued us, saying, "Honestly, I wish I could have read the other groups' [comics] and seen what they did with their projects."

Based on the student responses we received, we believe the heavy amount of scaffolding we assigned throughout the semester for this particular project contributed to its success. Additionally, the students' abilities to have a say in the rubric helped students become even more invested in the project; the final gallery day also had this effect, as the students were aware that they had a "real" audience of peers for their work. We recommend building more time into the semester for peer reviews and comic book revisions and that the last week of class is devoted to showcasing each of the comic books rather than allocating only a few minutes for brief gallery-style viewings.

Notes

1. The "podcast groups" are carry-overs from an earlier assignment. We put students into groups early in the semester to help them bond over time and become comfortable with each other. We use the same groups for various projects to help students build confidence in working as teams (George 323; Blumenfeld et al. 38).

2. At the beginning of the course, we asked for and secured signed consent forms from students to share their thoughts and comic books.

Works Cited

Aoki, Keith, James Boyle, and Jennifer Jenkins. *Bound by Law? Tales from the Public Domain.* Durham,: Duke Center for the Study of the Public Domain, 2006. Web. 17 June 2013.

Blumenfeld, Phyllis C., Ronald W. Marx, Elliot Soloway, and Joseph Krajcik. "Learning with Peers: From Small Group Cooperation to Collaborative Communities." *Educational Researcher* 25.8 (1996): 37–40. Print.

George, Diana. "Working with Peer Groups in the Composition Classroom." *College Composition and Communication* 355.3 (1984): 320–236. Print.

McCloud, Scott. *Understanding Comics: The Invisible Art.* New York: William Morrow Paperbacks, 1993. Print.

Wysocki, Anne Frances, and Dennis A. Lynch. *DK Handbook,* 2d ed. New York: Pearson Longman, 2011. Print.

Critical Analysis of Student Ethnography

Abby Wilkerson

Supplementary Materials

- Rationale
- Scaffolding Activities
  - Using the BEAM Schema in Research Workshops
  - Critical Annotated Working Bibliography
  - Peer Review of Paper Drafts
- Student writing sample
- Appendix: Introduction to Ethnographic-Style Research Project: Alternatives to "Constant Convenience Consumerism"

Critical Analysis Project (101–2 pp., 75/300 total points for the semester)

Set up your research and analysis: Choose one of the ethnographic-style projects—your own, or another—to study (it's your "exhibit" source).

Identify interesting key findings involving participant practices and their meanings. Develop a specific research question through several revisions, exploring some aspect of the findings in light of relevant published qualitative research. You may focus on relevant findings of the entire ethnographic paper or a subset of them. Your question should in some way incorporate relevant positionality/social group factors (as explained in the ethnographic assignment), due to their significance for qualitative research on food as societal dynamics that can significantly influence people's lives.

Explore these factors' relationships to the participants' practices and experiences. Address some combination of race, ethnicity, nationality, immigrant status, gender, sexuality, economic class, age, religion, region, urban/rural/suburban status, physical or mental ability, and/or specific social roles. As we've discussed, these factors' influence may vary and shift—as the categories themselves can do as well.

Develop an interpretive framework as a lens for analyzing the exhibit source. Situate the original paper's findings in relation to those of other relevant ethnographic studies. Use one or more critical terms or conceptual frameworks from one or more course readings, plus additional academic sources and other material as appropriate for your focus. Use this interpretive framework to develop your analysis. Use your sources to assemble a scholarly and intellectually informed conversation that will provide a context and impetus for your own contribution. Consider multiple perspectives.

Tailor your analysis to the needs and expectations (including use of terms, types of evidence, style, and so on) of a specific audience who can benefit from the knowledge you will produce. Make sure this audience includes relevant types of scholars.

Draft the paper:

- Research requirements:
    - relevant and appropriate sources for your specific inquiry (a sufficient number to allow thorough engagement with academic analysis, including several articles from academic journals—usually at least six to eight sources)
    - including several ethnographic sources
    - and one or more course readings that provide critical analytic terms useful in exploring your research question
    - sources used for Exhibit, Argument, and Method functions according to the BEAM categories [(Bizup)]
    - multiple and contrasting perspectives on your focus
    - academic sources focusing on the cultural, social, and/or political dimensions of food should play a significant role in the overall analysis
    - multiple academic sources that address positionality/social group factors as appropriate to your focus (including original participant characteristics/settings)
- Introduction: lay out the research question, convey the thesis, and set up the kinds of material being used (including the original project) and its purpose(s) for your project.
- Provide a clear and detailed picture of your object of study. Use ample quotations and other details.

- Contextualize sources: discuss each of your main sources in some detail, including necessary context such as the type of work it is (including the disciplinary field for scholarly works); its overall argument, or its overall purpose if it is not an argumentative source; and what kind of evidence supports it, so your readers can see how the authors arrived at their conclusions.
- Use plenty of quotations: integrate quotations into the paper by introducing them clearly and thoroughly, and commenting on their significance.[1]

Rationale[2]

First-year writing courses at George Washington University's University Writing Program (UWP) are theme-based. Students choose from a wide variety of themes, taught by faculty from various fields and disciplines. As my UWP colleague Sandie Friedman notes, this opportunity "may be one of the few times in the course of a goal-focused, pre-professional college career when students can explore something that interests them for its own sake—for reasons of intellectual curiosity, rather than because it is a step towards acquiring a necessary skill or credential" (79). The shared theme of a class also "enable[s] students to begin to develop expertise in a particular field or topic" (78–79).

I have been teaching food-based course themes for some time now, most recently "The Good Food Revolution: Food Movements and Rhetorics of Social Change."[3] Food is a provocative subject for first-year students, many of whom are away from home for an extended period for the first time in their lives. The absence of familiar dishes, meals, and family foodways gives rise to reflections and critical perspectives that might not emerge as readily at another time. In the first major project of the semester, students collaborate in small groups to produce ethnographic-style research on food provisioning, preparation, production, politics, or activism.[4]

Ethnographic-style research allows first-year students to generate rich and complex material in a relatively short time, which poses a significant critical thinking challenge—framing and organizing the material, and formulating a thesis statement that does justice to its richness. These student-produced texts eventually become the objects of study for the final project of the course (and the subject of this essay). Since the course explores relationships between people's social circumstances and their access to food, as well as organized efforts to promote "food justice" (Alkon and Ageyman 5), students are expected to situate the results of their research in relation to positionality or social group categories. The overall method of this Critical

Analysis assignment could be applied to other types of student-produced texts, especially those providing rich experiential material—for example, literacy narratives, a standard feature of many composition courses.

The Critical Analysis project facilitates students' experience of themselves and their classmates as emerging scholars, and of the classroom as a space of intellectual community, as they work together from a common pool of material they have generated and engage with one another's work in a variety of ways. The metaphor of scholarly writing as conversation becomes literal as students take up one another's texts, testing and debating the ideas and arguments of the earlier projects. The project positions students as experts, treating their own and their peers' writing as worthy of study, as "legitimate scholarship" (Downs et al. 121). Students whose texts are taken up by others have the experience of "having their writing *read* rather than judged, evaluated, analyzed, diagnosed, or corrected," as is more typical (Downs et al. 122).

I set up the course blog and Blackboard site to give students access to a pool of texts from all three sections of the class. Students choose from their classmates' or their own ethnographic-style texts, and analyze the findings of that earlier project in light of relevant scholarship.

The process serves to introduce students to scholarly writing and guides them to continually refine their research questions and use sources to pose new ones, rather than simply seek information or find ways to support a predetermined thesis. Ultimately, research becomes a tool for shedding new light on familiar experiences.

Shortly before we discuss this assignment in class, the UWP provides a context that facilitates this work, through our University Writing and Research Conference, where selected student authors from the previous semester present their projects to current students who have not yet begun their own. Presenters are asked to convey their argument and how it evolved through their writing process. For student attendees, the conference positions them and their peers as intellectuals. More specifically, presenters writing in response to this particular assignment are deeply engaged in student texts, encapsulating a semester-long conversation and demonstrating one version of the serious intellectual accomplishments possible for first-year students.

Seeing ambitious research projects modeled by peers before launching their own projects can help students shift from typical high school models of researching to support a thesis to more sophisticated inquiry-based research processes. It's one thing to hear a professor claim that drastically revising an argument, a thesis statement, or research question can often be useful or even necessary. When the same advice comes from a peer who has experienced the frustrations of starting over, as well as the satisfactions of meeting the challenge, the message is much more meaningful. I often hear students recall—or remind one another of—this vivid lesson later during their own difficult moments in the research process.

The Critical Analysis assignment has generated a gratifying level of engagement both with scholarship and with student peers' ideas and arguments; the research gains immediacy and relevance because it involves experiences that have exerted a palpable presence over the classroom all semester. For example, students have pursued projects arising from classmates' grandmothers' or other relatives' efforts to sustain cultural food traditions while adapting to changing circumstances. One semester, several students independently explored questions raised by a student ethnography of her Seattle aunt's farmers' market and community garden participation. Not only does working with classmates' texts heighten the immediacy of the issues being addressed and a sense of how specific people's lives are affected, this process also sharpens students' sense of audience, since they are writing and thinking about people whose relative or friend may be critiquing their work—and who may even read the work themselves.

The earlier ethnographic-style research allows students to conduct and synthesize one kind of research done by scholars. This paper allows them to develop their own perspective in conversation with those of their peer authors whose work they are analyzing, including these original authors' interpretations and analyses of the interview material they have produced. Authors of the new paper, the critical analysis, test their own analysis of the material produced earlier both with those of their peer authors, and with relevant work of published writers, experiencing the dialogue that characterizes academic discourse.

The assignment advances several crucial rhetorical goals in the transition to university-level writing: approaching source use rhetorically; clearly distinguishing one's own ideas from others'; quoting, paraphrasing, and attributing ideas in ways that are both appropriate and effective for specific contexts; and grasping the rhetorical purposes of documentation in academic discourse. In the process, students gain greater awareness of the range of purposes that outside sources serve in scholarship.

Charles Paine and John D. Miles, editors of the collection *Teaching with Student Texts: Essays Toward an Informed Practice*, remind us of "a well-known principle in teaching writing, that what we *say* about student texts is less important than what we *do* with them" (247). Since I created this assignment, students are noticeably taking their research and the drafting and revision of the resulting texts more seriously. They know that their ethnographic projects are potential objects of study, not only for students in their own class, but in two other classes as well. Through the final project, the critical analysis, students are gaining a deeper appreciation for the responsibilities involved in representing others and their experiences, and the importance of the choices involved.

The design of the critical analysis paper itself and the overall semester's supporting work are predicated on both a course load and student cap within each section that allow faculty sufficient time to review student drafts, prepare feedback, and conduct small-group workshops. The Conference on College Composition and Communication states in its "Principles for the Postsecondary Teaching of Writing": "No more than 20 students should be permitted in any writing class. Ideally, classes should be limited to 15." Yet, as many institutions retreat from their commitment to ensure the working conditions necessary for the rigorous instruction they aspire to provide, many of us in the profession face the sacrifice of crucial elements of our pedagogies.

Our profession must continue to challenge the "do more with less" neoliberal spirit that prevails in higher education now, even as we find ourselves in a conflicted position, working collectively for the future while facing piles of drafts that won't read themselves. What I can do here is to suggest two potential adaptations for addressing—if by no means resolving—faculty workload challenges with this assignment or others with similar goals. First, for this particular assignment, if the two-paper sequence of ethnography and critical analysis is impractical, consider incorporating a limited version of the critical analysis functions—using scholarly sources to contextualize and analyze the results of the ethnography—into the original collaborative paper in stages. Use a course blog and/or discussion board for students to post their abstracts and suggest useful sources for one another. (The second suggestion involves instructor and peer review of drafts, which I will take up in a later section.) These modifications promote student engagement with one another's texts while addressing other assignment goals, if not to the same degree as the original assignment, particularly in its positioning of students as authoritative researchers.

Scaffolding Activities

Using the BEAM Schema in Research Workshops

In "BEAM: A Rhetorical Vocabulary for Teaching Research-Based Writing," Joseph Bizup proposes a schema for approaching research-based writing (both the reading and the production of it) rhetorically. This schema affords students a more nuanced understanding of source use, in ways that push them beyond approaching materials as simple information sources (whether for published authors or themselves) to recognize the complex relationships writers can have to source materials. "Background" source use is taking something up as factual, agreed-upon, in ways that assume readers need not question the information. "Exhibit" source use involves putting a source on display within a piece of writing, to analyze and interpret it. "Argument" sources are those a writer engages with as such, whether to refute, refine, defend, or extend (and more) another author's argument. "Method" sources are those used to create an interpretive framework or some other way of proceeding in a piece or in the original research a piece of writing presents. Sources used in this way might provide keywords or critical terms, or methodological processes.

Students come to us with varying degrees of awareness of these categories. The schema is based on how a source is being used in a particular context, rather than on any static properties of it. Thus, the schema first and foremost provides tools for thinking about source use as serving a range of purposes. Background use is familiar and straightforward to students. Most are also familiar with argument use, having written "thesis and support" papers using sources to argue with and, often, against. First-year students tend to be familiar with exhibit usage (if not Bizup's term for it) through literary papers for high school English classes, but are less familiar with it outside that context. Thinking of "exhibit" as a type of usage allows them to consider how a way of using sources in one field corresponds to a standard use pattern in another field that looks very different on the surface (an English paper analyzing a Naomi Shihab Nye poem, versus a lab report on the effects of soil acidity on tomato plants). "Method" source use is the least familiar, and an important move for students to make as they shift into university-level writing and the need to use published authors' work not simply for information, as argument, or as object of study, but as a building block in constructing an interpretive framework or method of analysis.

Over several class meetings, my instructional librarian partners, Cathy Eisenhower and Dolsy Smith of GWU's Gelman Library,[5] and I help students to finalize their chosen exhibit sources from the class ethnographic projects and draft and revise research questions about what they intend to explore based on these texts. At the same time, we work with them to grasp the BEAM schema, identify instances of the categories in specific student and professional texts (chosen to advance additional pedagogical goals also related to the assignment), and use the schema to structure their own anticipated inquiry as they assemble working bibliographies. The schema challenges them to push the complexity of their thinking and writing by using sources for "method" purposes—especially critical analytic terms—that ground their interpretation of their "exhibit" sources and the broader significance of that earlier project's findings. During this period, their homework each day involves finding a new source of potential use for their project, and creating a citation and annotation stating a brief overview of the source and discussing how they would use it in terms of BEAM functions. (This work is in the

Informal Writing and Preparation category of course requirements, which amounts to 30 of the 300 points possible for the course.)

Critical Annotated Working Bibliography (4–5 pp., 25/300 points)

As many of my UWP colleagues do, I challenge students to use sources above all to ask, rather than primarily to answer, questions—to look for sources that will help them to *ask new questions* about their focus, rather than simply provide information. This represents a shift away from most students' high school research experiences. I explain that this is one of the most crucial ways of using sources in academic discourse, both for established scholars and for students.

This process of application and extrapolation[6] is difficult for many students, yet it is important for even the most sophisticated and talented first-year writers to consciously process so they may understand how academic discourse works, respond effectively to future writing challenges in college, and generally advance the complexity of their thinking. The BEAM schema can be used in facilitating the shift from picking sources that provide factual information or support an argument, to *exploring* how some of the work they encounter might raise questions for their own inquiry. In this way, the schema helps re-orient students to research as a trial and error process of revising and adjusting one's research questions as one proceeds.

The bibliography assignment requires at least seven sources:

- The chosen object of study (the original paper/exhibit source)
- Four or more articles from academic journals that students find (at least three of which should be in ethnography, for this particular assignment)
- One or more academic readings from the course that provide a useful critical term for the student's context
- One or more academic books
- And among these, sources that could serve Exhibit, Argument, and Method functions, based on how students consider using them

In their annotations, students provide these BEAM categorizations for each potential source, giving an overview of each work that explains its purpose and argument, as well as its relevance for their own context, and how they might use it, including its BEAM functions based on these plans. This assignment allows students to practice introducing and beginning to use their main sources, and to receive guidance about selecting and working with them.

Peer Review of Paper Drafts (set of peer critique letters, 12/300 points)

Students upload their own drafts on the course website and download those of their assigned workshop group members.[7] They are asked to print, read, and mark the drafts in specific ways, then compose a letter to the author of each paper discussed in their workshop group (usually a total of four to five students). I cancel classes for the week to conduct the workshops; I lead discussion, asking questions to guide students in responding to one another's drafts, assessing specific features. The goal is to prompt students to identify how to advance the strengths of each draft and more fully accomplish both the authors' purposes and specific assignment goals.

As students prepare by reading each draft, they are to identify how sources are being used by marking passages focusing on the original paper—the object of study, or "exhibit source" according to Bizup's BEAM schema—with EXH. They also are to mark passages focusing on the main new sources (those not in the original paper) as either NS/ARG for those used for argument functions, or NS/METH for those used for method purposes. Because many first-year students can stand to gain greater awareness of the distinction between describing and interpreting an exhibit source, and the reasons for these activities in research-based writing, I also have them mark passages accordingly, using the designations DESCR. or INTERP., as appropriate. They are also asked to underline what they have identified as the thesis statement and to circle passages they have questions about.

In letters of at least 300 words, students address whether the paper overall is clearly *about* the exhibit source (the original paper); the effectiveness of the research question (including its complexity); how clearly the new sources are contextualized and developed; what they learn overall about the original paper's participants' practices as a way of life, their meanings, and their significance; and their own sources' effectiveness for illuminating the direct experience of the participants—practices, meanings, motivations, and how the setting(s) and circumstances (including relevant social group categories) influence these. Students are also asked to note their questions about particular passages, assess the overall balance in the draft between coherence and complexity, and make suggestions about how to strengthen that balance.

A possible workload-based adaptation: ensure that students receive feedback at many stages by increasing more peer responses while reserving instructor feedback on individual drafts for the most crucial stages. To make this modification as effective as possible, train students thoroughly in preparing and giving effective feedback, and modify goals as needed for different stages and activities of the project; launch simultaneous group peer-review discussions by setting up review goals together as a class first. I emphasize the benefits of peer review for reviewers themselves: enhanced understanding of assignment goals and course concepts in a context detached from their own papers, which in turn can facilitate new perspectives on their own writing. When instructors are not commenting on individual drafts, they might give general feedback to the class based on spot-review of selected drafts, perhaps incorporating this advice into initial class discussions before small-group review.

Student Writing Sample

One of the most compelling responses to the assignment was Kelsey Genuino's paper, "Meat, Men, and Masculinity: The Causes and Effects of Familial Relationships on Vegetarians," an analysis of her classmates', Jack Nobel and Jesse Lederman's, ethnographies of three vegetarians—Nobel's father, Lederman's mother, and a friend of Lederman's, a teenage girl. As Genuino explains, Nobel and Lederman's "paper focuses on the lives of three, white, American vegetarians ranging in age and relationship with their family" (1). Genuino summarizes the results of their research: "The authors concluded, '... the older subjects received support and acceptance from their children, who are notably peers of' the teenage participant (Lederman and Nobel 14)" (2). She also reports that the teenager experienced "animosity," not

> "from her peers, but from her adult parents and grandparents, who are closer in age to the older subjects" (Lederman and Nobel 14-15). Thus, the overall relationships among the families are not attributed to the generational difference between teenagers and the parents of teenagers; however, [... a] vegetarian's experience can be influenced based on interaction with children versus with older adults, and with male family members versus female family members (2).

Genuino's project, then, is to explore just these factors in the lives of vegetarians. First, using popular culture sources, published qualitative research, an undergraduate senior thesis, and an American Studies analysis, she establishes cultural perceptions in the U.S. of vegetarianism as odd or ideologically hostile to the mainstream and then situates the "animosity" faced by one participant within this larger context. She then takes up dynamics of gender, age, and family role in qualitative studies. One of these, addressing "the psychosocial variables that affect an individual's belief in vegetarianism" (6), finds that meat tends to be "an imperative aspect of a male's life and normativity" (Genuino 7).

Genuino takes up scholarly sources not only for their qualitative findings, but for keywords or critical terms that she uses in constructing her interpretive framework, including "masculinity" and "heteronormativity" (8). Based on her review of these sources, she identifies:

> notable trends ...men typically are less receptive to vegetarianism than women are. They also consider the environmental/health factors of vegetarianism less seriously than females do. On the other hand, females are more likely to embrace vegetarianism. They are also more likely to address the moral issues behind eating meat through vegetarianism. Children are the most tolerant [...] and typically do not condemn meat eaters or vegetarians [11].

Based on her survey of scholarship, Genuino also reports that "vegetarians are chastised by their male family members more than by their female family members, and it can give them a bad home dining experience with their diet" (11). Moreover, "vegetarians are well received by female family members, and their support brings the family closer together" (11). Genuino is careful to acknowledge, however, that statistics and trends are not reliable predictors of every individual's experience: "Vegetarians cannot be generalized into either a loving home or a divided household. There is a complex relationship that exists for every vegetarian and their family" (11).

Genuino concludes by calling for additional research on gender dynamics in attitudes to vegetarianism, then summarizing her own findings and identifying their broader implications:

> In this paper's research, the severity of a general population of males' opposition to vegetarianism and their emphasis on meat culture is significant. Some see the importance of meat as a symbol of masculinity through heteronormativity or socio-economic normativity. In families with males who hold this viewpoint towards vegetarian relatives, the vegetarians can be negatively affected and hurt by that, and it is imperative to realize the extent of interaction on familial relationships (11).

The following semester, when it came time to plan for the University Writing and Research Conference, I invited the authors of the two papers to present their work as a panel, with Lederman and Nobel presenting first, followed by Genuino. They surprised me by working as a team to create a single presentation spanning both projects. They spoke at the conference to a packed room. It became clear that their title and subject matter had drawn a number of students who were vegetarian or otherwise engaged in the issues. Yet the nonvegetarian students there also became caught up in the discussion, some even reporting previously having no strong feelings about the issues beyond liking to eat meat, but finding themselves needing to reflect and engage further due to the presentation, particularly about the social dynamics of eating or not eating meat.

This was one session of the conference in which there was no need for a faculty moderator to pose questions or direct the conversation, as students effectively claimed several forms of expertise in order to collectively explore the focus: the authority the first authors gained by following a rigorous ethnographic research process to document, and then frame, the experience of three vegetarians known to two student authors; the expertise gained by the other student author through a rigorous research process; and the authority of all students in the conversation—including the student authors—drawn from personal experience and observation. These three modes of knowledge then were effectively integrated in ways directly fostered by the assignment, and augmented by the University Writing and Research structure—an experience that offered both a culmination of their project to the three student authors (and an advanced form of peer review, similar to what scholars experience at conferences), and an exciting model of inquiry to the current students in the audience.

Appendix: Introduction to Ethnographic-Style Research Project: Alternatives to "Constant Convenience Consumerism" (13–14 pp. for groups of two, 15–16 pp. for groups of three)

Ethnography (first developed by anthropologists) involves detailed description of everyday habits and practices in a specific cultural setting, to uncover underlying social values and norms. Ethnographic techniques such as participant observation, interviews, and case studies are based on the assumption that expertise in a culture and its values resides in those who belong to the culture. In this form of research, we formulate an over-arching open-ended question that allows us to learn from participants, rather than testing a hypothesis. Ethnography is a form of qualitative research, which explores subjective aspects of experience to investigate social interactions and practices. This context provides the range of choices for a successful project, from preparing for and conducting interviews, to drafting, revising, and editing the paper.

This is a collaborative project with significant individual components. Groups will consist of two to three students. Focus on a well-defined set of participants (one per group member) who share a common or related practice involving the preparation or production of food, or food politics or activism in their daily lives—practices and experiences that in some way constitute alternatives to what Sandor Katz calls "constant convenience consumerism" (Katz 1). All participants must be actively engaged with these processes. If you have the relevant experience, you can serve as your own participant by following auto-ethnographic methods (work based on the researcher's personal experience), or one group member can interview another.

You will explore your participants' social worlds through their stories, especially how these experiences relate to cultural standards and patterns of meaning-making and how people follow, challenge, modify, or depart from these patterns. This in turn will allow you and your readers to become more aware of these (often implicit) norms and standards, to gain insight into the cultural and political dimensions of food practices.

As one way to situate people's experiences within their settings, ethnographers generally explore the relationships of social group categories and demographics (also referred to as positionalities) to their practices. Ethnographers closely study factors such as race, ethnicity, nationality, gender, sexuality, economic class, age, religion, geography, and physical or mental ability because of their impact in specific social contexts. Scholars recognize, however, that these factors' influence may vary and shift—as the categories themselves can do as well—so one thing that ethnography can do is to trace and reflect these shifts over time and across different settings. Your research, within its very specific focus, can contribute to the broader ethnographic project of exploring both continuity and change in foodways, as you consider the influence of social group categories in your participants' experiences.

The purpose of your research *process* is to explore your participants' experiences (habits, routines, and stories), not to test a hypothesis. The purpose of your *paper* is to present descriptions of these experiences framed with your analysis or interpretation of their significance; after completing and reviewing the interviews, you will organize the paper around a clear argumentative thesis—one that emerges from the interviews, rather than being pre-determined. Watch for patterns and commonalities, as well as distinctions between different participants' experiences. Sometimes conflicts or contradictions emerge within a participant's experiences that may point the way to broader cultural norms or social forces that conflict with one another—which can be very significant both ethnographically and politically. These patterns, commonalities, distinctions, and contradictions are what you will analyze.

Each group member will take the lead in drafting and polishing one interview or auto-ethnography, which will be one section of the larger collaborative paper. The lead author of each section will receive feedback specific to that section, though all group members have significant responsibility for the entire paper. Each member must participate equally in planning, interviewing, drafting, revising, and editing, rather than splitting up these tasks. To frame these sections, the paper will include a fully collaborative introduction and conclusion. The paper as a whole determines a range within which each individual group member's grade will fall. Keep a log of how many hours you personally are putting in weekly, from start to finish, since you will be asked periodically to specify the amount of time you have spent working on the project, both on your own and with your group.

NOTES

1. Citation and other formatting specifications have been omitted.
2. The author is grateful to Cathy Eisenhower, Patrick McGann, Pamela Presser,

and Karen Sosnoski for thoughtful responses to drafts of the critical analysis assignment and this essay.

3. I borrow this course title from food justice leader Will Allen's book of the same name.

4. The introduction to this ethnographic-style assignment (and to ethnographic research in general) is reproduced here as an appendix to this essay.

5. In 2014, Gelman Library was recognized by the Association of College & Research Libraries as an "Exemplary Program" in "Information Literacy Best Practices" for its instructional librarian/faculty collaboration program (Association).

6. This process is discussed in the highly influential pedagogical work of Joseph Harris, among others.

7. This workshop follows earlier ones reviewing drafts of the ethnographic-style essay and of the critical bibliography, requiring peer critiques worth 12 and 6 of the total 300 points for the course, respectively.

Works Cited

Alkon, Alison Hope, and Julian Ageyman. "Introduction: The Food Movement as Polyculture." *Cultivating Food Justice: Race, Class, and Sustainability*. Ed. Alison Hope Alkon and Julian Ageyman. Cambridge: MIT Press, 2011. 1–20. Print.

Allen, Will, with Charles Wilson. *The Good Food Revolution: Growing Healthy Food, People, and Communities*. New York: Gotham, 2013. Print.

Association of College & Research Libraries. "Information Literacy Best Practices: Exemplary Programs." *American Library Association*. 2015. Web. 10 Sept. 2014.

Bizup, Joseph. "BEAM: A Rhetorical Vocabulary for Teaching Research-Based Writing." *Rhetoric Review* 27.1 (2008): 72–86. Print.

Conference on College Composition and Communication. "Principles for the Postsecondary Teaching of Writing." *Conference on College Composition and Communication*, March 2015. Web. 30 Nov. 2015.

Downs, Doug, Heidi Estrem, and Susan Thomas, with Ruth Johnson, Claire O'Leary, Emily Strasser, and Anita Varma. "Students' Texts Beyond the Classroom: *Young Scholars in Writing*'s Challenges to College Writing Instruction." *Teaching with Student Texts: Essays Toward an Informed Practice*. Ed. Joseph Harris, John D. Miles, and Charles Paine. Logan: Utah State University Press, 2010. 119–128. Print.

Friedman, Sandie. "This Way for Vampires: Teaching First-Year Composition in 'Challenging Times.'" *Currents in Teaching and Learning* 6.1 (2013): 77–84. PDF.

Genuino, Kelsey. "The Role of Male and Female Family Members on Vegetarians." George Washington University, University Writing 1020: The Good Food Revolution, Prof. Abby Wilkerson, 2013. TS.

Harris, Joseph. *Rewriting: How to Do Things with Texts*. Logan: Utah State University Press, 2006. Print.

Katz, Sandor. *The Revolution Will Not Be Microwaved: Inside America's Underground Food Movements*. White River Junction, VT: Chelsea Press, 2006. Print.

Lederman, Jesse, and Jack Nobel. "Make It or Break It: An Ethnographic Study into the Familial Relationships of Vegetarians." George Washington University, University Writing 1020: The Good Food Revolution, Prof. Abby Wilkerson, 2013. TS.

Paine, Charles, and John D. Miles. "Afterword: Notes toward an Informed Practice." *Teaching with Student Texts: Essays Toward an Informed Practice*. Ed. Joseph Harris, John D. Miles, and Charles Paine. Logan: Utah State University Press, 2010. 242–255. Print.

About the Contributors

Melissa **Bender** is a lecturer in the university writing program at the University of California, Davis. Her recent publications and conference presentations concern visual rhetoric, the rhetoric of disability, history writing, and popular culture. Her courses include Writing in Science, Writing in the Health Professions, Technical Writing, Writing in History, Visual Rhetoric, and a graduate seminar on teaching expository writing.

M. Ann **Brady** is a professor of rhetoric and technical communication at Michigan Technological University, where she directs the undergraduate program in scientific and technical communication. Her research interests are in technical communication, the history and theories of rhetoric, interdisciplinary theory, feminist theory, and qualitative research methods and methodologies.

Nicole I. **Caswell** is an assistant professor of English and the director of the university writing centers at East Carolina University. She teaches research methods and enjoys thinking through ethical research issues with students as time and technology evolve.

Jodie **Childers** is a documentary filmmaker and writer. Her research and creative work are primarily concerned with twentieth century American dissidence as expressed through cultural production. She wrote and produced the documentary film *The Other Parade*, and she is co-directing a second film about folk legend Pete Seeger's environmental legacy. She is a PhD student in American studies at the University of Massachusetts, Amherst.

Elisa **Cogbill-Seiders** is a PhD student in English at the University of Nevada, Las Vegas. She has taught an advanced composition course that uses blogging platforms as well as introductory writing courses and world literature surveys. As an Information Literacy Fellow at the Lied Library at UNLV in 2014, she explored the correlation between themed-writing classes and student success, as well as the influence and effectiveness of library sessions on research-based writing courses.

Barbara J. **D'Angelo** is a clinical associate professor of technical communication at Arizona State University, where she is also the graduate advisor for the technical communication program and coordinates a multi-section professional writing course for nurses. She has presented on writing and communication at several national conferences and is the recipient of the 2011 Francis W. Weeks Award of Merit from the Association for Business Communication.

About the Contributors

Christine **Denecker** is the chair and professor of English at the University of Findlay, where she also serves as director of the Center for Teaching Excellence. Her research interests include multimodal composition, digital storytelling, and concurrent enrollment, and her articles have appeared in journals and edited collections such as *Composition Studies*, *The Journal of Faculty Development*, *The Writing Instructor*, *Computers and Composition Online*, and *Stories That Speak to Us*.

Jason W. **Ellis** is an assistant professor of English at the New York City College of Technology, CUNY. As a Marion L. Brittain fellow at the Georgia Institute of Technology, he taught English composition, technical communication, and science fiction, and directed the Digital Pedagogy Research and Development Lab (DevLab). With Massod Ashraf Raja and Swaralipi Nandi, he was co-editor of *The Postnational Fantasy: Postcolonialism, Cosmopolitics and Science Fiction*.

Sarah K. **Gunning** is an assistant professor in the English and professional writing programs at Towson University. Her research interests involve knowledge management, collaborative writing, and financial literacy.

Jim **Henry** has published widely on writers and writing pedagogies in professional writing, technical writing, and first-year writing. He founded the University of Hawai'i's Writing Mentors program, which places graduate students in first-year writing courses to coach students to perform to the best of their abilities

Dalyn **Luedtke** is an assistant professor of English and communications at Norwich University, the oldest private military college in the United States, where she has taught courses in first-year writing, advanced composition, the rhetoric of popular culture, and professional and technical writing. Her research focuses on television, digital writing, and pedagogy, and she is at work on a project that argues for the pedagogical use of reality television in the writing classroom.

Gerald **Maki** is an assistant professor of English at Ivy Tech Community College. His research has focused on postcolonialism, theory and cultural studies, and film. He previously worked as a faculty support specialist for developmental educators and has published essays on the topics of international cinema and educational philosophy.

Gracemarie **Mike** is a PhD candidate in English at Purdue University with a concentration in rhetoric and composition. Her research interests include composition pedagogy, professional writing, writing across the curriculum, second language studies, and histories of writing instruction. Her work has appeared in the *CEA Critic* and *Connexions*.

Erin Dee **Moore** earned a PhD in interdisciplinary humanities and an MA in literature from Florida State University. She teaches English composition at the Los Angeles Film School.

Ed **Nagelhout** is a professor of rhetoric and writing at the University of Nevada, Las Vegas. He has served as a co-editor of the *ATTW Bulletin* (2003–2010), a Stage I Reviewer for CCCC, and a reviewer for the *Online Writing Instructor*, *IEEE Transactions on Professional Communication*, and the *Journal of Business and Technical Communication*.

About the Contributors

Lori **Ostergaard** is an associate professor and the chair of the Department of Writing and Rhetoric at Oakland University. Her archival research examines the history of composition-rhetoric at Midwestern normal schools and high schools. Her articles have appeared in *Rhetoric Review, Composition Forum, Studies in the Humanities, Issues in Writing,* and *Peitho.*

Gwendolynne **Reid** is a doctoral candidate in communication, rhetoric, and digital media at North Carolina State University. She is a former lecturer and assistant director of a first-year writing program. She has presented at a number of conferences, including CCCC, Computers and Writing, and the Council of Writing Program Administrators.

Katherine **Robbins** is a PhD candidate at the University of Nebraska, Lincoln, specializing in instructional technology. She has taught writing, literature, and film at various universities and community colleges in Virginia and Nebraska. In addition to her academic pursuits, she works for TalentSprout by Sykes, which designs curricula that emphasize active learning, blended classroom environments, and multimodal components.

Denise **Tillery** is an associate professor of rhetoric and writing at the University of Nevada, Las Vegas. She has published and presented on topics including environmental communication, gender and rhetoric, and program design and administration. An editorial board member and reviewer for the journal *Technical Communication Quarterly*, she is also a reviewer for *Technical Communication Quarterly, IEEE Transactions on Professional Communication,* and *Science Communication.*

Melissa **Vosen Callens** is an assistant professor of practice in the Department of Communication at North Dakota State University, Fargo. Cullens' research and teaching interests include collaborative writing, popular culture, and online education, and her writing can be found in *Rhetoric Matters: Language and Argument in Context, A Sense of Community: Essays on the Television Series and Its Fandom,* and *English Journal,* among other publications.

Karma **Waltonen** is a senior lecturer in the university writing program at the University of California, Davis, and teaches for Sacramento City College. She has taught courses on style in the essay, advanced composition and rhetoric, writing in the health professions, developmental writing, and writing in the fine arts, among others. She was the winner of the 2015 Academic Federation Excellence in Teaching Award.

Courtney L. **Werner** is an assistant professor of English at Monmouth University, where her work in writing-center studies fuels her academic life. Her research interests include multimodal writing and rhetoric, teaching digital composition, and playing with digital design.

Abby **Wilkerson** is a philosopher and associate professor of writing at the George Washington University. Her publications include *The Thin Contract: Social Justice and the Political Rhetoric of Obesity* (forthcoming) and *Diagnosis: Difference: The Moral Authority of Medicine* (1998). She co-edited the award-winning "Desiring Disability: Queer Theory Meets Disability Studies," a special issue of *GLQ: A Journal of Lesbian and Gay Studies,* with Robert McRuer.

Index

abstract 71, 262
Adkins, Christine 150
advertisement 4, 39, 101, 133, 138, 148, 164–5, 167–8, 174–5
Affordable Care Act 167, 223
Ageyman, Julian 259, 270
Alexander, Bryan 56, 59
Alexie, Sherman 37
Alkon, Alison Hope 259, 270
Allen, Will 270
animation 49, 137, 140, 168
annotation 231, 234–243, 263; annotated bibliography 4, 132, 134, 136–7, 153–8, 160, 162, 201, 257, 263–4
Aoki, Keith 256
Armstrong, Lance 211
Artman, Margaret 193, 202
Association of College & Research Libraries 270
AT&T 211
attention deficit/hyperactivity disorder (ADHD) 197
Atwood, Margaret 43

Bacon, Francis 148
Ball, Cheryl 176
Bankrate.com 110, 115, 117
Banksy 147, 149–152
Barr, Brittany 176
Barthes, Roland 18
Bartholomae, David 182
Batchelor, Ray 11, 19
BEAM schema (background, exhibit, argument, method) 257–8, 263–5, 270
Bean, J.C. 11, 19
Bean, John 2, 68–9
Berger, John 36, 39, 41, 44
Berrett, Dan 170, 177
Berthoff, Ann E. 40, 44
Bizup, Joseph 258, 265, 270
Black, Alison 109, 117
Blackwell, Unita 212

Blake Yancey, Kathleen 215
Blakely, Barbara J. 120, 129
Blekle Rat 145, 149
blog(s) 3, 12, 42, 45–59, 232, 260, 262
Blue, Bennis 182, 189
Blumenfeld, Phyllis C. 256
Bomb It! 145, 149
Borton, Sonya C. 176
Bosley, Deborah S. 30, 33
Bound by Law? Tales from the Public Domain 245, 250
Bourdieu, Pierre 17
Bowles-Terry, Melissa 193
Boyle, James 256
Brady, Ann 24, 33
Breton, André 148
brochure 2, 20, 25, 29–31 163, 218
Brokaw, Tom 91
Broken Windows Theory 144–5, 147
Brooke, Robert 120, 129
Brooks, Kevin 218
Brueggemann, Brenda Jo 182, 189
Buck, Amber 55, 59
Burnett, Rebecca E. 105

Carrithers, D. 11, 19
CARS model 154, 156, 158
case study 132–4, 247, 268
Castro, Fidel 212
Chapette, Patrick 177
Clark, J. Elizabeth 55, 59
Clifford 207, 215
Clouse, Abby 19
Cohen, Noam 196
Coley, Soraya M. 64, 69
collage 7, 11, 12–5, 18–19, 95, 102, 138, 212
College Board 110, 117
Comaneci, Nadia 212
Conference on College Composition and Communication (CCCC) 184–5, 205, 262, 270
Connors, Robert J. 183, 189

276 Index

Connors, Sean P. 91
contract 3–4, 62, 106–11, 114–6; group or team 28, 134, 141–2
contrastive rhetoric 30
Cooper, Marilyn 119–20, 129
copyright 48, 58, 133, 138, 202; *see also* fair use
counter argument 226–7
CRAAP (currency, relevancy, authority, accuracy, purpose) test 199
C.R.A.P. (contrast, repetition, alignment, proximity) principles 158, 161, 224
Crosling, Glenda 77, 91
Cross, Tom 196
Csikszentmihalyi, Mihaly 19
Cuban missile crisis 211–2

Daily Mail 212
Daley, Elizabeth 38, 44, 91
Dali, Salvador 148
Darell, Richard 52, 59
Dautermann, Jennie 30, 33
Davies, Matthew 209
Davies-Wilson, Dennis 78, 79, 91
Da Vinci, Leonardo 201
Davis, Erin 193
Davis, Fred 19
Davis, Matthew 215
Dawkins, Richard 234
Dee, Jonathan 196
description 28–9, 30, 37, 39, 42–3, 72, 94, 144–6, 148–9, 166, 168, 179–80, 183–4, 186, 194–5, 207, 211, 221, 223, 225, 247–8, 251, 268–9
Diagnostic and Statistical Manual of Mental Disorders 197
digital literacy 24, 54, 56–7, 81, 170, 193, 204, 246
digital media 55, 170, 176, 182
digital natives 169, 177–8, 193, 202
disability studies 180
discourse analysis 246–7
discourse community 4, 56–7, 59, 153–6, 206–7
Dix, Otto 148
Django Unchained 211
DK Handbook 247
Dobrin, Sidney 120, 129
document design 5, 109–11, 217, 219–221
Donnelly, Liza 177
Donovan, Jennie 177
Downs, Douglas 155, 163, 260, 270
Dytham, Mark 105n2

Ebert, Samuel H. 128, 130
Eisenhower, Cathy 263
Elbow, Peter 12–13, 182
Ellsworth-Jones, Will 151
Elmborg, James K. 193
Encyclopedia of the U.S. Presidency: A Historical Reference 197

Estrem, Heidi 260, 270
ethics 107, 110, 132–4, 144, 147, 150
ethnography 5, 153, 154, 247, 257, 259–69
Exit Through the Gift Shop 147
expressivism 180
Eyman, Douglas 177

fair use 48, 133, 138–9, 202, 250; *see also* copyright
Fairey, Shepard 149–150
Faith47 145, 149
feminist methodology 246–7
Fifty Shades of Grey 211
Fischer, Katherine 206–7, 215
flier, flyer 71, 138, 217–18
flowchart 140
focus groups 4, 246–7
Fordism/Fordist theory 16–7
Franken, Al 233
Frazee, Andy 105
free writing 80, 164, 170–1
Friedman, Sandie 259, 270
Frisicaro-Pawloski, Erica 193

"Gangnam Style" 211
Garden, Mary 55, 59
Garfinkel, Simon L. 195–6
genre 2, 22, 24–5, 38, 45, 52, 54–6, 65–6, 101, 112–3, 118, 126, 137, 144–6, 156, 159–61, 163, 201, 245; conventions 25, 93, 221; theory 204, 206–7
Genuino, Kelsey 266, 270
George, Diana 256
Gibson, David 111, 117
Gibson, William 99, 105
Giles, Jim 196
Girard, Brian J. 209
Goggin, Maureen Daly 183, 189
Grattan, George 123, 130
Greckyte, R. 176
Griffith, Eric 52, 59
Grobman, Laurie 121, 130
Guerrilla Girls 149

Hall, Carla 111, 117
Hanggi, Kathleen 105
Haniford, Lauren C. 209
Harris, Joseph 270
Harris, Sylvia 111, 117
Hawisher, Gail 213, 215
Head, Alison 193
Heagney, Margaret 77, 91
health literacy 216–7, 219, 221–3
Henderson, Felicity 56, 59
Henry, Jim 121, 129
heteronormativity 267
HIPPA (Health Insurance Portability and Accountability Act) 219
Holliday, Wendy 202

Hoover, Eric 91
Horgan, John 233
Howe, Neil 78–9, 91
Hu, Jinming 103–5
Huff Bruland, Holly 121, 129
Huot, Brian 176
Hurlbert, Claude 120, 129
Hurricane Katrina 211

IDA (interpretation, decisions, and action) model 209, 212
ill-defined problem 11, 20, 21
industry 24, 107–8, 116, 132, 136–7, 182, 218
infographics 52, 101, 132–4, 137–142, 142n1
information literacy 169, 193, 202–3, 270–1
international students 3, 20–33
interview 4, 109, 122, 128, 132–8, 140–1, 145, 149, 155, 157, 247, 261, 268–9; mock 137

Jenkins, Jennifer 256
Johnson, Ruth 260, 270
Jordan, Barbara 212
José, Laurence 24, 33
Judd, Terry 193

Katz, Sandor 268, 270
Kawaharada, Dennis 123, 130
Kennedy, Gregor 193
Kennedy, John F. 197, 212
Kent State University Department of English 177
Kerns, Richard 91
Klein, Astrid 105n2
Klinenberg, Eric 234
Krakcik, Joseph 256
Kruschev, Nikita 212
Kugel, Seth 175, 177

lab report 263
Lamott, Anne 37, 44
Ledbetter, Lehua 121, 129
Lederman, Jesse 266, 270
Lindgren, Tim 123, 130
Ling, T. 11, 19
literature review 57, 181, 186–7, 247–9
logical fallacy 212, 228, 230
Lutkewitte, Claire 177
Lynch, Dennis A. 247, 256

Macleod, D. 176, 178
Madden, Amanda 105
Magnuson, Korinne 87–90
Marback, Richard 11, 19
Markel, Mike 22–3
Marsee, Mickey 78, 79, 91
Marshmallow challenge 141, 142n2
Martin, Malissa 91
Marx, Ronald W. 256
masculinity 267

Mastrangelo, Lisa 184–5, 189
Mathieu, Paula 123, 130
Mauk, Johnathon 120, 129
McCloud, Scott 255–6
McIntosh, Jason 120, 129
McKee, Heidi A. 177
McLuhan, H. Marshall 100–1, 104–5, 207
Medina, John 98, 102, 105
memo 9, 20, 25, 31, 61–2, 141, 228–30
Miles, John D. 261, 270
Miller, Carolyn R. 136, 142
Miller, Daniel 19
Miller, Nan 178
Miller, Scott L. 182, 189
Mills, C. Wright 16
Mirabelli, Tony 163, 163
Mirel, Barbara 24, 33
mock debate 196–7
Mockford, Emma 188–9
mock-up 139–140
Mona Lisa 148
Monaco, Michele 91
Mondrian, Piet 148
Monet, Claude 148
Monge, Robert 193
Mookini, Esther T. 128, 130
Moore, Erin 177
Moore, Michael R. 177
Moss, Pamela A. 209

narrative 34, 35, 62, 90, 109, 145, 176, 249–251; literacy 5, 62, 109, 156, 260; personal 3, 4, 34–4, 180
National Council of Teachers of English (NCTE) 177, 181
New London Group 170
new media 34, 100–1, 180, 185, 194
New Media Consortium 170, 178
Nielson, Jakob 109, 117
Nobel, Jack 266, 270
The Non-Designer's Design Book 224
Nordstrom, Georganne 122, 130
Norgaard, Rolf 193

The Oatmeal 234
Obama, Barack 167
Obama Hope 150
O'Brien, Annemaree 177
Okamura, Jonathan Y. 121, 130
O'Keefe, Patrick 77, 91
O'Leary, Claire 260, 270
Organization of the American States 212
Osborne, Helen 219, 221–3
Owens, Derek 120, 130

Pagnac, Susan B. 120, 129
Paine, Charles 261, 270
Paiz, Joshua 177
parataxis 12

participant observation 268
Pedersen, Anne-Marie 137, 142
Pew Research Center 91
Picasso, Pablo 148
Pitbull 88
plagiarism 143, 149–150, 101, 229, 231, 253
plain language principles 219–221, 223
podcast 182, 232, 251–2, 256
Pollock, Jackson 148
popular culture 12, 144, 147, 266
Prensky, Marc 169, 177–8
Presentation 122, 163, 182, 214–5, 232, 267
Presley, Elvis 87
process pedagogy 3, 180
procrastination 103, 140–1
professional writing 6, 20–33, 135, 142, 180, 182, 218
professionalization 30, 101–2, 131–2, 135–6, 138, 180, 206, 216
Project Information Literacy 193
Psy (Park Jae-sang) 211
public service announcement 138, 178
public space 148–9, 175
Pukui, Mary Kawena 128, 130
Purdy, James 11, 19

readability 47, 113, 219, 223
reverse outline 158–9, 193
Reynolds, Nedra 120, 128–129
rhetorical analysis 54, 143–150, 184, 191, 211–2, 216, 220, 229, 246–7
rhetorical appeals 4, 98, 165–8, 174–5, 185, 228; ethos 16, 64, 66, 98, 145, 147, 166, 177, 185, 200, 226–7; kairos 98, 185; logos 69, 98, 166, 176–7 185, 227–8; pathos 69, 98, 166, 176–7, 185, 208, 227–8
rhetorical purpose 191, 199–201, 261
rhetorical situation 2, 45, 47, 51–2, 56, 59, 65, 76–7, 87, 102, 162, 192, 227
Rice, Doug 170, 178
Ritter, Kelly 183
Robert Hooke's London 56, 59
Romlein, Jeanne 188
Rosenau, Matt 177
Roth, Philip 196
Rothko, Mark 149
Ruppel Shell, Ellen 19

St. Amant, Kirk 30, 33
Sano-Franchini, Jennifer 121, 129
satire 147, 229
Scheinberg, C.A. 64, 69
Schön, Donald A. 24, 33
Schrock, Kathy 177
self-sponsored writing 180
Selfe, Cynthia 79, 81, 83, 91, 170, 177, 207, 213, 215
Selfe, Richard J. 170, 178
Shepherd, Deneen M. 182, 189

Shihab Nye, Naomi 263
Shipka, Jody 38, 44
Shultz, Stacy 123, 130
The Simpsons 147
Skinner, Carolyn 137, 142
Smith, Dolsy 263
Soloway, Elliot 256
Spigelman, Candace 121, 130
Steinberg, Avi 52, 59
Sterling, Elspeth P. 128, 130
Stiff, Paul 109, 117
Stolley, Karl 177
storyboard 35–6, 39, 41, 75–6, 80–3, 140, 159, 244, 247, 249–251
Strasser, Emily 260, 270
Strauss, William 78–9, 91
Sullivan, Racheal 91
Summers, Catherine C. 128, 130
Supiano, Becky 110, 117
surveys 4, 31, 111, 170, 177, 215, 246–7, 267
Swales, John 154, 156, 158, 163
Sweeney, Julia 234
Sweeny, Richard T. 91

Takayoshi, Pamela 79, 91
Teaching with Student Texts: Essays Toward an Information Practice 261
technical writing 20–33, 60–74, 135–6,
Thaler, Richard 110, 117
thick description 247
think aloud protocol 109, 246–7
Thomas, Liz 77, 91
Thomas, Susan 260, 270
Thompson, Elizabeth 77–8, 80, 91
Thrush, Emily 22, 30, 33
Tulley, Christine 213, 215
Turner, Patrick 77–8, 80, 91
Turner, Tim 177

U.S. Naval Academy 212
usability, usability testing 3, 20–24, 27–28, 31–32, 46, 49, 106–10, 117, 134, 218
Usability.gov 109, 117
user-centered design 24

Van Gogh, Vincent 148
Varma, Anita 260, 270
vegetarianism 266–7
visual rhetoric 4, 145, 147–8, 177, 204–6, 208, 211–2

Waiteman, F. 178
Waller, Robert 109, 117
Wardle, Elizabeth 11, 19, 155, 163
warrants 226, 228–9
Waters, Sue 56, 59
Weaver, Travis 124
web design 4, 46–50, 58, 154, 159, 182, 213
Weeks, Linton 14

Weida, Stacy 177
Weiss, John 149
Weisser, Christian R. 120, 129
Werthiem, Margaret 233
Wilhoit, Stephen 150, 152
Williams, George 177
Williams, Robin 219, 221
Wilson, Charles 270
Wisheu, Karen 177
Witmer, Andrew 205, 215
Wolfe, Johanna 108, 116–7
Wong, Jamie 123

Wright brothers 194
Writing-About-Writing 155, 194
Writing Across the Curriculum (WAC) 181
Writing in the Disciplines (WID) 2, 181, 194
Writing Program Administrators (WPA) 181
Wujec, Tom 142n2
Wysocki, Anne Frances 247, 256

Yancey, Kathleen Blake 37–8, 44, 54, 59, 170, 177–8, 205, 209, 215

Zezão 147, 149

www.ingramcontent.com/pod-product-compliance
Ingram Content Group UK Ltd.
Pitfield, Milton Keynes, MK11 3LW, UK
UKHW021844140426
5217IPUK00022B/1581